S0-AXR-506

THE EDITOR

JACK D. FORBES has won wide recognition as an authority on American Indians, Mexican-Americans, and on Indian–European relations. His research projects in Mexico, Spain, and the American Southwest have resulted in two books, *Warriors of the Colorado* and *Apache, Navaho and Spaniard*. A frequent contributor to historical and anthropological journals, Dr. Forbes has been awarded fellowships by the Social Science Research Council and the John Simon Guggenheim Memorial Foundation; he was twice elected to the Executive Committee of the American Indian Ethnohistoric Conference. He received his doctorate from the University of Southern California and is currently a professor of history at San Fernando Valley State College.

◆ ◆

THE
INDIAN
IN
AMERICA'S PAST

◆ ◆

EDITED BY
JACK D. FORBES

A SPECTRUM BOOK

PRENTICE-HALL, INC.
ENGLEWOOD CLIFFS, N.J.

To my parents
George T. Forbes and Dorothy Rufener Forbes
My debt to them is without measure

◆ ◆

Current printing (last digit):

11 10 9 8 7

Copyright © 1964 by Prentice-Hall, Inc.

ENGLEWOOD CLIFFS, N.J.

All rights reserved. No part of this book may be reproduced in any form, by mimeograph or any other means, without permission in writing from the publishers. Library of Congress Catalog Card Number 64-17608. Printed in the United States of America (C). 45688-P; 45689-C.

CONTENTS

SEVEN   UNITED STATES POLICY, 1789-1870   98

INTRODUCTION

WHAT IS AN INDIAN?

In 1954 the California State Senate Interim Committee on Indian Affairs held a series of hearings throughout the state to determine the effect of several bills then pending in the United States Congress relative to "terminating" federal services for California Indians. The committee, after hearing many hours of testimony, was finally forced to grapple with the question: "What is an Indian?"

Senator Charles Brown: Speaking of Indians, what is your definition of an Indian?

Mrs. Jane Penn (of Morongo, California, Reservation): Briefly, I would say a person who is half could be either one, but when you get less than half you are more of one than you are of the other.

Senator Brown: I just wanted to know; that question came up (in the hearings) before.

Mrs. Penn: For different purposes the government classifies them as one-eighth, one-quarter, without giving us a true definition. . . . I believe a person more than half, would be that, but in our case (on our reservation) we have one-sixteenth (and one-thirty-second).

Senator A. W. Way: What is the proper definition of an Indian who will come under this act (termination)?

Mr. Leonard M. Hill (Sacramento Area Director, Bureau of Indian Affairs): To answer that, Senator, there is no definition contemplated under this act. I think that I mentioned at Redding the other day that the government itself has that question before it, trying to find some definition of an Indian. There was a bill presented to Congress last session which made a definition that anyone with less than half-blood was not an Indian and would not be entitled to any services. They are still talking about it in the Department of Interior, and in the congressional committees, as to how to define an Indian. . . . and it is not possible under our multiplicity of laws and regulations to define it. You have to look to the purpose for which you're trying to define an Indian. . . . for some purposes . . . he must be a quarter-blood and live on trust land. For educational purposes . . . he must be a quarter-blood or more. . . . I just don't think there is any definition that you can give to an

1

Indian. . . . He is an Indian for some purposes and for other purposes he isn't an Indian, so there just isn't any clear definition.

Senator Way: I think that we should have a definition of an Indian who would come within this act.

Mr. Hill: Well, sir, a definition in . . . the act defines a tribe or group of Indians and I believe it states those Indians who reside on or have an interest in trust property.

Senator Way: I still don't know what is a person who is described as an Indian. . . .

Mr. Hill: I am sorry, I cannot make a definition. . . . We in the Indian Bureau are concerned with it also. We don't know how to define an Indian.[1]

What is an Indian? How can one discuss the role of the Indian in America's past if the United States Bureau of Indian Affairs and various other governmental agencies cannot agree upon a definition for the term "Indian"? Whatever one's answer may be, it is obvious that any study dealing with indigenous Americans must first confront certain semantic problems.

In attempting to find a definition from the point of view of the Americas as a whole one immediately confronts a serious difficulty. There are large numbers of so-called East Indians residing in the former British West Indies and Guiana, as well as in the United States. The presence of thousands of Asian Indians in the Americas brings to the fore an old semantic problem: ever since it was learned that Columbus failed to reach the Indies (India), it has been necessary to distinguish between the Indians and the natives of the Americas (whom Columbus mistakenly called Indians), and much confusion has resulted.

Many Europeans avoided the problem for several centuries by ignoring Columbus's mistake. They referred to the American natives simply as Americans.[2] This was a logical resolution of the issue until British colonists established the United States of America. Not wishing to call themselves "Unitedstatesians," the Anglo-Europeans gradually began to appropriate the term "American" as one belonging exclusively to themselves. The natives could no longer be referred to as Americans by these "New Americans" (especially as the natives were often their enemies). However, it should be noted that European writers occasionally continued to do just that, being aware as they were of the presence of Indians in the Indian subcontinent of Asia.[3]

Further confusion has resulted from the practice in Spanish and Portuguese America of using the term "Indian" (as well as *indígena* and *natural*) to refer not to an ethnic stock, but to a person following a tribal or folk way of life. Thus in Mexico, a Nahuan Indian who moves away from his village and subsequently behaves in the same manner as the majority of Mexicans ceases to be an Indian. He becomes simply a Mexican, in spite of the fact that racially speaking he is still an indigenous American. South of the Rio Grande *Indio* has often had a derogatory connotation—implying backward and childlike behavior and inferior capabilities.

In the United States confusion also reigns because the term "Indian" is variously used to refer to a racial group, a legal concept, a sociocultural group, and a caste. In this connection, it should be pointed out that the greatest reservoir of Native American ancestry in the United States is not contained within the group usually referred to as "Indians," but among the perhaps 6,000,000 Mexican-Americans and so-called Spanish-Americans. A high percentage of the latter are of relatively unmixed native ancestry, and yet it is maintained that they are not "Indians" (although many of them were "Indians" in Mexico—Taraumaras, Yaquis, Tepehuanes, etc.). As a matter of fact, many states legally classify Mexican-Americans as "White," and the federal census does not enumerate them as Indians.

Although the average person may tend to think of an Indian as being the member of a unique ethnic group (with high cheek bones, a prominent eagle-beak nose, reddish brown skin, etc.), these characteristics are not considered by the Bureau of Indian Affairs or the federal census. An Indian to the latter is a person who resides on a reservation (trust land) or whose name appears on a "tribal roll." This person may be a pure-blood native or he may be one-quarter, one-eighth, or even less. During certain periods some pure-blood Whites married to Indians or mixed-bloods were effectively classified as Indians. Thus, according to the federal government not all Indians are of unmixed ethnic stock—at least one-half of the Indians counted in the census are actually mixed-bloods.

In order to avoid confusion, I will henceforth refer to the group classified as Indians by the government as Tribal Americans, such these people owe their uniqueness to their tribal connections (keeping in mind that many modern "tribes" are creations of the government) and since they are, by any definition, Americans.

In contrast to the half-million Tribal Americans are the many millions of other Americans of native or part-native ancestry. These people are not usually classified as Indians, and indeed they should not be. (I have become convinced that the term "Indian" should be reserved for the people of India.) Nevertheless, as indicated above there is more Native American "blood" to be found among Mexican-Americans than among Tribal Americans. Likewise, many persons classified by the census as English-speaking Whites are actually part Native American (I personally know of some who are at least half Native American); almost all Puerto Ricans have some degree of native ancestry; many French Canadians are actually American-European hybrids; and perhaps one of every three so-called Negroes is part Native American.[4] Conservatively, it would seem that at least 10,000,000 residents of the United

States are part Native American, and actually the figure could easily be pushed up to 16,000,000 or more.

In dealing wth the role of the native in America's past it is necessary to avoid the fiction which denominates one pure Native American as an Indian and another equally pure as a White, or the fictions which lead the census to enumerate certain persons as being part-native while classifying other part-natives as "Whites" or as "Negroes." In attempting to understand the dynamics of European-American and African-American relations over four centuries, it is necessary to regard all Native Americans as belonging to a single stock whether they happen to speak Cherokee or Spanish. Likewise, the role of persons of part-Native-American ancestry will be considered whether they adhere to a tribal group or become identified with a nontribal community, as long as their status is relevant to an understanding of European-African-native relationships in the United States.

Some readers may object to my including materials dealing with Spanish-speaking groups, especially since almost every other work that has been written about Indians in the United States ignores the Native American of Mexican origin. Of the many arguments against such objections, two stand out. First, any work purporting to deal with all indigenous Americans residing in the United States must include at least some reference to the numerous persons of Mexican origin; and second, one cannot understand the discrimination that has been visited upon Mexican-Americans without taking into account the color of their skin and the fact that they look like Native Americans or part Native Americans.

In answer then to the question, "What is an Indian?", I would state that an Indian is a person whose ancestors lived in India. In my vocabulary, persons whose ancestors were indigenous to America are simply native Americans; European–Native American hybrids are Eurindians; African–Native Americans are Afro-Indians, and African-European–Native Americans are Afro-Eurindians. Persons who are affiliated with a tribal group are Tribal Americans, regardless of their social background.

The major purpose of this work is to explore the dynamics of inter-ethnic relations by examining interactions of Americans with Europeans and Africans in the United States. This study of the confrontation of groups has a relatively modern beginning—it should be borne in mind that the native Americans were themselves the result of ancient inter-ethnic relations, and that they were not a uniform group when the Europeans arrived. Not only were the indigenous Americans divided into a number of diverse linguistic and cultural groups, but these groups also had distinctive physical characteristics. There was, for example, very little similarity between a heavily bearded, round-faced central California native and a lightly bearded, sharp-featured plains dweller. Variations in color, facial type, beardedness, height, body build, and other features were very pronounced, especially in certain regions; and changes could be observed within short distances.

Thus, the Native Americans themselves may represent a process of amalgamation of diverse stocks which was not yet complete at the time of European contact. On the other hand, they may originally have been a relatively uniform people who formed separate groups through the processes of isolation, genetic drift, and differential re-amalgamation. We cannot be sure of their history over 20,000 or more years, but we can assume a healthy quantity of inter-ethnic interactions both in the Americas and, presumably, in their earlier home in Eurasia.

Of much more significance to the student of human behavior—because there is more data available on this period—are the last 400 years of the Native Americans' history; and I hope that this work will serve to awaken a greater interest in this area of investigation.

Notes

1. *Progress Report to the Legislature by the Senate Intermim Committee on Indian Affairs* (Sacramento: California State Senate, 1955) pp. 241-2, 407-8.
2. Thus in 1650 one section of a work dealing with New Netherland was entitled "Of the Americans or Natives, their Appearance, Occupations, and Means of Support." See J. Franklin Jameson, ed., *Narratives of New Netherland* (New York: Charles Scribner's Sons, 1909) p. 300. As late as the 1780's Frenchmen were referring to the natives of the Pacific Coast as Americans. See Hubert Howe Bancroft, *History of California* (San Francisco: Bancroft, 1890) Vol. I, p. 429 n.
3. For example, Charles Maclaren (a Scotsman), writing an article about America about 1880, referred to "the American race," "the color of the Americans," "the American nations," and "the Americans," by all of which he meant "the Americans of indigenous races." See "America," in *Werner Encyclopedia* (Akron: The Werner Company, 1909) Vol. I, pp. 602-604.
4. See Melville J. Herskovitz's excellent studies: *The American Negro* (New York: Alfred A. Knopf, Inc., 1928), and *The Myth of the Negro Past* (New York: Harper & Row, Publishers, 1958).

ONE

WHEN WORLDS COLLIDE

In the year 458 A.D. five Buddhist priests of Ki-piu (Afghanistan) sailed from China, going 12,000 li to Japan, 7,000 li to the north to "Wen-shin," 5,000 li to the east to "Ta-han" and then 20,000 li eastward to the "kingdom of Fu-sang," which lay due east of China. The expedition apparently (if we are to accept the accounts as accurate) followed the Japanese current, a route used frequently later by drifting Japanese junks and Spanish galleons. It seems quite possible that Wen-shin is the Alaska region and Ta-han the Californias. The people of the latter area had no weapons and did not carry on warfare, characteristics that agree in general with the peaceful nature of most California natives described later.

The kingdom of Fu-sang was apparently Mexico or Guatemala. The land was named after the fu-sang (maguey) plant, which:

> sprouts forth like the bamboo, and the people eat the shoots. Its fruit resembles the pear, but is red; the bark is spun into cloth for dresses, and woven into brocade. . . . The (people) use characters and writing, making paper from the bark of the fu-sang. . . . The king of this country is termed Yueh-ki. . . . When the king goes abroad he is preceded and followed by drummers and trumpeters. . . . Iron is not found in the ground, though copper is; they do not prize gold or silver, and trade is conducted without rent, duty or fixed prices. . . . In olden times they know nothing of the Buddhist religion, but . . . [in 458] five beggar priests went there. They traveled over the kingdom, everywhere making known the laws, canons, and images of that faith. Priests of regular ordination were set apart among the natives, and the customs of the country became reformed . . . [in 499] a shaman priest named Hwui Shin arrived at King-chau (a Chinese city on the Yangtze River) from the kingdom of Fu-sang and he related the above, which was duly recorded in the Imperial Archives.

There is considerable evidence to support the above testimony, although not every detail of Hwui Shin's report agrees with what we know of conditions in Mexico at that time. Nevertheless, it is certain that between 1774 and 1880, when literate observers were present, some

6

forty to sixty Japanese ships drifted to the American coast. Survivors from these ships came ashore as far north as Sitka and as far south as Santa Barbara. Furthermore, Chinese artifacts have been found in British Columbia and ancient Japanese-like pottery in Ecuador. At various Maya and Toltec sites elements of Asian art associated with Buddhism (such as symbols for the lotus, the foliated cross, reclining or cross-legged figures, and a picture of an elephant) have been found. These appear about 700 A.D., during the same general period when Quetzalcoatl was introducing a reformed religion in Mexico. Some scholars have suggested that there may be a connection between the journey of Hwui Shin and Quetzalcoatl; however, little evidence is available to support such a thesis.[1]

In any case, it is clear from this and other evidence that the Native Americans may well have had extensive contacts with Asians over the centuries, and these contacts may well have affected the physical and cultural characteristics of some groups living along the Pacific Coast.

THE FIRST EUROPEAN MOVEMENT WESTWARD

In the ninth century, Iceland was occupied by Norse adventurers who made raids upon Britain and Ireland. By the beginning of the eleventh century Norse colonies had also been established in Greenland. There, the Norsemen found ruins and broken kayaks but no Eskimos. Thus there was apparently no direct confrontation between Europeans and Native Americans until the Scandinavians actually penetrated to the North American mainland.

In 1007 a party of Norse-Celtic settlers, led by Leif Ericson, make friendly contact with the "Skraelings" (the Norsemen's name for all people they encountered in North America). The Skraelings were described as swarthy and ugly, with coarse hair, large eyes, and broad cheeks. Friendly trading took place until the bellowing of a European bull frightened the natives and hostilities developed. Although the Scandinavians possessed metal weapons, the superior numbers of the Americans forced them to return to Greenland.

A number of Norse expeditions seem to have reached the Labrador–Nova Scotia area between 1007 and 1347 (when a ship was blown to Iceland after having sailed from Greenland to the North American mainland), and considerable fighting with the Skraelings is recorded. In the 1300's the Americans finally assumed the offensive and attacked the Scandinavians' "western settlement" in Greenland, destroying some ninety farms and three churches. The Norsemen tried to counterattack from their "eastern settlement" but could not locate the Skraelings.

The subsequent history of Greenland is shrouded in mystery. In 1448 Pope Nicholas V wrote that:

. . . about thirty years ago . . . a barbarous and pagan fleet from neighboring shores invaded the island [Greenland] laying waste the land with fire and sword, and destroying the sacred temples. Just nine parish churches [of fifteen] were left standing. . . . These churches are left intact, because being situated in the mountain fastnesses, they were inaccessible to the barbarian hordes, who, after completing their work of destruction, led captive to their shores the unfortunate inhabitants of both sexes, and more particularly those who seemed best able to bear the hardships of servitude and tyranny. But . . . many of these captives, after a time, returned to their native land.[2]

In the 1490's Pope Alexander VI deplored the fact that it had been eighty years since a vessel had touched at Greenland and that "we are informed" that the former Catholics, without any resident priest among them, had forgotten Christianity. A cleric was appointed Bishop of Greenland; however, he appears never to have reached his destination.[3] The Eskimo succeeded in conquering all of inhabited Greenland, and the Englishman John Davis found no Norsemen when he visited the area in 1585.

Thus the first European attempt to penetrate the Americas, although lasting some 400 years, ultimately failed. This failure is all the more surprising when one notes that during the same general period Norsemen succeeded in conquering large sections of Scotland, Ireland, and France, and that descendants of Norsemen conquered England and southern Italy. However, the northern Europeans were not yet technologically advanced and politically unified enough to overcome the Native Americans' numerical superiority in the latter's homeland.

The Second European Intrusion

At about the same time that Pope Alexander VI was appointing a bishop for Greenland, Christopher Columbus sailed westward to what he assumed was the coast of Asia. After reaching the Bahamas Columbus sailed along the coast of Cuba, where he:

found innumerable small villages and a numberless population, but nought of ruling authority. . . . I understood sufficiently from other Indians whom I had already taken (in the Bahamas), that this land. . . . was an island. . . .

Then they sailed eastward to Haiti, where

there is a population of incalculable number. . . . The people of this island, and of all the others that I have found and seen, or not seen, all go naked, man and woman, just as their mothers bring them forth; although some women cover a single place with a leaf of a plant, or a cotton something which they make for that purpose. They have no iron or steel, nor any weapons; nor are they fit thereunto; not because they be not a well-formed people and of fair stature, but that they are most wondrously timorous.

They have no other weapons than the stems of reeds in their seeding state, on the end of which they fix little sharpened stakes. Even these, they dare not use; for many times has it happened that I sent two or three men ashore to some village to parley, and countless numbers of them sallied forth, but as soon as they saw those approach, they fled away in such wise that even a father would not wait for his son. And this was not because any hurt had ever been done to any of them:—on the contrary, at every headland where I have gone and been able to hold speech with them, I gave them of everything which I had, as well cloth as many other things, without accepting aught therefor;—but such they are, incurably timid. It is true that since they have become more assured, and are losing that terror, they are artless and generous with what they have, to such a degree as no one would believe but him who had seen it. Of anything they have, if it be asked for, they never say no, but do rather invite the person to accept it, and show as much lovingness as though they would give their hearts. . . . And they knew no sect, nor idolatry; save that they all believe that power and goodness are in the sky, and they believed very firmly that I, with these ships and crews, came from the sky; and in such opinion, they received me at every place where I landed, after they had lost their terror. And this comes not because they are ignorant: on the contrary, they are men of very subtle wit, who navigate all those seas, and who give a marvelous good account of everything, but because they never saw men wearing clothes nor the like of our ships. And as soon as I arrived in the Indies, in the first island that I found, I took some of them by force, to the intent that they should learn [our speech] and give me information of what there was in those parts. . . . They have in all the islands very many canoas, after the manner of rowing-galleys, some larger, some smaller; and a good many are larger than a galley of eighteen benches. They are not so wide, because they are made of a single log of timber, but a galley could not keep up with them in rowing, for their motion is a thing beyond belief. And with these, they navigate through all those islands, which are numberless and ply their traffic. I have seen some of those canoas with seventy and eighty men in them, each one with his oar. In all those islands, I saw not much diversity in the looks of the people, nor in their manners and language. . . . Nor have I been able to learn whether they held personal property, for it seemed to me that whatever one had, they all took share of, especially of eatable things. Down to the present I have not found in those islands any monstrous men, as many expected, but on the contrary all the people are very comely; nor are they black like those in Guinea, but have flowing hair. . . . In another island, which they assure me is larger than Española, the people have no hair. In this there is incalculable gold; and concerning these and the rest I bring Indians with me as witnesses. . . . their Highnesses may see that I shall give them as much gold as they may need . . . and slaves as many as they shall order to be shipped,—and these shall be from idolators. . . .[4]

The Spaniards were eminently fitted for the conquest of the Americas. A warrior class had developed during the civil wars in Spain between Christians and Moslems, and under Ferdinand of Aragon the entire Iberian Peninsula, excepting Portugal, was unified. Thus Spaniards were able to proceed to the "new world" adequately armed with diverse military experiences, and backed by an aggressive, powerful state. Religious zeal and a great desire for wealth provided the psychological incentives necessary for the transference of Spanish authority.

The natives of the West Indies were for the most part a peaceful people who possessed no earthly way of resisting the designs of hardened European soldiers. Treated with great cruelty and attacked by new diseases, the Americans died in great numbers. For example, the population of Borinquén (Puerto Rico) declined from more than 200,000 in 1508 to 20,000 in 1511; and that of Haiti dropped from over 200,000 in 1492 to 60,000 in 1508 and 40,000 in 1509. Many committed suicide rather than serve as slaves, and mothers refused to have children, a reaction seen in other native groups under similar circumstances at a later date.

While the West Indies were being depopulated Spaniards began searching elsewhere for the legendary wealth of Asia. Various expeditions soon reached Florida, Panama, Yucatan and Mexico; and from the latter area new groups of adventurers set forth to locate still greater riches in what is now the United States. These conquistadores were told:

> You must explain to the natives of the land that there is only one God in heaven, and the emperor on earth to rule and govern it, whose subjects they must all become and whom they must serve.[5]

The Spaniards, therefore, never thought that the American natives had a right to self-determination and self-government. The Americans were to be brought under the authority of God and King, peacefully if possible, by the sword if necessary. There were no other alternatives.

Soon other Europeans began to reach North America, their goal being principally the area of Newfoundland. From the early sixteenth century onward this area was visited annually by Portuguese, English, French, and other vessels which engaged in fishing, fur-trading, and slave-gathering. This European invasion, although not so destructive initially as that of the Spanish, nevertheless had the effect of weakening the native population. By 1583, when Sir Humphrey Gilbert visited St. John's Harbor, he found no inhabitants, "which by all likelihood have abandoned these coasts, the same being so much frequented by Christians." [6]

Many of the Europeans who reached America in the sixteenth and early seventeenth centuries were men who could not have been expected to respect the rights of any native people; however, the more enlightened of their contemporaries were scarcely any more tolerant of alien societies. In 1583 Sir George Peckham, an advocate of English expansion, wrote:

that the "savages" are to be brought from falsehood to truth, from darkness to light, from the highway of death to the path of life, from superstitious idolatry to sincere Christianity, from the devel to Christ, from hell to heaven. . . . Beside the knowledge how to till and dress their ground, they shall be reduced from unseemly customs to honest manners, from disordered, riotous routs and companies to a well-governed commonwealth, and withal shall be taught mechanical occupations, arts, and liberal sciences.[7]

Peckham's interest in making Englishmen of Americans (for that is what he really had in mind) may have been laudable enough; however, his a priori condemnation of Native American culture reflects a continuing theme in European-American relations. Most Europeans and Euro-Americans, instead of attempting to "coexist" with native groups, have sought to forcibly alter the latter's way of life, a practice naturally conducive to hostile relations.

The first impressions made by Native Americans upon Englishmen who actually visited America were not unfavorable. In 1584, Arthur Barlow recorded the following on his visit to North Carolina:

The next day there came unto us divers boates, and in one of them the Kings brother, accompanied with fortie or fiftie men, very handsome and goodly people, and in their behaviour as mannerly and civil as any of Europe. His name was Granganimeo, and the king is called Wingina, the countrey Wingandacoa and now by her Majestie Virginia. The maner of his coming was in this sort: hee left his boates altogether as the first man did a little from the shippes by the shore, and came along to the place over against the shippes, followed with fortie men. When hee came to the place his servants spread a long matte upon the ground on which he sate downe, and at the other ende of the matte foure others of his companie did the like, the rest of his men stood round about him, somewhat a farr off: when wee came to the shore to him with our weapons, hee never mooved from his place, nor any of the other foure, nor never mistrusted any harme to be offred from us, but sitting still he beckoned us to come and sit by him, which wee performed: and being set hee made all signs of joy and welcome, striking on his head and his breast, and afterwardes on ours, to shew wee were all one, smiling and making shewe wee were all one, smiling and making shewe the best he could of all love, and familiaritie. . . .

A day or two after this, we fell to trading with them, exchanging some things that wee had, for Chamoys, Buffe, and Deere skinnes: when wee shewed him all our packet of merchandize, of all things that hee sawe, a bright tinne dish most pleased him, which hee presently tooke up and clapt it before his breast, and after made a hole in the brimme thereof and hung it about his necke, making signes that it would defende him against his enemies arrowes: for those people maintaine a deadly and terrible warre, with the people and King adjoyning: Wee exchanged our tinne dish for twentie skinnes, woorth twentie Crownes, or twentie Nobles: an a copper kettle for fiftie Crownes. They offered us good exchange for our hatchets and axes, and for knives and would have given any thing for swords: but wee would not depart with any. . . . They are of colour yellowish, and their hair black for the most part, and yet wee saw children that had very fine aburne and chestnut couloured haire.[8]

Given the anarchy of European affairs and the constant desire of Europeans to conquer and mistreat each other, it did not really make any appreciable difference whether Americans were as "mannerly and civil as any of Europe" or not. The aggressive tendencies of the age made conquest a normal feature of human existence, and the Americas, made up of a multitude of small, loosely organized, democratic or semi-democratic states, were ripe for the picking—or so it seemed. Thus commenced the long struggle between Redman and White, which was to change Europe as well as America.

Notes

1. Charles Morris and Oliver H. G. Leigh, eds., *The Great Republic* (New York: R. S. Belcher Co., 1902) Vol. I, pp. 14, 19-21. See also Gordon Elcholm, "Asia and North America—Transpacific Contacts," in *Memoirs of the Society for American Archaeology*, No. 9, 1953.
2. Letter of Nicholas V, 1448, in Julius E. Olson and Edward Gaylord Bourne, eds., *The Northmen, Columbus and Cabot, 985-1503*, in Early Narratives of American History Series (New York: Charles Scribner's Sons, 1906) pp. 73-4.
3. *Ibid.*, p. 74.
4. Letter from Columbus to Luis Santangel, *Ibid.*, pp. 264-270.
5. George P. Hammond and Agapito Rey, *Narratives of the Coronado Expedition, 1540-1542* (Albuquerque: University of New Mexico Press, 1940) p. 60. Reprinted by permission of the University of New Mexico Press.
6. J. A. Doyle, *English Colonies in America* (New York: Henry Holt and Co., 1882) Vol. I, p. 50.
7. *Ibid.*, p. 54.
8. Arthur Barlow's Narrative, in Olson and Bourne, *op. cit.*, pp. 230-233.

TWO

THE EUROPEAN SEES THE NATIVE

The "image" that the members of one ethnic group come to have of members of another ethnic group is very important in understanding confrontations of the two groups. If a certain image comes to dominate the thinking of one group about the other, it may lead to the development of attitudes and policies that are based wholly or in part upon mythology rather than reality. And if the image is a derogatory one it may lead to actions that are damaging to the people to whom it is applied.

As the following selections will show, the first Europeans in America possessed no single "image" of the Native American. Nevertheless, later —especially in the minds of the Anglo-American masses—a stereotype of the "Redskin" as a savage, cruel, and almost irredeemable enemy became very strong. True, this image was often partially offset in those areas removed from actual confrontation by the stereotype of the native as a "noble of the forest"; however, this viewpoint was apparently effective only at the literary and intellectual level and was seldom applied to a living Indian. Thus, many easterners in the nineteenth century developed a real sympathy for "book" Indians, but this did not appreciably alter the actual treatment of the remnants of eastern native groups, nor did it really ameliorate conditions on the western frontier, where actual warfare and conquest were then in progress and where the negative image of the native dominated.

In more recent times Anglo-American attitudes have become more complex, but in general the image of the native as a "noxious savage" has become less prevalent. Attitudes at present range from viewing the native as a lazy and backward incompetent to seeing him as the noble creator of a rich and valuable culture, with most Anglo-Americans possessing an ambiguous set of images largely determined by motion pictures and other mass media.

The image of Native Americans of Mexican origin in many regions, such as California, is usually more derogatory than that of the Tribal American (this varies, of course, among individuals). Thus a young pupil of Navaho ancestry in Los Angeles suffered from discrimination because he was mistaken for a Mexican-American, but as soon as his Anglo-American teacher and fellow pupils learned he was a Navaho their attitude changed and discrimination ceased. An appreciable number of natives of Mexican origin and Eurindians have gained some relief by posing as Spanish-Americans (Hispanos) or by referring to themselves as Latin Americans. A very few others have sought to cultivate their Aztec, Mayan, or other indigenous background, thus improving the image that they present to their Anglo-American associates. Needless to say, the second approach is probably the more healthy one, since it is based upon an affirmation of real ancestry rather than upon an escape through a false or misleading statement of ancestry (such as calling oneself "Spanish").

In the final analysis, it is not possible to generalize meaningfully about the ways in which Europeans and Euro-Americans have visualized the Native American; however, the selections that follow should provide some insight into the subject.

FIRST VIEWS—A DIVISION OF OPINION

Very early in the period of European expansion contrary views of the character of the Native American developed. Of the two selections that appear below, the first records a favorable view of the aborigines, while the second is very unfavorable. It is interesting to note that the former was based upon firsthand contact with natives, and the latter was based upon hearsay.

Arthur Barlow, 1584

The Englishman who accompanied Barlow and Philip Amidas to Roanoke, North Carolina found the natives to be:

◆◆ . . . as mannerly and civil as any in Europe. The English were entertained with all love and kindness, and with as much bountie (after their manner) as they possibly could devise. . . . we found the people most gentle, loving, and faithful, void of all guile and treason, and such as live after the manner of the golden age.[1] ◆◆

William Bradford, 1617

When the English Puritans in the Netherlands decided to leave that country:

◆◆ The place they had thoughts on was some of those vast and unpeopled countries of America, which are fruitfull and fitt for habitation, being devoid of all civill inhabitants, wher ther are only salvage and brutish men, which range up and downe, little otherwise then the wild beasts of the same. . . . [They would, however,] be in continuall danger of ye salvage people, who are cruell, barbarous, and most trecherous, being most furious in their rage, and merciles wher they overcome; not being contente only to kill, and take away life, but delight to tormente men in ye most bloodie manner that may be; fleaing some alive . . . , cutting of ye members and joynts of others by pees-meale, and broiling on ye coles, eate ye collops of their flesh in their sight whilst they live; with other cruelties horrible to be related.[2] ◆◆

Three years prior to their arrival at Plymouth, therefore, the Pilgrims had already acquired a collection of antinative prejudices based upon hearsay. What might be termed "the Calvinistic view" of the "Tawny Devil" was, then, not a product of actual contact (at least not initially). Regarding the natives as "brutes" and "savages," as they did, the Pilgrims could hardly have failed to eventually obtain responses that would serve to confirm their biases; and this is especially true since the Englishmen refused to allow their friendships with "good Indians" to subvert the image of the native as a "Tawny Serpent" of the Devil. It should be noted here that many devout European Christians, both Calvinist and Catholic, actually believed that the American natives were worshiping Satan when they prayed to their own deities. As devil-worshipers the natives were hardly worthy of consideration by the Calvinists. The Catholic response, not based upon the doctrine of predestination, was of course quite different.

THE NEGATIVE APPROACH: NATIVES AS SAVAGES AND ENEMIES

Father Luis Velarde, ca. 1716

The following was written by a Jesuit missionary in northern Sonora; in it, Father Velarde betrays a tendency to value Spanish imperial interests above Christian brotherhood.

◆◆ And truly it has been due to the particular providence of our Lord, that this nation [the friendly Pimas of Arizona-Sonora] has been diminished due to continuous epidemics; for because of their pride there are not lacking among them people who are restless and troublesome.[3] ◆◆

An anonymous Franciscan, 1769

To this Franciscan the natives of California in 1769, when the Spaniards first established themselves there, were:

◆◆ . . . without religion, or government, [having] nothing more than diverse superstitions and a type of democracy similar to
that of ants. Each village recognizes a leader [whom they obey very
little]. From this [stem] their continuous debates and factions.[4] ◆◆

The Spanish priests, coming as they did from an authoritarian society,
were much opposed to the democratic tendencies of most Native American groups. Fray Pedro Font (1775) commented that "since the Indians
[of the Colorado River] are so free and live so like animals and without
civilization" they do not obey their leaders.[5]

Mrs. D. B. Bates, 1851

Mrs. Bates, a new arrival in California from New England, apparently
expected to meet James Fenimore Cooper Indians in California. Instead,
she met natives near Yuba City who had been in steady contact with
European influences for many years and who had suffered from epidemics, warfare, and loss of land.

◆◆ It is universally conceded that the California Indians
possess but few, if any, of those nobly daring traits of character which
have distinguished the savage tribes of the Atlantic States. . . . The
extreme indolence of their nature, the squalid condition in which they
live, the pusillanimity of their sports, and the general imbecility of their
intellects, render them rather objects of contempt than admiration.[6] ◆◆

Louise Clappe, 1852

Louise Clappe voiced similar sentiments about the natives of northeastern California:

◆◆ Viewed in the most favorable manner, these poor
creatures are miserably brutish and degraded, having very little in common with the lofty and eloquent aborigines of the United States. It is
said that their entire language contains but about twenty words.[7] ◆◆

Frederick Law Olmsted, 1856

In South Texas Olmsted came upon a camp of Lipan Apaches with
a few Mescaleros and Tonkawas:

◆◆ Here . . . was nothing but the most miserable
squalor, foul obscenity, and disgusting brutishness, if there be excepted
the occasional evidence of a sly and impish keenness. We could not find

even one man of dignity; the universal expression towards us was either a silly leer or a stupid indifference. . . . The faces of both sexes were hideously streaked with paint, the features very course, nose large, and cheek-bones particularly prominent. . . .[8] ◆◆

Near the Brazos River Olmsted met an Anglo-Texan and they discussed the possibility that the United States might acquire additional Mexican territory. The Texan then said:

◆◆   Mexico! What the hell do we want of it? It isn't worth a cuss. The people are as bigoted and ignorant as the devil's grandchildren. They haven't even the capacities of my black boy [Negro slave]. Why, they're most as black as niggers any way, and ten times as treacherous. . . . You go any further into Mexico with your surveyor's chains, and you'll get Mexicans along with your territory; and a dam'd lot of 'em too. What are you going to do with 'em? You can't drive them out, because there ain't nowhere to drive 'em. No, sir! There they've got to stay, and it'll be fifty year before you can out vote 'em.[9] ◆◆

Charles Maclaren (Fellow of the Royal Society, Edinburgh), 1875

◆◆   The indigenous population of America presents man under many aspects, and society in various stages, from the regular but limited civilization of Mexico and Peru, to savage life in its most brutal state of abasement. . . . The intellectual faculties of this great family appear to be decidedly inferior, when compared with those of the Caucasian or Mongolian race. The Americans are not only averse to the restraints of education but are for the most part incapable of a continued process of reasoning on abstract subjects. . . . Their inventive and imitative faculties appear to be of very humble capacity, nor have they the smallest taste for the arts and sciences.[10] ◆◆

During the 1880's "friend" and foe alike seemed to share a similar view of native character. In 1881 General John Pope asserted, "It is idle to talk of civilizing the Mescalero Apaches. They are savages, pure and simple."[11]

J. B. Harrison, 1881

Six years later, J. B. Harrison in his "The Latest Studies on Indian Reservations" (published by the Indian Rights Association) stated: "The Indians as a race are, of course, far inferior to white men in intellectual capacity."[12]

Frederick Schwatka, 1891

This military explorer in Alaska said in a similar vein: "The Innuits' [Eskimos'] . . . intelligence is of a low order and the race is apparently diminishing. . . ." [13]

Captain J. Lee Humfreville (an officer in the United States Army), 1897

◆◆ Our savage Indians had no idea of the ownership of land, either individually or collectively. . . . The idea propagated by some modern sentimentalists that in resisting the march of civilization the wild Indians were fighting for their homes and firesides belongs to fiction rather than to fact. . . . they had no home and no fireside, in the civilized sense of these terms.

Like all other savage people, his [the Indian's] intellectual gifts were limited. . . . There was in the Indian nature a trait of intractability not found in any other portion of the human race. . . . [He has shown] himself incapable of even a veneer of civilization. He might be brought up in the midst of civilized surroundings and educated, but at the first opportunity he would relapse into his original barbarism.

Coupled with his barbarous instincts . . . was his natural inclination to cruelty. It has been truly said that all savage races are like children, in that they have no adequate conception of suffering or pain suffered by others. They were entirely devoid of sympathy. The controlling instinct of the Indian was to kill.

It may seem strange that a people so vicious and murderous should pray,—nevertheless the custom obtained among nearly all Indians. . . . The Indian could hardly be said to have possessed any moral nature. In the first place, he had no abstract ideas. He could understand nothing unless it appeared to him in the concrete. There were no words in his language to express moral ideas. . . . He was naturally distrustful. . . . Of all the savage races the Indian was the only one who never tried to imitate the white man. . . . Any one knowing his character would not trust him in any way. . . . He was the very impersonation of duplicity. . . . Occasionally, it is true, the Indian evinced some commendable traits of character. But these were the exception to the rule.

It is difficult to place the Indian intellectually. Other savage races when brought within the environment of civilization have afforded brilliant instances of individual effort, but the Indian never. . . . He was animal in his instincts, and he neither knew nor cared about anything not connected with his material wants. . . . In conversation, . . . all Indians were obscene to a degree unknown to any other people. They seemed to have no conception of vulgarity, obscenity, or decency. . . .

Morality, as we understand it, was unknown among them. Having no conception of right and wrong, murder was not considered a crime. . . . All Indians are lazy and thievish, work being considered degrading. . . . vindictiveness and ferocity . . . is a part of Indian nature.[14] ◆◆

Commissioner of Indian Affairs, W. A. Jones, 1903

◆◆ It is probably true that the majority of our wild Indians have no inherited tendencies whatever toward morality or chastity, according to an enlightened standard. Chastity and morality among them must come from education and contact with the better element of the whites.[15] ◆◆

THE POSITIVE APPROACH: THE NATIVE AS A PERSON

The examples of a positive approach to the native American presented here vary from selections that attempt to treat the native simply as an ordinary human being to extremely laudatory passages. The reader will also note that many of these selections contradict assertions presented in the previous section.

Benjamin Franklin, 1784

◆◆ Savages we call them, because their manners differ from ours, which we think the perfection of civility, they think the same of theirs. . . . Our laborious manner of life, compared with theirs, they esteem slavish and base; and the learning, on which we value ourselves, they regard as frivolous and useless.[16] ◆◆

Thomas Jefferson, 1785

◆◆ . . . I am safe in affirming that the proofs of genius given by the Indians of North America place them on a level with whites in the same uncultivated state. The North of Europe furnishes subjects enough for comparison with them, and for a proof of their equality, I have seen some thousands myself, and conversed much with them, and have found in them a masculine, sound understanding. . . . I believe the Indian to be in body and mind equal to the white man.[17] ◆◆

Governor Pedro Fages of California, 1787

◆◆ It is well-known to all of the first discoverers of this country, and to those who have come since, that the Indians located from this place [Ventura] as far as the mission of San Luis [Obispo] have a type of civility and manners that has not been observed in the rest. They are bright, hard workers, and from particular industries it can be said that [they] are of a quality midway between gente de razon [hispanicized persons] and the other Indians.[18] ♦♦

Alexander Ross, 1811

♦♦ The Oakinacken [Okanagan] Indians of Washington . . . are a sedate and docile people, and very susceptible of improvement, and could, with comparatively little trouble, I am confident, be brought round to a state of civilization. Their superstitions seem to be the only barrier between them and the attainment of a more refined state.[19] ♦♦

John D. Hunter (who resided among several tribes for many years), 1823

♦♦ . . . no doubt remains in my mind, if we average the perfections and imperfections, that the Indians will bear a comparison in their physical conditions, with any other great division of the human family. . . . they display, according to the opportunities presented by circumstances and modes of their lives, as great energy of mental powers . . . as any other people ever have. . . . In reasoning, their judgement and perceptions are clear and quick, and their arguments ingenious and cogent. They resort much to figures, which are generally poetic, bold, and appropriate . . . and their orators [are] far more numerous, in proportion to numbers, than is common among any class of people on the globe. . . . But enough, in my opinion, has been said on the subject, to convince all unprejudiced and reflecting minds; and for those who think differently, if volumes were to be written in support of this position it is probable their opinions would remain unaltered.[20] ♦♦

George Catlin, 1832-1839

Catlin, a remarkable man for his day, traveled extensively among the natives of the central United States and Florida painting portraits of leading persons for his gallery of the North American Indian. As the following selection shows, in addition to being an artist he was a social scientist and anthropologist even before this discipline had appeared on the scholarly scene in the United States.

♦♦ The Indians (as I shall call them), the savages or red men of the forests and prairies of North America, are at this time a subject of great interest and some importance to the civilised nations of the earth. A numerous nation of human beings, whose origin is beyond the reach of human investigation,—whose early history is lost—whose term of national existence is nearly expired—three-fourths of whose country has fallen into the possession of civilised man within the short space of 250 years—twelve millions of whose bodies have fattened the soil in the meantime; who have fallen victims to whiskey, the small-pox and the bayonet; leaving at this time but a meagre proportion to live a short time longer, in the certain apprehension of soon sharing a similar fate. . . .

The world know generally, that the Indians of North America are copper-colored, that their eyes and their hair are black, etc.; that they are mostly uncivilised, and consequently unchristianised; that they are nevertheless human beings, with features, thoughts, reason, and sympathies like our own. . . .

The Indians of North American . . . —are less than two millions in number—were originally the undisputed owners of the soil, and got their title to their lands from the Great Spirit who created them on it,—were once a happy and flourishing people, enjoying all the comforts and luxuries of life which they knew of, and consequently cared for;—were sixteen millions in numbers, and sent that number of daily prayers to the Almighty, and thanks for His goodness and protection. Their country entered by white men, but a few hundred years since; and thirty millions of these are now scuffing for the goods and luxuries of life, over the bones and ashes of twelve millions of red men; six millions of whom have fallen victims to the small-pox, and the remainder to the sword, the bayonet, and whiskey; all of which means of their death and destruction have been introduced and visited upon them by acquisitive white men; and by white men, also whose forefathers were welcomed and embraced in the land where the poor Indian met and fed them with "ears of green corn and with pemican." Of the two millions remaining alive at this time, about 1,400,000 are already the miserable living victims and dupes of white man's cupidity, degraded, discouraged, and lost in the bewildering maze that is produced by the use of whiskey and its concomitant vices; and the remaining number are yet unroused and unenticed from their wild haunts or their primitive modes, by the dread or love of white man and his allurements.

It has been with these, mostly, that I have spent my time, and of these, chiefly, and their customs, that the following Letters treat. Their habits (and theirs alone) as we can see them transacted, are native, and such as I have wished to fix and preserve for future ages. . . .

The reader . . . should forget many theories he has read in the books of Indian barbarities, of wanton butcheries and murders; and divest himself, as far as possible, of the deadly prejudices which he has carried from his childhood, against this most unfortunate and most abused part of the race of his fellow-man.

He should consider, that if he has seen the savages of North America without making such a tour, he has fixed his eyes upon and drawn his conclusions (in all probability) only from those who inhabit the frontier; whose habits have been changed—whose pride has been cut down—whose country has been ransacked—whose wives and daughters have been shamefully abused—whose lands have been wrested from them—whose limbs have become enervated and naked by the excessive use of whiskey—whose friends and relations have been prematurely thrown into their graves—whose native pride and dignity have at last given way to the unnatural vices which civilised cupidity has engrafted upon them, to be silently nurtured and magnified by a burning sense of injury and injustice, and ready for that cruel vengeance which often falls from the hand that is palsied by refined abuses, and yet unrestrained by the glorious influences of refined and moral cultivation.—That if he has laid up, what he considers well-founded knowledge of these people, from books which he has read, and from newspapers only, he should pause at least, and withhold his sentence before he passes it upon the character of a people, who are dying at the hands of their enemies, without the means of recording their own annals—struggling in their nakedness with their simple weapons, against guns and gunpowder—against whiskey and steel, and disease, and mailed warriors who are continually trampling them to the earth, and at last exultingly promulgating from the very soil which they have wrested from the poor savage, the history of his cruelties and barbarities, whilst his bones are quietly resting under the very furrows which their ploughs are turning.

So great and unfortunate are the disparities between savage and civil, in numbers—in weapons and defences—in enterprise, in craft, and in education, that the former is almost universally the sufferer either in peace or in war; and not less so after his pipe and his tomahawk have retired to the grave with him, and his character is left to be entered upon the pages of history, and that justice done to this memory which, from necessity, he has entrusted to his enemy. . . .

Some writers, I have been grieved to see, have written down the character of the North American Indian, as dark, relentless, cruel and murderous in the last degree; with scarce a quality to stamp his existence of a higher order than that of the brutes:—whilst others have given them a high rank, as I feel myself authorised to do, as honourable and highly-intellectual beings; and others, both friends and foes to the red man, have spoken of them as an "anomaly in nature"! . . .

From what I have seen of these people I feel authorised to say, that there is nothing very strange or unaccountable in their character; but that it is a simple one, and easy to be learned and understood, if the right means be taken to familiarise ourselves with it. Although it has its dark spots; yet there is much in it to be applauded, and much to recommend it to the admiration of the enlightened world. And I trust that the reader, who looks through these volumes with care, will be disposed to join me in the conclusion: that the North American Indian in his native state is an honest, hospitable, faithful, brave, warlike, cruel, revengeful, relentless,—yet honourable, contemplative and religious being. . . .

I am fully convinced, from a long familiarity with these people, that the Indian's misfortune has consisted chiefly in our ignorance of their true native character and disposition, which has always held us at a distrustful distance from them; inducing us to look upon them in no other light than that of a hostile foe, and worthy only of the system of continued warfare and abuse that has been for ever waged against them.

There is no difficulty in approaching the Indian and getting acquainted with him in his wild and unsophisticated state, and finding him an honest and honourable man; with feelings to meet feelings, if the above prejudice and dread can be laid aside, and any one will take the pains, as I have done, to go and see him in the simplicity of his native state, smoking his pipe under his own humble roof, with his wife and children around him, and his faithful dogs and horses hanging about his hospitable tenement.—So the world may see him and smoke his friendly pipe, which is invariably extended to them; and share, with a hearty welcome, the best that his wigwam affords for the appetite, which is always set out to a stranger the next moment after he enters.

But so the mass of the world most assuredly will not see these people; for they are too far off, and approachable to those only whose avarice or cupidity alone lead them to those remote regions, and whose shame prevents them from publishing to the world the virtues which they have thrown down and trampled under foot. . . .

I have roamed about from time to time during seven or eight years, visiting and associating with some three or four hundred thousand of these people, under an almost infinite variety of circumstances; and from the very many and decided voluntary acts of their hospitality and kindness, I feel bound to pronounce them, by nature, a kind and hospitable people. I have been welcomed generally in their country, and treated to the best that they could give me, without any charges made for my board; they have often escorted me through their enemies' country at some hazard to their own lives, and aided me in passing mountains and rivers with my awkward baggage; and under all of these circumstances of exposure, no Indian ever betrayed me, struck me a blow, or stole from me a shilling's worth of my property that I am aware of.

This is saying a great deal (and proving it too, if the reader will believe me) in favor of the virtues of these people; when it is borne in mind, as it should be, that there is no law in their land to punish a man for theft—that the commandments have never been divulged amongst them; nor can any human retribution fall upon the head of a thief, save the disgrace which attaches as a stigma to his character, in the eyes of his people about him.

And thus in these little communities, strange as it may seem, in the absence of all systems of jurisprudence, I have often beheld peace and happiness and quiet, reigning supreme, for which even kings and emperors might envy them. I have seen rights and virtue protected, and wrongs redressed; and I have seen conjugal, filial and paternal affection in the simplicity and contentedness of nature. I have, unavoidably, formed warm and enduring attachments to some of these men which I do not wish to forget—who have brought me near to their hearts, and in our final separation have embraced me in their arms, and commended me and my affairs to the keeping of the Great Spirit. . . .

I cannot help but repeat, before I close this Letter, that the tribes of the red man of North America, as a nation of human beings, are on their wane; that (to use their own very beautiful figure) "they are fast travelling to the shades of their fathers, towards the setting sun;" and that the traveller, who would see these people in their native simplicity and beauty, must needs be hastily on his way to the prairies and Rocky Mountains, or he will see them only as they are now seen on the frontiers, as the basket of dead game,—harassed, chased, bleeding and dead; with their plumage and colors despoiled, to be gazed amongst in vain for some system or moral, or for some scale by which to estimate their true native character, other than that which has too often recorded them; but a dark and unintelligible mass of cruelty and barbarity. . . .

Of the dead, to speak kindly, and to their character to render justice, is always a praise worthy act; but it is yet far more charitable to extend the hand of liberality, or to hold the scale of justice, to the living, who are able to feel the benefit of it. Justice to the dead is generally a charity, inasmuch as it is a kindness to living friends; but to the poor Indian dead, if it is meted out at all, which is seldom the case, it is thrown to the grave with him, where he has generally gone without friends left behind him to inherit the little fame that is reluctantly allowed him while living, and much less likely to be awarded to him when dead. Of the thousands and millions, therefore, of these poor fellows who are dead, and whom we have thrown into their graves, there is nothing that I could now say, that would do them any good, or that would not answer the world as well at a future time as at the present; while there is a debt that we are owing to those of them who are yet living, which I think justly demands our attention, and all our sympathies at this moment. . . .

If the great family of North American Indians were all dying by a scourge or epidemic of the country, it would be natural, and a virtue, to weep for them; but merely to sympathise with them (and but partially to do that) when they are dying at our hands, and rendering their glebe to our possession, would be to subvert the simplest law of Nature, and turn civilised man, with all his boasted virtues, back to worse than savage barbarism.

Justice to a nation who are dying, need never be expected from the hands of their destroyers; and where injustice and injury are visited upon the weak and defenceless, from ten thousand hands—from Governments —monopolies and individuals—the offence is lost in the inseverable iniqıity in which all join, and for which nobody is answerable, unless it be or their respective amounts, at a final day of retribution. . . .

For their government, which is purely such as has been dictated to hem by nature and necessity alone, they are indebted to no foreign, naive or civilised nation. For their religion, which is simply Theism, they are indebted to the Great Spirit, and not to the Christian world. For their modes of war, they owe nothing to enlightened nations—using only those weapons, and those modes which are prompted by nature, and within the means of their rude manufactures. . . .

As I have in a former place said, cruelty is one of the leading traits of the Indian's character; and a little familiarity with their modes of life and government will soon convince the reader, that certainty and cruelty in punishments are requisite (where individuals undertake to inflict the penalties of the laws), in order to secure the lives and property of individuals in society.

In the treatment of their prisoners also, in many tribes, they are in the habit of inflicting the most apalling tortures, for which the enlightened world are apt to condemn them as cruel and unfeeling in the extreme; without stopping to learn that in every one of these instances, these cruelties are practised by way of retaliation, by individuals or families of the tribe, whose relatives have been previously dealt with in a similar way by their enemies, and whose manes they deem it their duty to appease by this horrid and cruel mode of retaliation.

And in justice to the savage, the reader should yet know, that amongst these tribes that torture their prisoners, these cruelties are practised but upon the few whose lives are required to atone for those who have been similarly dealt with by their enemies, and that the remainder are adopted into the tribe, by marrying the widows whose husbands have fallen in battle, in which capacity they are received and respected like others of the tribe, and enjoy equal rights and immunities. And before we condemn them too far, we should yet pause and inquire whether in the enlightened world we are not guilty of equal cruelties—whether in the ravages and carnage of war, and treatment of prisoners, we practise any virtue superior to this; and whether the annals of history which are familiar to all, do not furnish abundant proof of equal cruelty to prisoners of war, as well as in many instances, to the members of our own respective communities. It is a remarkable fact, and one well recorded in history, as it deserves to be, to the honour of the savage, that no instance has been known of violence to their captive females, a virtue yet to be learned in civilised warfare.

If their punishments are certain and cruel, they have the merit of being few, and those confined chiefly to their enemies. It is natural to be cruel to enemies; and in this, I do not see that the improvements of the enlightened and Christian world have yet elevated them so very much above the savage. To their friends, there are no people on earth that are

more kind; and cruelties and punishments (except for capital offences)
are amongst themselves entirely dispensed with. No man in their com
munities is subject to any restraints upon his liberty, or to any corpora
or degrading punishment; each one valuing his limbs, and his liberty to
use them as his inviolable right, which no power in the tribe can deprive
him of; whilst each one holds the chief as amenable to him as the mos
humble individual in the tribe.

On an occasion when I had interrogated a Sioux chief, on the Upper
Missouri, about their government—their punishments and tortures of
prisoners, for which I had freely condemned them for the cruelty of the
practice, he took occasion when I had got through, to ask me some ques
tions relative to modes in the civilised world, which, with his comment
upon them, were nearly as follow; and struck me, as I think they mus
every one, with great force.

> "Among white people, nobody ever take your wife—take your children—take
> your mother—cut off nose—cut eyes out—burn to death?" No! "Then you no
> cut off nose—you no cut out eyes—you no burn to death—very good."

He also told me he had often heard that white people hung their crimi
nals by the neck and choked them to death like dogs, and those their
own people; to which I answered, "yes." He then told me he had learned
that they shut each other up in prisons, where they keep them a grea
part of their lives because they can't pay money! I replied in the affirma
tive to this, which occasioned great surprise and excessive laughter, even
amongst the women. He told me that he had been to our Fort, at Coun
cil Bluffs, where we had a great many warriors and braves, and he saw
three of them taken out on the prairies and tied to a post and whipped
almost to death, and he had been told that they submit to all this to ge
a little money. "Yes."

He said he had been told, that when all the white people were born
their white medicine-men had to stand by and look on—that in the In
dian country the women would not allow that—they would be ashamed
—that he had been along the Frontier, and a good deal amongst the
white people, and he had seen them whip their little children—a thing
that was very cruel—he had heard also, from several white medicine-men
that the Great Spirit of the white people was the child of a white woman
and that he was at last put to death by the white people! This seemed to
be a thing that he had not been able to comprehend, and he concluded
by saying, "The Indians' Great Spirit got no mother—the Indians no
kill him, he never die." He put me a chapter of other questions, as to
the trespasses of the white people on their lands—their continual corrup
tion of the morals of their women—and digging open the Indian's grave
to get their bones, etc. To all of which I was compelled to reply in the
affirmative, and quite glad to close my note-book, and quietly to escape

from the throng that had collected around me, and saying (though to myself and silently), that these and a hundred other vices belong to the civilised world, and are practised upon (but certainly, in no instance, reciprocated by) the "cruel and relentless savage." . . .

To each other I have found these people kind and honourable, and endowed with every feeling of parental, of filial, and conjugal affection, that is met in more enlightened communities. I have found them moral and religous; and I am bound to give them great credit for their zeal, which is often exhibited in their modes of worship, however insufficient they may seem to us, or may be in the estimation of the Great Spirit.

I have heard it said by some very good men, and some who have been preaching the Christian religion amongst them, that they have no religion—that all their zeal in their worship of the Great Spirit was but the foolish excess of ignorant superstition—that their humble devotions and supplications to the Sun and the Moon, where many of them suppose that the Great Spirit resides, were but the absurd rantings of idolatry. To such opinions as these I never yet gave answer, nor drew other instant inferences from them, than, that from the bottom of my heart, I pitied the persons who gave them.

I fearlessly assert to the world (and I defy contradiction), that the North American Indian is everywhere, in his native state, a highly moral and religious being, endowed by his Maker with an intuitive knowledge of some great Author of his being, and the Universe; in dread of whose displeasure he constantly lives, with the apprehension before him, of a future state, where he expects to be rewarded or punished according to the merits he has gained or forfeited in this world. . . .

Morality and virtue, I venture to say, the civilised world need not undertake to teach them; . . .

Of their extraordinary modes and sincerity of worship, I speak with equal confidence; and although I am compelled to pity them for their ignorance, I am bound to say that I never saw any other people of any colour, who spend so much of their lives in humbling themselves before, and worshipping the Great Spirit, as some of these tribes do, nor any whom I would not as soon suspect of insincerity and hypocrisy.

Self-denial, which is comparatively a word of no meaning in the enlightened world; and self-torture and almost self-immolation, are continual modes of appealing to the Great Spirit for his countenance and forgiveness; and these, not in studious figures of rhetoric, re-sounding in halls and synagogues, to fill and astonish the ears of the multitude; but humbly cried forth from starved stomachs and parched throats, from some lone and favourite haunts, where the poor penitents crawl and lie with their faces in the dirt from day to day, and day to day sobbing forth their humble confessions of their sins, and their earnest implorations for Divine forgiveness and mercy.[21] ◆ ◆

28   THE EUROPEAN SEES THE NATIVE

Lt. A. W. Whipple, 1849

◆◆ They [the Quechan or Yuma Indians] are a noble race, well formed, active and intelligent. . . . To this day, among the Yumas, I have never seen anger expressed by word or action, nor known of one of their women to be harshly treated; they are sprightly, full of life, of gaiety and good humor.²² ◆◆

Carl Meyer (an educated Swiss traveler), 1851

◆◆ The Allequas [Yuroks of Trinidad, California] seemed to me to be the most beautiful and intelligent Indians of California. . . . Although the Allequa has no knowledge of morals in the abstract he practices a strict moral code by harmonizing his life with nature. He is slightly conscious of having this advantage in life over civilization. That is why he has such a bad opinion of the whites whom he calls "palefaces" or "weak ones" because of the color of their skins. . . . Contemptuously he and his wife punish the bold, lewd "palefaces." A dark red blush covers the cheeks of the maiden when the white man makes his lewd jokes about her naked body and stares lustfully at her. . . .
The Americans . . . wished to have nothing to do with the Indians, saying that they are not human. . . . Therefore the Indian hates the American, yes he despises him. . . . He has learned to consider the Americans the worst of all as they have been the most heartless to him. . . . I saw with my own eyes how the Americans stole their wives and daughters and treated them like slaves, how they brutally forced the men to serve as guides and burden-bearers.²³ ◆◆

Franklin A. Buck, 1852

◆◆ There is a large rancheria of Indians here [at Colusa in California] and, in fact, there are more Indians than whites in the place. . . . These are the best specimens of the Diggers to be seen in the country. They are all clothed and the men work discharging the boats and the girls are employed as servants in the Public Houses and they do first-rate. At Hall's Ranch they wait on the table and are clean and neat. . . . The Mountain Diggers are another race, perfectly wild and untamable. . . . They waylay and murder all they can and the whites shoot every Indian that shows himself. A short time ago they killed a Mr. Anderson from this place, close by town. A party of men went out, discovered the rancheria, surrounded it and killed 140 Indians. They brought in one squaw and a little boy. Their destiny is to be exterminated.
[At Weaverville] The poor Indians have been treated with great

cruelty, I always thought, by our forefathers at home, but they have been killed off in this State like some wild animals, without the slightest cause and driven to actual starvation. Moreover, these Indians in the mountains are not so mean a race as those in the valley. They are larger and possess more intelligence and are easier civilized than any other Indians I have ever seen. There are five boys in town who are as bright and smart as any white boys. Enough said about the Diggers.[24] ◆◆

George Bird Grinnell (a sympathetic student of the Plains Indians), 1888

◆◆ Few and rapidly diminishing in numbers as are the Pawnee people, I have yet confidence that by the innate strength of their character their decline may be checked, and their race may rise again. It can never do so in its old purity. It must take to itself fresh blood from other stocks, and thus renew its vitality. What I hope for the Pawnee, to-day and in the future, is that the native vigor of the race, the strong heart and singleness of purpose, which in ancient times led the wild brave to success on his warpath, and gave his tribe so high a place among the savage warriors of the plains, may now be exercised in the pursuits of peace; and that the same qualities may give to these earnest toilers, as they tread new paths, strength, courage, and endurance to hold a front rank among those Indians, who, to-day so far behind, are nevertheless resolutely setting their steps toward a place with civilized people.

But whatever the fate of the Pawnee people—whether, like so many other native stocks, it shall dwindle away and disappear, leaving behind it no reminder of its existence, or whether its native force shall enable it under its new conditions to survive and make some mark—we may remember it always as a race of strong, brave people, whose good qualities are deserving for more than a passing tribute.

It was the last day of my stay at the Pawnee agency. I had seen many an old friend; had laughed and joked with some over incidents of former years, and with others had mourned over brave warriors or wise old men who were no longer with us. My visit had been full of pleasure, and yet full of pain. When I had first known the tribe [1870] it numbered more than three thousand people, now there are only a little more than eight hundred of them. The evidences of their progress toward civilization are cheering. They are now self-supporting. They no longer die of hunger. But the character of the people has changed. In the old barbaric days they were light-hearted, merry makers of jokes, keenly alive to the humorous side of life. Now they are serious, grave, little disposed to laugh. Then they were like children without a care. Now they are like men, on whom the anxieties of life weigh heavily. Civilization, bringing with it some measure of material prosperity, has also brought to these people

care, responsibility, repression. No doubt it is best, and it is inevitable,
but it is sad, too.[25]   ◆◆

Ernest Thompson Seton and Julia M. Seton, 1937

Seton was a naturalist and student of the Native American. His interest
in the outdoor "lore" of the Indian has exercised a great influence on
American youth through the Woodcraft Rangers, Boy Scouts and other
organizations.

          ◆◆   The Civilization of the Whiteman is a failure; it is
visibly crumbling around us. It has failed at every crucial test. No one
who measures things by results can question this fundamental statement.
      Apparently, the money-madness is the main cause of it all. We know
that such a thing was unknown among the Indians. Their big menace
was failure of food supply, and against this they prepared by a storage
plan that was effectual.
      What is Civilization? Literally, it is a system by which men can live
in a large group (a city, or *civitas*) and enjoy all the benefits without
suffering the evils that result from such association. . . .
      How are we going to appraise the value of a Civilization? By certain
yard measures that are founded on human nature, and which remorse-
lessly investigate the fundamentals of the man-mind and the man-needs.
      First of these is: Does your Civilization guarantee to you absolute free-
dom of action so long as you do not encroach on the equal right of your
neighbour to do the same thing?
      Does your system work for the greatest happiness of the greatest num-
ber?
      Is your Civilization characterized by justice in the courts and gentle-
ness in the streets?
      Are its largest efforts to relieve suffering and misery?
      Does your Civilization grant to every individual the force and rights of
humanhood?
      Does your system guarantee absolute freedom of religion?
      Is everyone in your community guaranteed food, shelter, protection,
dignity, so long as your group has these things in its gift?
      Does your system guarantee the tribal control of tribal interests?
      Does your system guarantee to each man one vote; but so much in-
fluence as his character can command?
      Does your system guarantee to each man the product of his industry?
      Does your system accept the fact that material things are of doubtful
or transient value, that the things of the spirit are all that are enduring
and worth while?
      Does your system set larger value on kindness than on rigorous justice?

Does your system discourage large material possessions in one man?

Does your system provide for the sick, the helpless, the weak, the old and the stranger?

Does your system guarantee the integrity of the natural group called the family?

Does your system recognize and further the fundamental thought that the chief duty of man is the attainment of manhood, which means the perfect and harmonious development of every part and power that goes to make a man; and the consecration of that manhood to the service of one's people?

By every one of these tests, the White Civilization is a failure.

How is it that we of the Whiteman's way have just as much food in the land as we ever had, just as much wealth as ever we had, just as much need for labour, just as much material of every kind, just as much readiness to work; and yet we are facing a breakdown because we cannot co-ordinate these things into effective action?

Our system has broken down—our Civilization is a failure. Wherever pushed to a logical conclusion, it makes one millionaire and a million paupers. There is no complete happiness under its blight.

Men of the White Race! We speak now as representative of the most heroic race the world has ever seen, the most physically perfect race the world has ever seen, the most spiritual Civilization the world has ever seen.

We offer you the Message of the Redman, the Creed of Manhood. We advocate his culture as an improvement on our own, if perchance by belated repentance, remorse, restitution, and justification, we may save ourselves from Divine vengeance and total destruction, as did the Ninevites in their final stance; so that we may have a chance to begin again with a better, higher thought.[26] ◆◆

John Collier, 1947

John Collier served as Commissioner of Indian Affairs from 1933 to 1945. He has been extremely active in promoting a positive approach in dealing with native societies. In the following selection Mr. Collier sets forth his view of Native American social organization and socioreligious orientation.

◆◆ They had what the world has lost. They have it now. What the world has lost, the world must have again lest it die. Not many years are left to have or have not, to recapture the lost ingredient.

This is not merely a passing reference to World War III or the atom bomb—although the reference includes these ways of death, too. These deaths will mean the end if they come—racial death, self-inflicted because we have lost the way, and the power to live is dead.

What, in our human world, is this power to live? It is the ancient, lost reverence and passion for human personality, joined with the ancient, lost reverence and passion for the earth and its web of life.

This indivisible reverence and passion is what the American Indians almost universally had; and representative groups of them have it still.

They had and have this power for living which our modern world has lost—as world-view and self-view, as tradition and institution, as practical philosophy dominating their societies and as an art supreme among all the arts.

By virtue of this power, the densely populated Inca state, by universal agreement among its people, made the conservation and increase of the earth's resources its foundational national policy. Never before, never since has a nation done what the Inca state did.

By virtue of this power, the little pueblo of Tesuque, in New Mexico, when threatened by the implacable destroying action of government some twenty-five years ago, starved and let no white friend know it was starving. It asked no help, determined only to defend its spiritual values and institutions and its remnant of land which was holy land.

If our modern world should be able to recapture this power, the earth's natural resources and web of life would not be irrevocably wasted within the twentieth century, which is the prospect now. True democracy, founded in neighborhoods and reaching over the world, would become the realized heaven on earth. And living peace—not just an interlude between wars—would be born and would last through ages. . . .

I believe that the answer will contain our fate. Their own answer, the Indians still living in their societies continue to affirm. Self-willed, self-wrought personality excellence, empowered by the whole social institution of the tribe and of the race, is more than a merely practical thing, according to their answer—according to their view of selfhood, society and the wide world. It is the very essence of cosmic survival and victory.

As we traverse Indian history from the Conquest down to their present-day strivings, and up and down the two continents, we come upon the Indian affirmative over and over again. We shall meet that affirmative—which this writer, at least, was so slow to understand—all through the record. For through all the slaughter of American Indian biological stocks, the slaughter of their societies and trampling upon their values, strange as it may seem, they have kept the faith. The inner core-value, complex and various, has not been killed.

And since it has not been killed, it never will be. Be it for now or a hundred years from now, or a thousand—so long as the race of humanity shall survive—the Indian keeps his gift as a gift for us all. . . .

The Indian knew the meaning of society as creator of personality and as organizer of man with universe, through many aeons before ever the white man came. He kept alive, and was made alive by, a multiplicity of contrasting societies.

The white conqueror, for reasons military, economic and religious, pronounced sentence of death on the Indian societies. Through century-long years of slavery, expropriation, physical decimation, and propaganda directed to the Indian against the Indian spirit, the conqueror worked hard to carry out the Indian's death sentence.

A broad view of Indian history from 1492 until recent years shows a death hunt against the Indian societies. To many of the societies, the death hunt brought annihilation, death everlasting. To others it brought wounds that seemed mortal; but with an astounding regenerative power they arose from the rubble. Harried into the wastes, secreted there for lifetimes, and starving, still the Indian grouphoods, languages, religions, culture systems, symbolisms, mental and emotional attitudes toward the self and the world, continued to live on. Not fossilized, unadaptive, not sealed into the past, but plastic, adaptive, assimilative, while yet faithful to their ancient values, these many societies somehow held their own. A few of them burgeoned right on through the centuries, and entered our own day with the noise and shine of waters gushing from their ancient sources. More, many more, sustained only a life covert, indrawn; but they sustained the core and genius of their way of life. When so very, very late, and perhaps for only a brief term of years (none can be sure, as yet) some of the white man's societies lifted their sentences of death from these all but invisible Indian societies, the response was a rush of human energy, a creativity industrial, civic, esthetic. How swiftly, with what flashing brilliance, with what terrible joy, these long-immured, suddenly reprieved little societies demonstrated the truth which our age has lost; that societies are living things, sources of the power and values of their members; that to be and to function in a consciously living, aspiring, striving society is to be a personality fulfilled, is to be an energy delivered into the communal joy, a partner once more in the cosmic life.

So the Indian record is the bearer of one great message to the world. Through his society, and only through his society, man experiences greatness; through it, he unites with the universe and the God, and through it, he is freed from all fear. Those who accept the Indian message and lesson will know how intense, even how awful, is the need for creators and creative effort in the field of understanding and discovery of the nature and meaning of the societies of mankind.[27] ◆ ◆

Notes

1. Arthur Barlow, in Doyle, *English Colonies in America*, pp. 57-58.
2. William Bradford, *History of Plimoth Plantation*, (Boston: Wright & Potter, 1898), pp. 32-34.
3. Luís Velarde, "Relación," translated and edited by Rufus Ray Wyllys, *New Mexico Historical Review*, Vol. VI, No. 2, April 1931, p. 138.

4. Informe de la mas peculiar de la nueva California, in Libro de Misión de Purisima, c-c 29, Bancroft Library, Berkeley, California. Printed by permission of the Bancroft Library.
5. Herbert E. Bolton, *Anza's California Expeditions,* (Berkeley: University of California Press, 1930) Vol. IV, pp. 100-101. Reprinted by permission of the University of California Press.
6. Mrs. D. B. Bates, *Four Years on the Pacific Coast,* (Boston: E. O. Libby, 1858) pp. 150-151.
7. From "Letters of Louise Clappe (The Dame Shirley Letters)" in *The Pioneer, or, California Monthly Magazine,* Vol. III, p. 360.
8. Frederick Law Olmsted, *A Journey Through Texas* (New York: Dix, Edwards & Co., 1857) pp. 289-290.
9. *Ibid.,* p. 126.
10. Charles Maclaren, *Werner Encyclopedia,* Vol. I, pp. 602, 604.
11. C. L. Sonnichsen, *The Mescalero Apaches* (Norman: University of Oklahoma Press, 1958) p. 208. Reprinted by permission of the University of Oklahoma Press.
12. *Ibid.,* p. 208.
13. Frederick Schwatka, *A Summer in Alaska* (St. Louis: J. W. Henry, 1894) p. 364.
14. J. Lee Humfreville, *Twenty Years Among Our Savage Indians* (Hartford: Hartford Pub. Co., 1897) pp. 52-53, 67-72, 85, 251, 370.
15. From *Annual Report of the Commissioner of Indian Affairs for 1903* (Washington: U.S. Government Printing Office, 1904) p. 9.
16. John Bigelow, ed., *The Works of Franklin* (New York: G. P. Putnam's Sons, 1904) Vol. X, pp. 385-6.
17. John P. Foley, ed., *The Jefferson Cyclopedia* (New York: Funk & Wagnall's Company, 1900) p. 422.
18. Pedro Fages, "Informe General sobre misiones," c-a 52, Bancroft Library, Berkeley, California, pp. 134-5. Reprinted by permission of The Brancroft Library.
19. Alexander Ross, *Adventures of the First Settlers on the Oregon or Columbia River* (London: Smith, 1849) p. 323.
20. John D. Hunter, *Manners and Customs of Several Indian Tribes* (Minneapolis: Ross & Haines, Inc., 1957) pp. 207, 210-212.
21. George Catlin, *The North American Indians* (Philadelphia: Leary, Stuart & Co., 1913) Vol. I, pp. 5-12; Vol. II, pp. 269-275.
22. A. W. Whipple, *Journal of an Expedition from San Diego to the Colorado River* (Washington: U.S. Government Printing Office, 1851) pp. 16-18.
23. Carl Meyer, *Bound for Sacramento* (Claremont: Saunder's Studio Press, 1938) pp. 166, 172-3. Reprinted by permission of the publisher.
24. Franklin A. Buck, *A Yankee Trader in the Gold Rush,* edited by Katherine A. White (Boston: Houghton Mifflin Co., 1930) pp. 99-100, 110. Reprinted by permission of Houghton Mifflin Company.
25. George Bird Grinnell, *Pawnee Hero Stories and Folk Tales* (Lincoln: University of Nebraska Press, 1961) pp. 406, 408.
26. Ernest Thompson Seton and Julia M. Seton, *The Gospel of the Redman: An Indian Bible* (London: Methuen & Co., Ltd., 1937) pp. 105-108. Reprinted by permission of Julia M. Seton. A new edition of this work (1958) is now available from Seton Village Press, Seton Village, Santa Fé, New Mexico.
27. John Collier, *Indians of the Americas* (New York: The New American Library, 1948) pp. 7-16. Reprinted by permission of the author.

THREE

THE LONG STRUGGLE

For four hundred years, from 1513 until the beginning of the twentieth century, Europeans and Native Americans fought a relentless series of wars to determine the ownership of what is now the United States. The struggle was, of course, unequal in many respects. The Europeans were overwhelmingly superior in numbers; the population of even the smallest of European states was probably greater than that of the entire aboriginal United States. Still further, of course, the Americans were divided into hundreds of rival tribes and local units, many of which allied themselves with Europeans. And finally, the Europeans were able to take advantage of the technological heritage of the Orient, the Middle East, North Africa and Europe itself.

Considering these odds, one might have expected to see European armies sweep across the continent like the ancient Macedonians or the Mongols of Genghis Khan, subjecting vast regions to their sway after brief campaigns. This did not occur, however, north of central Mexico. On the contrary, the Europeans showed a singular inability at conquest —decades and even centuries had to be expended before single native groups could be subdued—the continent had to be conquered mile by mile and league by league.

The heroic struggle of the Native American—one of the great dramas of all time—was of extreme importance in the creation of the United States of America. It was in many ways the anvil upon which Anglo-American character was forged, and it has given us the image of the red warrior, the "noble savage." On the other hand, it might have been better (from the viewpoint of those who value life per se over heroic death) if the natives had been less freedom-loving, less independent, less inclined to fight to the death. For if they had been conquered by a few epic campaigns they would probably have survived in greater numbers (albeit as "subjects" and slaves) and they might even have absorbed their conquerers through miscegenation and assimilation.

The struggle in the United States was, however, long and cruel and destructive. It was also complex, sometimes involving warfare between rival European groups as well as between rival tribes, sometimes pitting partially Europeanized natives and mixed-bloods against natives, and occasionally witnessing the mixed-blood's struggle against Europeans.

The following selections are designed to provide some understanding of the active phases of the struggle. They are, however, selective and tend to emphasize the effect of the European upon the native rather than that of the native upon the European.

The expedition of Francisco Vásquez de Coronado, 1539-1542

The Army of Coronado arrived among the Pueblo Indians of New Mexico and began acting in a highhanded manner, seizing Indians as captives and forcibly appropriating clothing and food. Finally a Spanish soldier raped a native woman and the Indians rebelled. Coronado ordered his soldiers ". . . not to take them alive, but to make an example of them so that the other natives would fear the Spaniards." A group of several hundred Indians surrendered after being promised pardon; however, Garcia López de Cardenas

♦♦ . . . ordered two hundred stakes to be prepared at once to burn them alive. Nobody told him about the peace that had been granted them . . . , not thinking that it was any of their business. Then when the enemies saw that the Spaniards were binding them and beginning to roast them, about a hundred men who were in the tent began to struggle and defend themselves with what there was there and with the stakes they could seize. Our men who were on foot attacked the tent on all sides . . . and then the horsemen chased those who escaped. As the country was level, not a man of them remained alive. . . .[1] ♦♦

The destruction of Acoma Pueblo, New Mexico, 1599

The Keres of Acoma were the first New Mexicans to resist with force the demands of Juan de Oñate's Spanish army for food and supplies. As a result they were to serve as an example for all of the other natives. On January 10, 1599, Oñate decreed that

♦♦ . . . inasmuch as we have declared war on them without quarter, you will punish all those of fighting age as you deem best, as a warning to everyone in this kingdom. All of those you execute you will expose to public view at the places you think most suitable. . . . If you should want to show lenience after they have been arrested, you should seek all possible means to make the Indians believe that you are doing so at the request of the friar with your forces. In this manner they will recognize the friars as their benefactors and protectors and come to love and esteem them, and to fear us. ♦♦

The Spanish army attacked the mesa of Acoma after the natives had refused to surrender their pueblo to be destroyed.

♦♦ In the attack of the preceding Thursday more than 300 men were killed, and from Saturday to Sunday, more than 200 more. We began to set fire to the pueblo and to destroy it, forcing them to retire to the strongest parts. The estufas [kivas] of the pueblo had been fortified until the first one was about as strong as the peñol [mesa] itself. . . . In good order [with two artillery-pieces], we forced the Indians to fight and they attacked with great fury. Twice we drew back, with them upon us, but they always fared badly. The result was that more than 800 persons died, and the prisoners taken numbered 500 women and children, and 80 men. The latter were tried and punished. With this the land was pacified, thanks to God our Lord. ♦♦

Juan de Oñate issued the following punishment, among others:

♦♦ The males who are over 25 years of age I sentence to have one foot cut off and to 20 years of personal servitude. The males between the ages of 12 and 25 I sentence likewise to 20 years of personal servitude.[2] ♦♦

The warfare initiated by Vásquez de Coronado and Oñate in the Southwest did not cease until many decades after the Spaniards had been ousted from Mexico. For over two centuries the northern frontier of the Spanish empire was a land of war, and eventually the Europeans suffered many setbacks. Regions from which the Spaniards hoped to gain great wealth were instead burdensome frontier outposts and the empire was constantly plagued by rebellions. Because of the fierce resistance of the Apaches and other independence-loving tribes the Spaniards were never able to consolidate their positions in what is now the United States. Thus native resistance in the Southwest helped to facilitate eventual Anglo-American conquest by weakening first the Spanish and then the Mexican positions.

The Virginia Assembly, 1619

An interesting feature of English colonization in many instances was the inability of the Europeans to conquer the natives coupled with a lack of willingness to assimilate with the latter. Thus a state of "coexistence" ensued during which the English attempted to hold the natives at arm's length for the most part, although also desiring the use of Indian labor and the conversion of American children to Christianity.

◆◆ As touching the instruction of drawing some of the better disposed of the Indians to converse with our people and to live and labor amongst them, the Assembly . . . counsel those of the colony, neither utterly to reject them nor yet to draw them to come in. But in case they will of themselves come voluntarily to places well peopled, there to do service in killing of deer, fishing, beating of corn and other works, that then five or six may be admitted into every such place, and no more. . . . for generally (though some amongst many may prove good) they are a most treacherous people. . . . for laying a surer foundation of the conversion of the Indians to Christian religion, each town, city, borough, and particular plantation do obtain into themselves by just means a certain number of the native's children to be educated by them in true religion and civil course of life. . . . It shall be free for every man to trade with the Indians, servants only excepted, upon pain of whipping. . . . That no man do sell or give any Indians any . . . arms . . . upon pain of being held a traitor to the colony, and of being hanged. . . .[3] ◆◆

The Pilgrims in Massachusetts, 1620-1621

◆◆ Being thus arrived at Cap-Cod. . . . they espied five or six persons with a dogg coming towards them, who were salvages; but they fled from them, and rane up into ye woods and ye English followed them. . . . but ye Indeans seeing them selves thus followed, they againe forsooke the woods, and rane away. . . . Afterwards [the English] . . . directed their course to come to the other shore . . . and by the way found . . . a good quantitie of clear ground wher the Indeans had formerly set corne, and some of their graves. And proceeding furder they saw . . . heaps of sand newly padled with their hands, which they, digging up, found in them diverce faire Indean baskets filled with corne. . . . they returned to the ship . . . and tooke with them parte of the corne . . . and showed their breethren; of which . . . they were marvelusly glad, and their harts incouraged. . . . the 6 of Desemr: they sente out their shallop againe . . . and as they drue near the shore they saw some 10 or 12 Indeans very busie aboute some thing. . . . Being landed, it grew late, and they made them selves a barricade. . . . But presently, all on the sudain, they heard a great and strange crie . . . and one of their company being abroad came running in and cried, 'Men, Indeans, Indeans'; and with all, their arowes came flying amongst them. . . . Afterwards they gave God sollamne thanks and praise for their deliverance, and gathered up a bundle of their arrows . . . and called that place the first encounter. . . . On Munday [December 11] they . . . marched into the land [at Plymouth], and found diverse cornfields, and little running brooks, a place (as they supposed) fitt for situation. . . . [the settlement was established].

All this while ye Indeans came skulking about them. . . . And once they stoale away their tools. . . . But about the 16 of Des^r a certaine Indean came bouldly amongst them and spoke to them in broken English. . . . he was not of these parts, but belonged to the eastrene parts, wher some English-ships came to fhish, with whom he was aquainted. . . . He became proftable to them in aquainting them with many things concerning the state of the cuntry in the east-parts. . . . His name was *Samaset;* he tould them also of another Indean whose name was *Squanto,* a native of this place, who had been in England. . . . their great Sachem, called *Massasoyt;* who, . . . came with the chiefe of his freinds and other attendance, with the aforesaid *Squanto.* With whom, after frendly entertainment . . . they made a peace with him (which hath now continued this 24 years). . . . *Squanto* continued with [the English], and was their interpreter, and was a spetiall instrument sent of God for there good beyond there expectation. He directed them how to set their corne, wher to take fish, and to procure other comodities . . . , and never left them till he dyed. . . .[4] ◆◆

Squanto not only showed them how to plant maize and how to "dress and tend it" but he instructed them in the technique of using fish for fertilizer. This was a crucial factor in the survival of the colony, for their English seeds did not sprout. Thus in Massachusetts, as in Virginia, English survival was dependent upon the friendship of the Americans and upon an assimilation to native methods of horticulture and to the use of new world crops.

Between 1607 and 1787 the English colonists, supplemented by Dutch, Scottish, Irish, French Huguenot, German, and Scandinavian settlers, expanded along the Atlantic seaboard, inundating tribe after tribe with disease, alcohol, and warfare. The Europeans were willing to become assimilated to America's crops—to America's physical environment—but not to America's people. Ironically, the Europeans left Europe not in order really to discover a new way of life, but to create little Europes all over again. And in their little Europes there were no places for Redmen.

Most of the natives who did not die were driven westward to a place from which they could be driven again and still again. Those who remained along the coast formed little enclaves isolated from each other and from the Europeans and Africans who surrounded them, except for some who, through miscegenation, disappeared into the general population.

In 1787 Benjamin Franklin wrote, "During the course of a long life . . . it has appeared to me that almost every war between the Indians and whites has been occasioned by some injustice of the latter towards

the former." [5] By the end of the eighteenth century a number of European-Americans had come to share this viewpoint; however, the forces
that drove the newcomers westward were too great to be stemmed or
made less harsh by the sentiments of a small intelligentsia. The average
Anglo-American had already become a restless, ambitious, aggressive
person—and nothing could long stand between him and his dream of
land and wealth.

Isaac Weld, an English traveler, 1795-1797

◆◆ . . . to conciliate their [the Indian's] affections to
the utmost, presents alone are not sufficient; you must appear to have
their interest at heart in every respect; you must associate with them;
you must treat them as men who are your equal, and, in some measure,
even adopt their native manners. . . . The old Indians still say, that
they never were so happy as when the French had possession of the
country. . . . The necessity of treating the Indians with respect and
attention is strongly inculcated on the minds of the English settlers
[in Canada] . . . but still they cannot banish wholly from their minds,
as the French do, the idea that the Indians are an inferior race of people
to them. . . . they all live together, however, on very amicable terms,
and many of the English on the frontiers have indeed told me, that if
they were but half as honest, and half as well conducted towards one
another as the Indians are towards them, the state of society in the
country would be truly enviable. . . .

On the frontiers of the United States little pains have hitherto been
taken by the government, and no pains by the people, to gain the good
will of the Indians; and the latter, indeed, instead of respecting the
Indians as an independent neighbouring nation, have in too many instances violated their rights as men in the most flagrant manner. The
consequence has been, that the people on the frontiers have been involved in all the calamities that they could have suffered from a vengeful
and cruel enemy. . . .

To the conduct of the States themselves alone, and to no other course,
is unquestionably to be attributed the continuance of the warfare between them and the Indians, after a definitive treaty of peace was signed
[1783]. Instead of them taking the opportunity to reconcile the Indians
. . . they still continued hostile towards them; they looked upon them
as indeed they still do, merely as wild beasts, that aught to be banished
from the fact of the earth; and actuated by that insatiable spirit of
avarice, and that restless and dissatisfied turn of mind, which I have so
frequently noticed, instead of keeping within their territories, where
millions of acres remained unoccupied, but no part, however, of which
could be had without being paid for, they crossed their boundary lines,

and fixed themselves in the territory of the Indians, without ever previously gaining the consent of these people.⁶ ◆◆

Thomas Forsyth, ca. 1818

◆◆ . . . The French being settled in Villages in all parts of the Country and most of these settlers of villages were composed of people who were married to Indian women and followed a life similar to that of the Indians themselves such as hunting, fishing & by which means the Frenchman's children were related to both parties and nothing could stir among the Indian nations, but those Indian women who were married to the French hunters would hear who would relate it to their husbands, and from them to the commandant and so on, by which means the Government had always time to prepare and frustrate many a deep design that was laid for their total ruin. The French being thus settled in villages, those who cultivated the earth, worked their land in a common field, upon a very small scale by which means there never was any misunderstanding between the Whites & Indians about lands. In the fall of the year the Frenchman and his family and the Indian and his family would paddle their canoes off together and chuse out a proper place to hunt the ensuing winter. They would hunt together, eat & drink together, as much so as if they were one & the same family, if the Frenchman was in want of any thing that the Indian had he would assist him and the Frenchman would do the same in return. . . .

At this day let a Frenchman come from Paris and meet an Indian, the Indian will shake hands with him, as cordially as if they had been acquainted for many years, will inquire about France as if he had relations there, indeed there is no people who takes the pains the French do to conciliate the friendship of the Indians. For instance we see many young French Canadians, the first year they winter among the Indians. They will eat, drink, sleep and be high fellow well met with the Indians, will learn in the course of a few months the Indian language by which means the Indians become attached to the Frenchman and the Frenchman to the Indians and the French always had & always will have more influence over the Indians than any other nation of White people—

The Spaniards who have been in this country have copied much after the French in their treatment towards the Indians, . . .

The settlers below this [St. Louis] on the St. Frances, Arkansaw are more mixed with the Indians, than those above and there are more conextions in trade, hunting etc., by which means those Indians viz Shawanois, Delawars, Cherekees, Choctaws etc. are somewhat civilized. . . . As respects their lands, the Spaniards used the same method as the French. . . . the Spaniards as well as the French always listened to the complaints of the Indians and rendered them satisfaction for any injuries done them by white people, as I said before the Spaniards copied much after the French mode of treating Indians and their building of villages among the Indians, their intermarrying with them etc. etc. that the same relationship existed between the Spaniards & Indians as between the French & Indians—

The British method of treating Indians are [sic] different to any other people. . . . No man is eligible for the place of agent but one who can talk some one of the Indian languages, from which it is supposed, that he must be acquainted with the Indian customes and manners. Indians visit any of the posts, they are plentifully supplied with all the[y] want such as Clothing, arms and ammunition &c. The agent pays particular attention to particular leading men among the different nations. There is [sic] no complaints about land, for when a tract of country is wanted, it is sold by the Indians, as it is of no use to them as the sale will not interfere with any of the Indians hunting grounds. The British Government are very sedulous in making up any misunderstanding that may take place between two different nations of Indians, they keep the Indians in strict alliance with each other, they have an amazing large belt of wampum which every Indian nation who visits the British post adds their proportion of wampum to it and acknowledges their assent to the grand alliance. This belt of wampum is always in the hands of the agent and when any strange nation arrives it is presented to them in council and they agree to add their nation to the alliance. This ceremony is done in presence of all the Chiefs (or as many as can be had) who have already agreed to the alliance. Any depredations committed against the Subjects of England by the Indians is [sic] generally paid for out of the Indian Store, any complaints made to the agent by the Indians against any white person the Indian gets full satisfaction. The British Indian Agents takes [sic] very great care not to deceive the Indians in any of their promises indeed they (the British) have brought their treatment of Indians to a perfect System—. . . .

Agents chosen as abovementioned are always able to know the characters of the different individuals of the different nations of Indians, and those agents so chosen are never above sitting, talking & smoking with the different Indian Chiefs by which means it makes them [the Chiefs] think more of themselves and have more authority over their warriours than otherwise—Our manner of treating Indians is very different from any of the beforementioned Nations every Governor of a Territory is Ex Officio Superintendent of Indian Affairs. The Governor may be chosen from the interiour of the U. States and perhaps never had an oppty [opportunity] of seeing an Indian untill he comes to the Territory he is to govern. Indians being always fond of variety, will visit the great chief on his arrival, but not receiving any mark of attention, not perhaps a pipe of tobacco to smoke nor even spoken to by the Governor they [the Indians] will leave the place with disgust and will acquaint all their people and other nations with the poor reception they met with from the Governor by saying that their new Father is a man of no sence and is not fond of his Indian Children: by which means all the Indians become prejudiced against the Gov. and all his warriours, indeed our frontier settlers do not use the Indians as well as they ought to do, for if they find an Indian hunting on their lands, they will not hesitate to tell him to go away or they will kill him etc.: by telling the Indian that that land, with all that is on it, is his: however, the Indians Complain more about the sale of their lands than any thing else, and I am sorry to say that the necessary precautions to get the proper Chiefs to sign the instruments of the sale of lands or even to get them to the Council is [sic] hardly ever taken, by which means disputes arise that hardly ever can be settled. . . .

I would recommend it strongly to establish villages of White people in different parts of the Indian Country after the manner or as near as possible to the French System, indeed, the advantage arising from those villages of White people in the Indian country is great. . . .[7] ◆◆

The Death of Osceola, the Seminole, January 30, 1838

◆◆   About half an hour before he died, he seemed to be sensible that he was dying; and although he could not speak, he signified by signs that he wished me to send for the chiefs and for the officers of the post, whom I called in. He made signs to his wives (of whom he had two, and also two fine little children by his side), to go and bring his full dress, which he wore in time of war; which having been brought in, he rose up in his bed, which was on the floor, and put on his shirt, his leggings and moccasins—girded on his war-belt, his bullet-pouch, and powder-horn, and laid his knife by the side of him on the floor. He then called for his red paint, and his looking-glass, which was held before him, when he deliberately painted on half of his face, his neck and his throat—his wrists—the backs of his hands, and the handle of his knife, red with vermillion; a custom practised when the irrevocable oath of war and destruction is taken. His knife he then placed in its sheath, under his belt; and he carefully arranged his turban on his head, and his three ostrich plumes that he was in the habit of wearing in it. Being thus prepared in full dress, he lay down a few minutes to recover strength sufficient, when he rose up as before, and with most benignant and pleasing smiles, extended his hand to me and to all of the officers and chiefs that were around him; and shook hands with us all in dead silence; and also with his wives and his little children; he made a signal for them to lower him down upon his bed, which was done, and he then slowly drew from his war-belt, his scalping-knife, which he firmly grasped in his right hand, laying it across the other, on his breast, and in a moment smiled away his last breath, without a struggle or a groan.[8] ◆◆

Peter H. Burnett, 1843-1848

◆◆ When we, the American emigrants, came into what the Indians claimed as their own country [Oregon], we were considerable in numbers, and we came, not to establish trade with the Indians, but to take and settle the country exclusively for ourselves. Consequently, we went anywhere we pleased, settled down without any treaty or consultation with the Indians, and occupied our claims without their consent and without compensation. . . . Every succeeding fall they found the white population about doubled, and our settlements continually extending, and rapidly encroaching more and more upon their pasture and camas grounds. . . . They instinctively saw annihilation before them. . . .[9] ◆◆

Trappers and Indians, 1849

A party of thirteen trappers reached the junction of the Colorado and Gila rivers. They chose to cross the river by themselves, without hiring Quechan Indians to help, as other travelers usually did.

◆◆ After all their traps, luggage, and horses had got across . . . one of the trappers noticed an Indian; wrapped in a blanket, squatting above his ammunition, an Indian who, on rising to go away, carried away the ammunition secreted under the blanket. The trapper waited until the redman got about seventy yards away, then cooly aiming his rifle, killed him, and deliberately walking up, recovered the stolen ammunition, with his knife removed the Indian's scalp, and from the still bleeding corpse's back cut a strip of skin twenty inches long by three inches wide for a razor strap.[10] ◆◆

The Gold Rush and the California Indians, E. Gould Buffum, 1848-1849

◆◆ We . . . started for the Yuba [River], and . . . about three miles from the river. . . . we stopped suddenly, dumbfounded, before two of the most curious objects that ever crossed my sight. They were two Indian women, engaged in gathering acorns. They were entirely naked, with the exception of a coyote skin extending from the waists to the knees. Their heads were shaved, and the tops of them covered with tarry paint, and a huge pair of military whiskers were daubed on their cheeks with the same article. . . . We followed in the direction which they had taken, and soon reached the Indian rancheria. . . . We were suddenly surrounded upon our entrance by thirty or forty male Indians, entirely naked, who had their bows and quivers slung over their shoulders, and who stared most suspiciously at us and our rifles. Finding one of them who spoke Spanish, I entered into a conversation with him. . . . This pleased him highly, and from that moment till we left, Pule-u-le, as he informed me his name was, appeared my most intimate and sworn friend. . . . Pule-u-le exhibited to me the interior of several of the wigwams, which were nicely thatched with sprigs of pine and cypress, while a matting of the same material covered the bottom. . . . [one of the women] brought me in a large piece of bread made of acorns. . . . Pule-u-le showed us the bows and arrows, and never have I seen more beautiful specimens of workmanship. The bows were some three feet long, but very elastic and some of them beautifully carved. . . . Pule-u-le told me that in the spring he thought they should all leave and go over the "big mountain" [Sierra Nevadas], to get from the sight of the white man. . . .

A report which afterwards proved to be strictly correct, came to the mill [at Coloma], that a party of Indians had descended to the camp of five white men on the North Fork [of the American River], . . . had broken the locks of their rifles which were in their tents, and then fallen upon and cruelly beaten and murdered them. A large party . . . was immediately mustered at the mill, and started in pursuit of the Indians, and tracked them to a large rancheria on Weaver's creek. This was attacked, and after killing about twenty of them, took thirty prisoners, and marched to the mill. . . . Six of them, having been proved to have been connected with the party who killed the white men, were sentenced to be shot. . . . Soon after this several expeditions were fitted out, who scoured the country in quest of Indians, until now a redskin is scarcely ever seen in the inhabited portion of the northern mining region. Their rancherias are deserted . . . and they have gone,—some of them to seek a home beyond the rugged crest of the Sierra Nevada, while others have emigrated to the valley of the Tulares, and the whole race is fast becoming extinct.[11] ◆◆

Charles E. Pancoast, 1850

◆◆ We had been there [Big Oak Flat, near Yosemite] only a few days when one night a band of Mountain Indians made a raid on some of the miners on the Flat and robbed them of a Horse and other valuables, killing one miner and wounding another with their arrows. The miners followed the Indians for 25 miles up into the mountains, where they found their settlement, and killed old men, squaws, and children, the Bucks having fled. I am thankful that I did not join them, as their acts were more foul than the Indians'. [One white man, L. Armstrong, helped some women and boys to escape, however].[12] ◆◆

Traveling along the Humboldt River, Nevada, 1850

◆◆   Rumors of depredations of the Indians today—one
wagon with which were three or four men, was pillaged by a party of
the scamps right before their eyes in open daylight. The emigrants have
resolved to shoot down every Indian that makes his appearance on this
river unless under peculiar circumstances.[13]   ◆◆

A massacre in Northern California, 1850's-1860's

A group of Whites in Northern California invited some 300 Wintoon
men, women and children to a feast

◆◆   ". . . and told them not to bring their arms. . . .
They had been there several days, feasting and dancing, when some
Num'soos from Trinity Center came and warned them of danger, telling
of a similar trick played on their people . . . , when many were
slaughtered. . . . The Indians began to slip away quietly until by the
eighth or tenth day only forty-five warriors remained. The chief then
noticed that whenever an Indian left the table, a soldier followed. This
alarmed him, so he watched his chance and slipped down to the river.
. . . The forty-five Wintoon warriors remaining at the table were all
massacred by the soldiers and volunteers. An old woman [in the early
1900's] . . . was a little girl at the time of this massacre and was there
with her parents. She escaped by hiding in the willows." [14]   ◆◆

*The Sand Creek Massacre, November 29, 1864—testimony of First
Lt. Connor*

First Lt. James D. Connor, New Mexico Volunteers, testified about
this massacre as follows:

◆◆   About day break on the morning of the 29th of
November we came in sight of the camp of the friendly Indians afore-
mentioned, and were ordered by Colonel Chivington to attack the same,
which was accordingly done. The command of Colonel Chivington was
composed of about one thousand men; the village of the Indians consisted of from one hundred to one hundred and thirty lodges, and, as
far as I am able to judge, of from five hundred to six hundred souls,
the majority of which were women and children; in going over the
battleground the next day I did not see a body of man, woman, or child
but was scalped, and in many instances their bodies were mutilated in
the most horrible manner—men, women, and children's privates cut
out, etc.; I heard one man say that he had cut out a woman's private

parts and had them for exhibition on a stick. . . . according to the best of my knowledge and belief these atrocities that were committed were with the knowledge of J. M. Chivington, and I do not know of his taking any measures to prevent them; I heard of one instance of a child a few months old being thrown in the feed-box of a wagon, and after being carried some distance left on the ground to perish; I also heard of numerous instances in which men had cut out the private parts of females and stretched them over the saddle-bows, and wore them over their hats while riding in the ranks. . . .[15] ◆◆

The Sand Creek Massacre—testimony of Lt. Cramer

◆◆ "We arrived at the Indian village about daylight. . . . Colonel Chivington moved his regiment to the front, the Indians retreating up the creek, and hiding under the banks. . . . White Antelope rant towards our columns unarmed, and with both arms raised, but was killed. Several other of the warriors were killed in like manner. The women and children were huddled together, and most of our fire was concentrated on them. . . . The Indian warriors, about one hundred in number, fought desperately; there were about five hundred all told. I estimated the loss of the Indians to be from one hundred and twenty-five to one hundred and seventy-five killed; no wounded fell into our hands and all the dead were scalped. The Indian who was pointed out as White Antelope had his fingers cut off. Our force was so large that there was no necessity of firing on the Indians. They did not return the fire until after our troops had fired several rounds. . . . I told Colonel Chivington . . . that it would be murder, in every sense of the word, if he attacked those Indians. His reply was, bringing his fist down close to my face, 'Damn any man who sympathizes with Indians.' . . . he had come to kill Indians and believed it to be honorable to kill Indians under any and all circumstances." [16] ◆◆

The resettlement of the Pawnee in Oklahoma, 1872-1888

◆◆ The project of removing the Pawnees from their reservation on the Loup River in Nebraska appears to have been first heard of in the year 1872. The Pawnee reservation was close to civilization, and the settlers moving west into Nebraska coveted the Indian's lands. It was the old story, the same one that has been heard ever since the rapacious whites first set foot on the shores of this continent.

The Pawnees were strongly attached to their home in Nebraska. They had always lived there, and were used to it. Their forefathers were buried there. Up to the winter of 1873-74 they had no idea of moving. But they were constantly being subjected to annoyances.

Settlers crowded in close to the Pawnee agency, and even located on it on the south and east, and in the most matter of fact way drove their teams into the Pawnee timber, and cut and carried off the Pawnee wood, on which the tribe depended for fuel and for building materials. This open robbery gave rise to constant disputes and bickerings between the Indians and the whites, in which the former were invariably worsted. On the south and east side of the reservation the crowding and the depredations were continuous. On the north and west the reservation was exposed to frequent incursions from the different bands of Sioux. . . . These attacks, though always successfully repelled by the Pawnees, were a continual source of annoyance and irritation to them, while their consistent desire to obey the rules laid down for their guidance by the Government prevented them from retaliating in kind upon their enemies. . . .

Shortly before the removal of the tribe to the Indian Territory in 1874, *Pi'ta Le-shar,* the Head Chief, was shot, and died from his wound. It has been stated, and generally believed, that his death resulted from the accidental discharge of his own pistol, but there are well-informed persons who believe that he was murdered. There is reason to believe that the shot did not come from his own weapon, but that he was shot by a white man in order to get rid of his influence, which was consistently exerted to keep the Pawnees in their northern home. . . .

During the first four years of their sojourn in the Indian Territory [Oklahoma] the condition of the Pawnees was most miserable.

They had left the high, dry, sandy country of the Loup, and come south into the more fertile, but also more humid country of the Indian Territory, where they found a region entirely different from that to which they had been accustomed. Soon after their settlement on their new reservation, they were attacked by fever and ague, a disease which had been unknown to them in their northern home, and many of them died, while all were so weakened by disease and so discouraged by homesickness that their nature seemed wholly changed. They lost their old spirit and their energy, and were possessed only by a desire to return to their northern home. This was, of course, impossible, since their old reservation had been thrown open to settlement, and in part occupied by the whites. During the first ten years of their sojourn in the Territory more than one of the agents appointed to look after the Pawnees were either incompetent or dishonest, so that the people suffered from lack of food, and some of them even starved to death. They were miserably poor, for they did not know how to work, and no one tried to encourage or help them to do so. The few horses which they had were stolen from them by white horse thieves. . . .

When Major [Frank] North and his brother Luther visited the agency in 1876, to enlist scouts for General Crook's northern campaign, they found the Pawnees in a pitiable condition. They were without food, without clothing, without arms and without horses. Their sole covering consisted of cotton sheets, which afforded no protection against cold and wet. It is not strange that under such circumstances the people died off fast. At this time Major North had orders to enlist only one hundred scouts, but he was greatly perplexed in selecting his men, for four hundred wanted to go with him. Every able-bodied man in the tribe, and many who were not able-bodied, tried to get their names on the muster roll. Each man, at any cost, sought to get away from the suffering of his present life; from the fever that made him quake, the chill that caused him to shiver, and above all from the deadly monotony of the reservation life. . . .

The wretched condition of the Pawnees continued up to about 1884 or 1885. Before this time the people had become in a measure acclimated in their new home, and had come to realize that it was absolutely necessary for them to go to work if the tribe was to continue to exist. They began to work; at first only a few, but gradually many, of the Skidi, and then the Chau-i and the Kit-ke-hank-i. Presently a point was reached where it was no longer necessary to issue them Government rations. They raised enough on their farms to support themselves. Each year of late they have done better and better. A drought one season, and a cyclone another, destroyed their crops, but, undiscouraged and undaunted, they push ahead, striving earnestly to become like white men. The Pita-hau-erats are the least progressive of the four bands, and many of them still live in dirt lodges, and cultivate patches of corn scarcely larger than those tilled in their old villages; but as the other bands advance, and as the results of manual labor are seen and understood by those who are more idle, they, too, will catch the spirit of progress, and will lay hold of the plow.

Last March [1888], as I drove along toward the agency, and as we came in sight of Black Bear Creek, I was surprised to see what looked like good farm houses dotting the distant bottom. A nearer and a closer investigation showed me that the most well-to-do of the Pawnees live in houses as good as those of many a New England land owner, and very much better than those inhabited by new settlers in the farther West. Many of them have considerable farms under fence, a barn, a garden in which vegetables are raised, and a peach orchard. They realize that as yet they are only beginning, but to me, who knew them in their old barbaric condition, their progress seems a marvel. Nowadays by far the greater number of the Pawnees wear civilized clothing, ride in wagons, and send their children to the agency school. They are making rapid strides toward civilization, just such progress as might be expected from the intelligent and courageous people that they are and always have been. The Pawnees receive from the Government a perpetual annuity of thirty thousand dollars, of which one-half is paid in money, and one-half in goods. Besides this they have a credit with the Government of about two hundred and eighty thousand dollars (the proceeds of the sale of their old reservation in Nebraska), on which they receive interest; and for some years past they have leased to cattlemen about one hundern and twenty-five thousand acres of their reservation, for which they receive about three thousand eight hundred dollars per annum. It will thus be seen that in addition to the crops which they raise, the tribe is fairly well provided with money. While a considerable part of this is, of course, wasted, being spent for trifles and for luxuries, it is nevertheless the fact that a certain proportion of it is invested by the Indians in tools, farming implements, and in furniture." [17]   ◆◆

Black Elk: The massacre of Wounded Knee, December 29, 1890

◆◆ We followed down the dry gulch, and what we saw was terrible. Dead and wounded [Indian] women and children and little babies were scattered all along where they had been trying to run away. The soldiers had followed along the gulch, as they ran, and murdered them in there. Sometimes they were in heaps because they had huddled together, and some were scattered all along. Sometimes bunches of them had been killed and torn to pieces where the wagon guns hit them. I saw a little baby trying to suck its mother, but she was bloody and dead.

When we drove the soldiers back, they dug themselves in, and we were not enough people to drive them out from there. In the evening they marched off up Wounded Knee Creek, and then we saw all that they had done there.

Men and women and children were heaped and scattered all over the flat at the bottom of the little hill where the soldiers had their wagon-guns, and westward up the dry gulch all the way to the high ridge, the dead women and children and babies were scattered. . . .

This is the way it was: . . . The women and children ran into the gulch and up the west, dropping all the time, for the soldiers shot them as they ran. There were only about a hundred warriors and there were nearly five hundred soldiers. The warriors rushed to where they had piled their guns and knives [previously]. They fought soldiers with only their hands until they got their guns. . . . It was a good winter day when all this happened. The sun was shining. But after the soldiers marched away from their dirty work, a heavy snow began to fall. The wind came up in the night. There was a big blizzard, and it grew very cold. The snow drifted deep in the crooked gulch, and it was one long grave of butchered women and children and babies, who had never done any harm and were only trying to run away.[18]   ◆◆

Disease, the European's secret weapon

From the West Indies to California and from Newfoundland to Oregon tens of thousands of Native Americans died from the effects of diseases introduced by the Europeans. Without the "aid" of this secret weapon the various European groups would have been hard-pressed indeed in their conquest of America.

Disease often weakened the ability of a native group to resist prior to the commencement of active hostility. For example, in 1621 the Pilgrims sent a party to visit Chief Massassoit and found

> ye people not many, being dead & abundantly wasted in ye late great mortalitie which fell in all these parts aboute three years before . . . wherin thousands of them dyed, they not being able to burie one another; there sculs and bones were found in many places lying still above ground.[19]

The natives of Massachusetts were severely weakened by an epidemic in 1633, and in the following year smallpox swept through Connecticut —at one village of a thousand persons less than fifty survived. The English, incidentally, were not affected by the epidemic, even though some helped care for sick Indians in Massachusetts.

On the Pacific Coast, as along the Atlantic, disease was a major factor in breaking native resistance. More than 200,000 Indians may have perished in California alone between 1769 and the 1870's, many tens of thousands of them dying in the Franciscan missions. One of the most destructive sicknesses in the missions was syphilis, which virtually destroyed the native population of Baja California and then was introduced into California in the mid-1770's.

> Rarely did a neophyte [mission convert] reach the age of sixteen without showing signs of the disease, while frequently the symptoms were present at birth, in such children as mothers did not, owing to their diseased condition, abort. Many of the friars themselves, notably those of the College of Guadalupe, were contaminated. . . .[20]

The nonmissionized Indians were also affected by disease introduced by Europeans. S. F. Cooke has estimated that the San Joaquin Valley's population declined by 75 per cent (from 83,820 to 19,000) between 1800 and 1850, largely owing to a malaria epidemic introduced by trappers from Oregon.[21]

The high death rate continued even after Anglo-American settlers and miners poured into the Far West. In fact, the new arrivals introduced new diseases and weakened the natives' ability to resist illness by depriving them of an adequate means of subsistence.

Charles Pancoast met an old Indian living near Shasta City, California in 1852.

> He related to me a distressing story of a visitation of cholera in the Sacramento Valley, I suppose in 1832. He said. . . . half the Indians of the Valley had died, and his own tribe had never recovered its numbers. He informed

me that there was then a disease among them [1852] which was sweeping them all away, and besought me to do something for them. . . . They were dying rapidly, and when I left the Old Chief was the only one remaining.[22]

Even after the United States Government obtained complete control over the Far West little was done to prevent epidemics or supply medical care for the natives. Many sicknesses swept through the reservations during the first quarter of the twentieth century with disastrous effect. In 1901 C. Hart Merriam wrote:

Most of the Luiseño [of southern California] have several children. . . . The old people are numerous and look strong and healthy. The children are very apt to develop tuberculosis and die between the ages of sixteen and twenty-five. The deaths greatly exceed the births. Most of the deaths are of young people, and many of the young men and women we saw were coughing sadly. . . . A girl recently returned from an Indian school at Carlisle, Pennsylvania, had a dreadful cough and apparently a short lease on life. She died the same year.[23]

Notes

1. Narrative of Pedro de Castañeda, translated by George P. Winship, in *Fourteenth Annual Report of the Bureau of American Ethnology* (Washington: U.S. Government Printing Office, 1896) pp. 496-7.
2. George P. Hammond and Agapito Rey, *Don Juan de Oñate, Colonizer of New Mexico* (Albuquerque: University of New Mexico Press, 1953) Part I, pp. 427, 459, 477. Reprinted by permission of the University of New Mexico Press.
3. "Proceedings of the First Assembly of Virginia, 1619," in *Colonial Records of Virginia, Senate Document Extra* (Richmond: Virginia State Senate, 1874).
4. Bradford, *History of Plimoth Plantation*, pp. 97-116.
5. Bigelow, ed., *The Works of Benjamin Franklin*, Vol. XI, p. 396.
6. Isaac Weld, *Travels Through the States of North America and Provinces of Upper and Lower Canada* (London: John Stockdale, 1800) pp. 433-5.
7. Thomas Forsyth, "The French, British and Spanish Methods of Treating Indians &c.," *Ethnohistory*, Vol. IV, No. 2, Spring 1957, pp. 210-216. Reprinted by permission of the Wisconsin State Historical Society.
8. Catlin, *The North American Indians*, Vol. II, p. 251n.
9. Peter H. Burnett, "Recollection and Opinions of an Old Pioneer," *Oregon Hist. Society Quarterly*, Vol. V, No. 1, March 1904, p. 97.
10. Benjamin B. Harris, *The Gila Trail*, edited by Richard H. Dillon (Norman: University of Oklahoma Press, 1960) p. 112. Reprinted by permission of the University of Oklahoma Press.
11. E. Gould Buffum, *Six Months in the Gold Mines* from *A Journal of Three Years in Upper and Lower California, 1847-1849* (Philadelphia: Lea and Blanchard, 1850), pp. 43-46, 100-101.
12. Charles E. Pancoast, *A Quaker Forty-niner* (Philadelphia: University of Pennsylvania Press, 1930), p. 298. Reprinted by permission of the University of Pennsylvania Press.

13. Irene D. Paden, ed., *The Journal of Madison Berryman Moorman, 1850-1851* (San Francisco: California Historical Society, 1948) p. 71. Reprinted by permission of the California Historical Society.

14. C. Hart Merriam, *Studies of California Indians* (Berkeley: University of California Press, 1955) pp. 20-21. Reprinted by permission of the University of California Press.

15. *U.S. Senate, Reports of Committees, 39th Congress, 2nd Session,* Serial 1279, Document No. 156, pp. 53, 73-4.

16. *Ibid.,* pp. 73-4.

17. Grinnell, *Pawnee Hero Stories and Folk Tales,* pp. 389-402.

18. John G. Neihardt, *Black Elk Speaks* (Lincoln: University of Nebraska Press, 1961) pp. 265-8. Reprinted by permission of the author and the University of Nebraska Press.

19. Bradford, *History of Plimoth Plantation,* p. 123.

20. Hubert Howe Bancroft, *California Pastoral* (San Francisco: History Co., 1888) Vol. I, p. 616.

21. Sherbourne F. Cooke, "Aboriginal Population of the San Joaquin Valley," *Anthropological Records* (University of California) Vol. XVI, No. 2.

22. Pancoast, *op. cit.,* p. 343. Reprinted by permission of the University of Pennsylvania Press.

23. Merriam, *op. cit.,* pp. 91-2. Reprinted by permission of the University of California Press.

FOUR

VOICES FROM NATIVE AMERICA

Public speaking was developed into a true art form by the Native American peoples, and their oratorical skills had a considerable impact upon Anglo-Americans. A. Irving Hallowell has noted that the speeches made by natives during treaty negotiations aroused much interest and were widely circulated in printed form.[1] Several generations of school children were exposed to the speeches of Logan and other famous chiefs, and oratory in the United States may well have been considerably embellished thereby. In 1812 Thomas Jefferson recalled from his own experience the impressive character of Indian elocution:

> Before the revolution, the Indians were in the habit of coming often and in great numbers to the seat of government [in Virginia] where I was very much with them. I knew much the great Outacite, the warrior and orator of the Cherokees; he was always the guest of my father, on his journeys to and from Williamsburg. I was in his camp when he made his great farewell oration to his people the evening before his departure for England. . . . his sounding voice, distinct articulation, animated action, and the solemn silence of his people at their several fires, filled me with awe and veneration, although I did not understand a word he uttered.[2]

In spite of the Native American's oratorical ability and the fact that many speeches were printed in works published in the United States, the native viewpoint has seldom been given much attention by Americans of European origin. Official "Indian" policies have largely been based upon either the interests, narrowly construed, of the government, or upon erroneous conceptions of what was "best" for the native. Very seldom have Native American views been seriously considered, and less often have they been incorporated into policies or actions.

The following selections illustrate Native American thinking in general and, more specifically, on the confrontation with Europeans.

Speech of Wahunsonacock (Powhatan) to John Smith at
Werowocomoco (in Virginia), 1609

54

◆◆ I have seen two generations of my people die. Not a man of the two generations is alive now but myself. I know the difference between peace and war better than any man in my country. I am now grown old, and must die soon; my authority must descend to my brothers, Opitchapan, Opechancanough and Catatough;—then to my two sisters, and then to my two daughters. I wish them to know as much as I do, and that your love to them may be like mine to you. Why will you take by force what you may have quietly by love? Why will you destroy us who supply you with food? What can you get by war? We can hide our provisions and run into the woods; then you will starve for wronging your friends. Why are you jealous of us? We are unarmed, and willing to give you what you ask, if you come in a friendly manner, and not with swords and guns, as if to make war upon an enemy. I am not so simple as not to know that it is much better to eat good meat, sleep comfortably, live quietly with my wives and children, laugh and be merry with the English, and trade for their copper and hatchets, than to run away from them, and to lie cold in the woods, feed on acorns, roots and such trash, and be so hunted that I can neither eat nor sleep. In these wars, my men must sit up watching, and if a twig break, they all cry out, "Here comes Captain Smith!" So I must end my miserable life. Take away your guns and swords, the cause of all our jealousy, or you may all die in the same manner.[3] ◆◆

Speech of Ketagustah (a Cherokee) at a Cherokee-British Conference, 1730

◆◆ We are come hither from a dark Mountainous Place, where nothing but Darkness is to be found; but [we] are now in a place where there is light. . . . We look upon you as if the Great King George was present: and we love you, as representing the Great King, and shall Dye in the same Way of Thinking. The Crown of our Nation is different from that which the Great King George wears, and from that which we saw in the Tower [of London], but to us it is all one, and the Chain of Friendship shall be carried to our People.

We look upon the Great King George as the Sun, and as our Father, and upon ourselves as his Children; for tho' we are Red, and you are white, yet our hands and Hearts are joined together.

When we shall have acquainted our People with what we have seen, our Children from Generation to Generation will always remember it.

In war we shall always be as one with you, the Great King George's Enemies shall be our enemies, his People and ours shall be always one, and dye together.

We came hither naked and poor, as the Worm of the Earth, but you have everything: and we that have nothing must love you, and can never break the Chain of Friendship which is between us.

ˋ Here stands the Governor of Carolina, whom we know; this small rope which we shew you, is all we have to bind our slaves with, and may be broken, but you have Iron Chains for yours; however, if we catch your slaves, we shall bind them as well as we can, and deliver them to our Friends again, and have no pay for it. . . .

Your White People may very safely build Houses near us, we shall hurt nothing that belongs to them, for we are the Children of one Father, the Great King, and shall live and Dye together.

This is our Way of Talking, which is the same thing to us, as your letters in the Book are to you; and to you, beloved Men, we deliver these Feathers, in Confirmation of all that we have said.⁴ ◆◆

Speech of Logan (a Mingo leader) at the conclusion of Lord Dunmore's War, 1774

◆◆ I appeal to any white man to say, if ever he entered Logan's cabin hungry, and he gave him not meat; if ever he came cold and naked, and he clothed him not.

During the course of the last long and bloody war, Logan remained idle in his cabin, an advocate for peace. Such was my love for the whites, that my countrymen pointed as they passed, and said, "Logan is the friend of white men." I had even thought to have lived with you but for the injuries of one man. Colonel Cresap, the last spring, in cold blood and unprovoked, murdered all the relations of Logan, not even sparing my women and children. There runs not a drop of my blood in the veins of any living creature. This called on me for revenge. I have sought it; I have killed many; I have glutted my vengeance. For my country, I rejoice at the beams of peace. But do not harbor a thought that this is the joy of fear. Logan never felt fear. He will not turn on his heel to save his life. Who is there to mourn for Logan?—Not one!⁵ ◆◆

Red Jacket's reply to Missionary Cram at Buffalo, New York, 1805

◆◆ Friend and brother, it was the will of the Great Spirit that we should meet together this day. He orders all things, and He has given us a fine day for our council. He has taken His garment from before the sun, and caused it to shine with brightness upon us; our eyes are opened, that we see clearly; our ears are unstopped, that we have been able to hear distinctly the words that you have spoken; for all these favours we thank the Great Spirit, and Him only.

Brother, this council fire was kindled by you; it was at your request that we came together at this time; we have listened with attention to what you have said; you requested us to speak our minds freely; this gives us great joy, for we now consider that we stand upright before you, and can speak what we think; all have heard your voice, and all speak to you as one man; our minds are agreed.

Brother, you say you want an answer to your talk, before you leave this place. It is right you should have one, as you are a great distance from home, and we do not wish to detain you; but we will first look back a little, and tell you what our fathers have told us, and what we have heard from the White people.

Brother, listen to what we say. There was a time when our forefathers owned this great land. Their seats extended from the rising to the setting sun. The Great Spirit had made it for the use of Indians. He had created the buffalo, the deer, and other animals for food. He made the bear and the beaver, and their skins served us for clothing. He had scattered them over the country, and taught us how to take them. He had caused the earth to produce corn for bread.

All this He had done for His Red children because he loved them. If we had any disputes about hunting grounds, they were generally settled without the shedding of much blood.

But an evil day came upon us; your forefathers crossed the great waters, and landed on this island. Their numbers were small; they found friends, and not enemies; they told us they had fled from their own country for fear of wicked men, and come here to enjoy their religion. They asked for a small seat; we took pity on them, granted their request, and they sat down amongst us; we gave them corn and meat; they gave us poison in return. The White people had now found our country, tidings were carried back, and more came amongst us; yet we did not fear them, we took them to be friends; they called us brothers; we believed them, and gave them a larger seat. At length their numbers had greatly increased; they wanted more land; they wanted our country. Our eyes were opened; and our minds became uneasy. Wars took place; Indians were hired to fight against Indians, and many of our people were destroyed. They also brought strong liquors among us; it was strong and powerful, and has slain thousands.

Brother, our seats were once large, and yours were very small; you have now become a great people, and we have scarcely a place left to spread our blankets; you have got our country, but are not satisfied; you want to force your religion upon us.

Brother, continue to listen. You say that you are sent to instruct us how to worship the Great Spirit agreeably to His mind, and if we do not take hold of the religion which you White people teach, we shall be unhappy hereafter; you say that you are right, and we are lost; how do we know this to be true? We understand that your religion is written in a book; if it was intended for us as well as you, why has not the Great

Spirit given it to us, and not only to us, but why did He not give to ou
forefathers the knowledge of that book, with the means of understandin
it rightly? We only know what you tell us about it; how shall we kno·
when to believe, being so often deceived by the White people?

Brother, you say there is but one way to worship and serve the Grea
Spirit; if there is but one religion, why do you White people differ s
much about it? Why not all agree, as you can all read the book?

Brother, we do not understand these things; we are told that you
religion was given to your forefathers, and has been handed down fro·
father to son. We also have a religion which was given to our forefather
and has been handed down to us, their children. We worship that wa·
It teaches us to be thankful for all the favours we receive; to love eac
other, and to be united; we never quarrel about religion.

Brother, the Great Spirit has made us all; but He has made a grea
difference between His White and Red children; He has given us a di
ferent complexion and different customs; to you He has given the arts; t
these He has not opened our eyes; we know these things to be true. Sinc
He has made so great a difference between us in other things, why may w·
not conclude that He has given us a different religion according to ou
understanding? The Great Spirit does right; He knows what is best fo
his children; we are satisfied.

Brother, we do not wish to destroy your religion, or take it from you
We want only to enjoy our own.

Brother, you say you have not come to get our land or our money, bu·
to enlighten our minds. I will now tell you that I have been at you·
meetings, and saw you collecting money from the meeting. I cannot tel
what this money was intended for, but suppose it was for your ministe·
and if we should conform to your way of thinking, perhaps you ma·
want some from us.

Brother, we are told that you have been preaching to White people i·
this place; these people are our neighbors, we are acquainted with them
we will wait a little while and see what effect your preaching has upo·
them. If we find it does them good, makes them honest, and less dispose·
to cheat Indians, we will then consider again what you have said.

Brother, you have now heard our answer to your talk, and this is all w·
have to say at present. As we are going to part, we will come and tak·
you by the hand, and hope the Great Spirit will protect you on you·
journey, and return you safe to your friends.[6]   ◆◆

Curly Chief's relation of the Pawnee's first contacts with Anglo-Americans
1800-1820

Curly Chief, a Pawnee, relates one of the early contacts between hi·
people and Europeans:

◆◆ I heard that long ago there was a time when there were no people in this country except Indians. After that the people began to hear of men that had white skins; they had been seen far to the east. Before I was born they came out to our country and visited us. The man who came was from the Government. He wanted to make a treaty with us, and to give us presents, blankets, and guns, and flint and steel and knives.

The Head Chief told him that we needed none of these things. He said, "We have our buffalo and our corn. These things the Ruler gave to us, and they are all that we need. See this robe. This keeps me warm in winter. I need no blanket."

The white men had with them some cattle, and the Pawnee Chief said, "Lead out a heifer here on the prairie!" They led her out, and the Chief, stepping up to her, shot her through behind the shoulder with his arrow, and she fell down and died. Then the Chief said, "Will not my arrow kill? I do not need your guns." Then he took his stone knife and skinned the heifer, and cut off a piece of fat meat. When he had done this he said, "Why should I take your knives? The Ruler has given me something to cut with."

Then taking the fire sticks, he kindled a fire to roast the meat, and while it was cooking, he spoke again and said, "You see, my brother, that the Ruler has given us all that we need, the buffalo for food and clothing; the corn to eat with our dried meat; bows, arrows, knives and hoes; all the implements which we need for killing meat, or for cultivating the ground. Now go back to the country from whence you came. We do not want your presents, and do not want you to come into our country."[7] ◆◆

Tecumseh's speech to Governor W. H. Harrison, Vincennes, August 12, 1810

In this speech, Tecumseh is repudiating an allegedly fraudulent purchase of Indian land.

◆◆ I am a Shawnee. My forefathers were warriors. Their son is a warrior. From them I take only my existence, from my tribe I take nothing. I am the maker of my own fortune, and Oh! that I could make that of my Red people, and of my country, as great as the conceptions of my mind, when I think of the Spirit that rules the universe. I would not then come to Governor Harrison to ask him to tear up the treaty, and to obliterate the landmark, but I would say to him: "Sir, you have liberty to return to your own country."

The Being within, communing with past ages, tells me that once, nor until lately, there was no Whiteman on this continent, that it then all belonged to the Redman, children of the same parents, placed on it by the Great Spirit that made them to keep it, to traverse it, to enjoy its productions, and to fill it with the same race, once a happy race; since made miserable by the White people, who are never contented but always encroaching.

The way, and the only way, to check and to stop this evil, is for all the Redmen to unite in claiming a common and equal right in the land, as it was at first and should be yet; for it was never divided, but belongs to all for the use of each. That no part has a right to sell, even to each other, much less to strangers—those who want all and will not do with less. The White people have no right to take the land from the Indians, because they had it first, it is theirs. They may sell, but all must join. Any sale not made by all, is not valid. The late sale is bad. It requires all to make a bargain for all. All Redmen have equal rights to the unoccupied land. The right to occupancy is as good in one place as in another. There cannot be two occupations in the same place. The first excludes all others. It is not so in hunting or travelling, for there the same ground will serve many, as they may follow each other all day, but the camp is stationary, and that is occupancy. It belongs to the first who sits down on his blanket or skins, which he has thrown upon the ground, and till he leaves it, no other has a right.[8] ◆◆

Tecumseh's speech to General Henry Proctor, 1812

In this speech Tecumseh urges the British officer to fight the Anglo-Americans.

◆◆ Father!—Listen to your children: you have them now all before you. In the old war our British father gave the hatchet to his red children when our old chiefs were alive. They are now dead. In that war our British father was thrown on his back by the Americans, and he took them by the hand without our knowledge. We are afraid our father will do so again this time. In the summer before last, when I came forward with my red brethren, and was ready to take up the hatchet in favor of our British father, we were told not to be in a hurry, for he had not yet determined to fight the Americans.

Listen!—When war was declared, our father stood up and gave us the tomahawk, and told us that he was then ready to strike the Americans; that he wanted our assistance; and that he would certainly get our lands back which the Americans had taken from us.

Father, listen!—The Americans have not yet beaten us by land, nor are we sure they have done so by water. We therefore wish to stay here and fight the enemy if they come. If they beat us, we will then retreat with our father. At the battle of the Rapids, in the last war, the Americans certainly defeated us, and when we retreated to our father's fort at that place, the gates were shut against us. We were afraid this would happen again; but, instead of this, we now see our British father preparing to march out of his garrison.

Father!—You have got the arms and ammunition which our great father sent for his red children. If you mean to go away, give them to us, and you may go and welcome. Our lives are in the hands of the Great Spirit. We are determined to defend our lands, and, if it be his will, we wish to leave our bones upon them.[9] ♦♦

Jatiñil, leader of the Kamia of Neji, Baja California, 1820-ca. 1870

Jatiñil here tells of his contacts with the Spanish and Mexicans between the 1820's and about 1870 (he died in 1877).

♦♦ I am called Jatiñil, and I am captain of this tribe [and have been] since [1822]. My father was captain before me, and before my father, [the captain] was my grandfather; in such a manner that the command of our tribe has always been the charge of my family, and for this reason the tribe carries my proper name. My father told me, that this land was to belong to the gente de razón [Spanish-speaking people] and that I should not go against them even as [my father and grandfather] had not gone against them; always we were friends of the whites, and so we, like them, do not like robbery nor was anyone killed without reason. I aided Father [Felix] Caballero in erecting the Mission of Descanso from its foundations until finished [1830]; but afterwards [1834] I left to campaign with [Ensign] Macedonio Gonzalez, against the Indians of Santa Catarina, the Quiliguas [Kiliwas] and Cucupa [Cocopas], who then were numerous; at my command were one thousand warriors, and we were all fighting in each clash against those tribes to the extent that the majority of my best warriors were killed, [however] we also killed a great many of them; . . . I entered into the war as much as I could and for this reason I am [sic] all wounded by arrows but fortunately they did not hit me in a good place. We went on fighting more than a year, until all of the rebel tribes were brought to peace, and then I came to help Father Felix in erecting the mission of Guadalupe from its foundations until finished [1834] and also I aided in the sowing of crops every year and with the harvests, and the father gave us what he wanted to: corn, barley and wheat, with which we sowed and raised ourselves; but not being content with this he [Father Caballero] sought various times to baptize us in order to have us locked up in the mission, and manage us as [he did] with the rest of the Indians.

After I saved the troops of Macedonio Gonzalez, who had plunged into the Sierra of Jacume [Jacumba] when Pedro Pablo, Martin and Cartucho rose in rebellion [1836], I retreated from the Sierra to the coast because the enemies that could attack me there were very numerous, and I came to build a fort at a watering-place which is on the mesa of Descanso, very appropriate for defending ourselves. . . . Father Felix [Caballero] thought that it was certain that I could not return to the Sierra, from fear [of the rebels], and that I was very weak, so that he could make of me and my people that which he desired; and then without remembering my services . . . , against the will of all of us, he commenced to baptize by force the people of my tribe who went to visit him as we were accustomed to do; this gave me much anger and for this reason I went to look for him at Guadalupe with the intention of killing him [1840]; I did not want to kill nor offend anyone else, but the people who went with me and whom I sent ahead, while I was detained by a little clash in the brush, were those who killed, without my orders, corporal Aranty and the Indians Francisco and Jose Antonio. Afterwards when I arrived nothing was done, and as I did not find Father Felix, I left the mission and did not take anything from it. From that time I returned to this village [Los Alamos] and I have not gone to any other places. Now, I am an old man, the major portion of my people died in war, others got excited and went to Upper California, during the gold rush [1849], and have not returned; now I see it, only a few families remain with me and all of us live by working without robbing from anyone."

Jatiñil further explained that his people wished to kill Fray Caballero because he ". . . baptized by force the people of my tribe in order to enslave them in the mission . . . and live the same as horses."[10] ◆◆

The "Historia" of Janitín, ca. 1878

Janitín was a kamia of Neji, Baja California, who was probably missionized between 1820 and 1830 at San Miguel Mission, south of San Diego.

◆◆ I and two of my relatives went down from the Sierra of Neji to the beach of el Rosarito, to catch clams for eating and to carry to the sierra as we were accustomed to do all the years; we did no harm to anyone on the road, and on the beach we thought of nothing more than catching and drying clams in order to carry them to our village.

While we were doing this, we saw two men on horseback coming rapidly towards us; my relatives were immediately afraid and they fled with all speed, hiding themselves in a very dense willow-grove which then existed in the canyon of the Rancho del Rosarito.

As soon as I saw myself alone, I also became afraid of those men and ran to the forest in order to join my companions, but already it was too late, because in a moment they overtook me and lassoed and dragged me for a long distance, wounding me much with the branches over which they dragged me, pulling me lassoed as I was with their horses running; after this, they roped me with my arms behind and carried me off to the

Mission of San Miguel, making me travel almost at a run in order to keep up with their horses, and when I stopped a little to catch my wind, they lashed me with the lariats that they carried, making me understand by signs that I should hurry; after much traveling in this manner, they diminished the pace and lashed me in order that I would always travel at the pace of the horses.

When we arrived at the mission, they locked me in a room for a week, the father [a Dominican priest] made me go to his habitation and he talked to me by means of an interpreter, telling me that he would make me Christian, and he told me many things that I did not understand, and Cunnur, the interpreter, told me that I should do as the father told me, because now I was not going to be set free, and it would go very bad with me if I did not consent in it; they gave me atole de mayz [corn gruel] to eat which I did not like because I was not accustomed to that food; but there was nothing else to eat.

One day they threw water on my head and gave me salt to eat, and with this the interpreter told me that now I was Christian and that I was called Jesus: I knew nothing of this, and I tolerated it all because in the end I was a poor Indian and did not have any recourse but to conform myself and tolerate the things they did with me.

The following day after my baptism, they took me to work with the other Indians, and they put me to cleaning a milpa of maize; since I did not know how to manage the hoe that they gave me, after hoeing a little, I cut my foot and could not continue working with it but I was put to pulling out the weeds by hand, and in this manner I did not finish the task that they gave me. In the afternoon they lashed me for not finishing the job, and the following day the same thing happened as on the previous day, every day they lashed me unjustly because I did not finish what I did not know how to do, and thus I existed for many days until I found a way to escape; but I was tracked and they caught me like a fox; there they seized me by lasso as on the first occasion, and they carried me off to the mission torturing me on the road; after we arrived the father passed along the corridor of the house, and he ordered that they fasten me to the stake and castigate me; they lashed me until I lost consciousness, and I did not regain consciousness for many hours afterwards. For several days I could not raise myself from the floor where they had laid me, and I still have on my shoulders the marks of the lashes which they gave me then. ◆◆

Manuel Rojo's description of Janitín, 1878

◆◆ Janitín is a very old man and he showed us the scars from the wounds that the lashes gave him, assuring us that he was never a Christian voluntarily, and that he knows no more of Christianity than they showed him, nothing but the slavery which they subjected him to, for which reason he fled later when he could, and he lived many years in the Sierra without coming down to the coast until after the missions were abolished [1840].[11] ◆◆

Speech of Black Hawk, the Sauk-Fox leader, at the conclusion of "Black Hawk's War," 1832

◆◆ You have taken me prisoner with all my warriors. I am much grieved, for I expected, if I did not defeat you, to hold out much longer, and give you more trouble before I surrendered. I tried hard to bring you into ambush, but your last general understands Indian fighting. The first one was not so wise. When I saw that I could not beat you by Indian fighting, I determined to rush on you, and fight you face to face. I fought hard. But your guns were well aimed. The bullets flew like birds in the air, and whizzed by our ears like the wind through the trees in the winter. My warriors fell around me; it began to look dismal. I saw my evil day at hand. The sun rose dim on us in the morning, and at night it sunk in a dark cloud, and looked like a ball of fire. That was the last sun that shone on Black Hawk. His heart is dead, and no longer beats quick in his bosom. He is now a prisoner to the white men; they will do with him as they wish. But he can stand torture, and is not afraid of death. He is no coward. Black Hawk is an Indian.

He has done nothing for which an Indian ought to be ashamed. He has fought for his countrymen, the squaws and papooses, against white men, who came, year after year, to cheat them and take away their lands. You know the cause of our making war. It is known to all white men. They ought to be ashamed of it. The white men despise the Indians, and drive them from their homes. But the Indians are not deceitful. The white men speak bad of the Indian, and look at him spitefully. But the Indian does not tell lies; Indians do not steal.

An Indian who is as bad as the white men, could not live in our nation; he would be put to death, and eat [sic] up by the wolves. The white men are bad school-masters; they carry false looks, and deal in false actions; they smile in the face of the poor Indian to cheat him; they shake them by the hand to gain their confidence, to make them drunk, to deceive them, and ruin our wives. We told them to let us alone; but they followed on and beset our paths, and they coiled themselves among us like the snake. They poisoned us by their touch. We were not safe. We lived in danger. We were becoming like them, hypocrites and liars, adulterers, lazy drones, all talkers, and no workers.

We looked up to the Great Spirit. We went to our great father. We were encouraged. His great council gave us fair words and big promises, but we got no satisfaction. Things were growing worse. There were no deer in the forest. The oppossum and beaver were fled; the springs were drying up, and our squaws and papooses without victuals to keep them from starving; we called a great council and built a large fire. The spirit of our fathers arose and spoke to us to avenge our wrongs or die. . . . We set up the war-whoop, and dug up the tomahawk; our knives were ready, and the heart of Black Hawk swelled high in his bosom when he led his warriors to battle. He is satisfied. He will go to the world of spirits contented. He has done his duty. His father will meet him there, and commend him.

Black Hawk is a true Indian, and disdains to cry like a woman. He feels for his wife, his children and friends. But he does not care for himself. He cares for his nation and the Indians. They will suffer. He laments their fate. The white men do not scalp the head; but they do worse— they poison the heart, it is not pure with them. His countrymen will not be scalped, but they will, in a few years, become like the white men, so that you can't trust them, and there must be, as in the white settlements, nearly as many officers as men, to take care of them and keep them in order.

Farewell, my nation. Black Hawk tried to save you, and avenge your wrongs. He drank the blood of some of the whites. He has been taken prisoner, and his plans are stopped. He can do no more. He is near his end. His sun is setting, and he will rise no more. Farewell to Black Hawk.[12] ◆◆

Black Elk, an Oglala Sioux holy man, on the invasion of his people's lands between 1863 and 1890

◆◆ I had never seen a Wasichu [white man] then, and did not know what one looked like; but every one was saying that the Wasichus were coming and that they were going to take our country and rub us all out and that we should have to die fighting. . . . Once we were happy in our own country and we were seldom hungry, for then the two-leggeds and the four-leggeds lived together like relatives, and there was plenty for them and for us. But the Wasichus came, and they have made little islands for us and other little islands for the four-leggeds, and always these islands are becoming smaller, for around them surges the gnawing flood of the Wasichu; and it is dirty with lies and greed. . . .

I was ten years old that winter [1873], and that was the first time I ever saw a Wasichu. At first I thought they all looked sick. . . .

That fall [1883], they say, the last of the bison herd was slaughtered by the Wasichus. I can remember when the bison were so many that they could not be counted, but more and more Wasichus came to kill them until there were only heaps of bones scattered where they used to be. The Wasichus did not kill them to eat; they killed them for the metal that makes them crazy, and they took only the hides to sell. Sometimes they did not even take the hides, only the tongues; and I have heard that fireboats came down the Missouri loaded with dried bison tongues. You can see that the men who did this were crazy. . . . ♦♦

In 1886 Black Elk journeyed east to Chicago and New York with a "wild west" show. He hoped to

♦♦ . . . learn some secret of the Wasichu that would help my people somehow. . . . I did not see anything to help my people. I could see that the Wasichus did not care for each other the way our people did before the nation's hoop was broken. They would take everything from each other if they could, and so there were some who had more of everything than they could use, while crowds of people had nothing at all and maybe were starving. They had forgotton that the earth was their mother. This could not be better than the old ways of my people. There was a prisoner's house on an island where the big water came up to the town, and we saw that one day. Men pointed guns at the prisoners and made them move around like animals in a cage. This made me feel very sad, because my people too were penned up in islands, and maybe that was the way the Wasichus were going to treat them.[13] ♦♦

Little Warrior, a Pawnee scout, 1879

In 1879 the Utes became involved in hostilities with the United States. Little Warrior, a Pawnee scout accompanying the U.S. forces, encountered a Ute leader and gave him the following advice:

♦♦ My friend, you and I have the same skin, and what I tell you is for your good. I speak to you as a friend, and what I say to you now is so that you may save your women and children. It is of no use for you to try to fight the white people. I have been among them, and I know how many they are. They are like the grass. . . . If you try to fight them they will hunt you like a ghost. Wherever you go they will follow after you, and you will get no rest. The soldiers will be continually on your tracks. Even if you were to go up on top of a high mountain . . . the soldiers would follow you, and get around you, and wait, even for fifty years. . . . There is one white man who is the chief of all this country, and what he says must be done. It is no use to fight him.[14] ♦♦

The funeral oration of Stephen Kelly, late 1920's

This oration of a Quechan was recorded by C. Daryll Forde:

♦♦ Oh, people! Our hearts are good and strong. We can work all day. This sickness does go away, I know it.

I myself go away alone in the house, I lie down on the bed and forget
   everything, all this fades away,
All the sick hearts of our people will change.
This day is passing away now,
We are all together now, we will think well now that we are all together
   in this place.
I tell you when we lose a strong man our hearts cannot be good,
So are we now but we must not think about it,
We must think about our being all together,
I will finish now. I will finish well.
We think about our being all together,
People, it will be well. This day is going
We commune with one another.
I will find our strength. I will find our good.
My body was not good when I lay down alone.
On that I rely.
Our thoughts are sick but our hearts will change.
I rely on that.
I will finish. Rightly we are thinking good things.[15] ◆◆

Narrative of Black Elk, 1930-1931

During 1930 and 1931 John G. Neihardt visited Black Elk, a *wichasha
wakon* (holy man) of the Oglala Sioux. Black Elk was over sixty, nearly
blind, and very much aware of the tragic condition of his people. Nevertheless, he was willing to communicate to Neihardt something of his life
and religious experiences and, in fact, he seemed to have anticipated
Neihardt's coming:

       ◆◆ As I sit here, I can feel in this man beside me a strong
desire to know the things of the Other World. He has been sent to learn
what I know, and I will teach him. . . . There is so much to teach you.
What I know was given to me for men and it is true and it is beautiful.
Soon I shall be under the grass and it will be lost. You were sent to save
it, and you must come back so that I can teach you. . . .

My friend, I am going to tell you the story of my life, as you wish;
and if it were only the story of my life I think that would not tell it; for
what is one man that he should make much of his winters, even when
they bend him like a heavy snow? So many other men have lived and
shall live that story, to be grass upon the hills.

It is the story of all life that is holy and is good to tell, and of us two-
leggeds sharing in it with the four-leggeds and the wings of the air and
all green things; for these are children of one mother and their father is
one Spirit. . . . now that I can see it all as from a lonely hilltop, I know
it was the story of a mighty vision given to a man too weak to use it; of

a holy tree that should have flourished in a people's heart with flowers and singing birds, and now is withered; and of a people's dream that died in bloody snow.

But if the vision was true and mighty, as I know, it is true and mighty yet, for such things are of the spirit, and it is in the darkness of their eyes that men get lost. . . .

But these four spirits [Of the four directions] are only one Spirit after all, and this eagle feather here is for that One [Wakon Tonka, the Great Mysterious One], which is like a father, and also it is for the thoughts of men that should rise high as eagles do. Is not the sky a father and the earth a mother, and are not all living things with feet and wings or roots their children? [16]   ◆◆

A prayer of Black Elk, 1930

◆◆   Grandfather, Great Spirit, you have been always, and before you no one has been. There is no other one to pray to but you. You yourself, everything that you see, everything has been made by you. The star nations all over the universe you have finished. The day, and in that day, everything you have finished. Grandfather, Great Spirit, lean close to the earth, a relative to all that is! Give me the eyes to see and the strength to understand, that I may be like you. . . .

Great Spirit, Great Spirit, my Grandfather, all over the earth the faces of living things are all alike. With tenderness have these come up out of the ground. Look upon these faces of children without number and with children in their arms, that they may face the winds and walk the good road to the day of quiet.

This is my prayer; hear me! The voice I have sent is weak, yet with earnestness I have sent it. Hear me! [17]   ◆◆

Black Elk's prayer from a mountaintop in the Black Hills, 1931

◆◆   Hey-a-a-hey! Hey-a-a-hey! Hey-a-a-hey! Hey-a-a-hey! Grandfather, Great Spirit, once more behold me on earth and lean to hear my feeble voice. You lived first, and you are older than all need, older than all prayer. All things belong to you—the two-leggeds, the four-leggeds, the wings of the air and all green things that live. You have set the powers of the four quarters to cross each other. The good road and the road of difficulties you have made to cross; and where they cross, the place is holy. Day in and day out, forever, you are the life of things.

Therefore I am sending a voice, Great Spirit, my grandfather, forgetting nothing you have made, the stars of the universe and the grasses of the earth.

You have said to me, when I was still young and could hope, that in difficulty I should send a voice four times, once for each quarter of the earth, and you would hear me.

Today I send a voice for a people in despair.

From the west, you have given me the cup of living water and the sacred bow, the power to make live and to destroy. You have given me a sacred wind and the herb from where the white giant lives—the cleansing power and the healing. The daybreak star and the pipe, you have given from the east; and from the south, the nations' sacred hoop and the tree that was to bloom. To the center of the world you have taken me and showed the goodness and beauty and the strangeness of the greening earth, the only mother—and there the spirit shapes of things, as they should be, you have shown to me and I have seen. At the center of this sacred hoop you have said that I should make the tree to bloom.

With tears running, O Great Spirit, Great Spirit, my Grandfather— with running tears I must say now that the tree has never bloomed. A pitiful old man, you see me here, and I have fallen away and have done nothing. Here at the center of the world, where you took me when I was young and taught; here, old, I stand, and the tree is withered, Grandfather, my Grandfather!

Again, and maybe the last time on this earth, I recall the great vision you sent me. It may be that some little root of the sacred tree still lives. Nourish it then, that it may leaf and bloom and fill with singing birds. Hear me, not for myself, but for my people; I am old. Hear me that they may once more go back into the sacred hoop and find the good red road, the shielding tree!

In sorrow I am sending a feeble voice, O Six Powers of the World. Hear me in my sorrow, for I may never call again. O make my people live! [18] ◆◆

Nipo Tach-num Strongheart (Yakima Nation), 1956

◆◆ Who was that person who said that Indians are pagans? That person and others like him should study the Bible more thoroughly, to learn *what* makes a Christian! a Bahai, a Buddhist, or any other person of faith. The Indian people are proud of their heritage and rightfully so! They are the true and faithful children of the GREAT MAKER and they are ever grateful for the gifts GOD gives to them. . . . The Indian people are CHRISTIAN in the full sense of the word. . . .[19] ◆◆

George D. Heron (Seneca Nation), 1960

Speaking to the Subcommittee on Indian Affairs of the House of Representatives about the construction of a dam on treaty-guaranteed Seneca land, George D. Heron said:

◆◆   My name is George D. Heron. I live on the Allegany Reservation in New York, and I am president of the Seneca Nation of Indians. . . . my friends from Pennsylvania have said that the Treaty of November 11, 1794, was abrogated when all Indians became citizens in 1924. I would like to point out that the 1794 Treaty was signed by the *Seneca Nation,* not by individual Seneca Indians, and the Nation has not yet become a citizen. It remains today exactly what it was 165 years ago—in the words of the courts as reported to us by our attorney, Mr. [Arthur] Lazarus, a "quasi-sovereign dependent nation." More important, our tribal lawyer tells me that the Supreme Court of the United States has held not once, but at least a dozen times, that the grant of citizenship does not affect any Indian treaty rights or in any other way change the special relationship of Indians and their property to the Federal government. I am not an educated man, but it seems very strange to me that these lawyers from Pennsylvania are willing to say that the Supreme Court ruled against the Senecas, when it did not even hear the case, while at the same time they are ignoring a whole series of actual Supreme Court decisions which go against their arguments.

I am proud to be an American citizen, and have four years in the United States Navy to prove it. I am just as proud to be a Seneca Indian. And I do not see any reason why I cannot be both. . . .

Lastly, I know it will sound simple and perhaps silly, but the truth of the matter is that my people really believe that George Washington read the 1794 Treaty before he signed it, and that he meant exactly what he wrote. For more than 165 years we Senecas have lived by that document. To us it is more than a contract, more than a symbol; to us, the 1794 Treaty is a way of life.

Times have not always been easy for the Seneca people. We have known and we still know poverty and discrimination. But through it all we have been sustained by a pledge of faith, unbroken by the Federal government. Take that pledge away, break our Treaty, and I fear that you will destroy the Senecas as an Indian community. . . .

On behalf of the Seneca Nation, may I thank you for granting us this hearing.[20] ◆◆

Anonymous, on the assimilation of the Mexican-American, 1961

◆◆   When a Mexican or a Mexican family comes from another state, he first seeks out the local colonia [Mexican neighborhood] and it is there that he hopes to find a place to live. He still feels a security that cannot be explained by words; perhaps, it is because here he can identify himself with the populace, whereas outside he may not. . . . Personally I believe that this problem will always exist and no matter how Anglicized a Mexican-American may become, he will always be thought of as a Mexican first and an American second. Yet, if one wants to be technical about the whole matter, the true American is the Mexican. Next to the Indians themselves the Mexican is the closest that an American can be. But it is not technicalities that will make him a part of the true social structure, it is the Anglo-American himself. In him rests the fate of the Mexican-American.[21] ◆◆

John B. Cummins, Chairman of the Crow Tribal Council, 1962

In an interview with a reporter of *Americas*, John B. Cummins said:

◆◆ We had a claim against the U.S. Government for thirty-three million acres of land that was once owned by the Crow Tribe and this was the basis for the settlement that we have just received. We are very fortunate that we have won this money from the U.S. Government. Now, when I say very fortunate, I mean that the Crow Indians are very poor. Today we are living among the white people who have immigrated onto the Crow Indian reservation. The Crow Indians have had to sell their land because they needed the money. If they had had financial help before, the Crow reservation today would have been intact. . . .

We have some [people] in business, some in farming, and some are in livestock. We know that we can't make farmers or livestock raisers out of all of them, but that is what most of them want to do. Very few of our Indian people have college educations, but those who do want to go into other businesses. . . .

We like to keep our identity as Indians. The objective and the policy of the present tribal government is education. We want education, we want to educate our children to know the ways of the white man, so that they can help themselves as well as helping the Crow Tribe in carrying on its own business. We know the Indian can be an equal to the white man if he has the education. For example, Mr. Real Bird is a college graduate, I finished eighth grade, and Mr. Bends is a high school graduate. But we don't like to see our Indians lose their traditions as Crow Indians. We want to be Crow Indians and at the same time we want to be equal to the white population in the rest of the United States. I don't know if you understand that being an Indian, I am proud to be an Indian.[22] ◆◆

Edison Real Bird, Vice Chairman of the Crow Tribal Council, 1962

◆◆ I'm certain we will continue to exist as American Indians. We are proud of our heritage, proud of our language, our dances and ceremonies. The population growth of the American Indian has been tremendous. On our reservation we have increased substantially, and now our lands are getting crowded, so we have to undertake new enterprises.[23] ◆◆

Francis Le Quier (Ojibwa), Chairman, Committee for the Great Council Fire, 1963

The following is the text of a proclamation posted on the Indian Reservation at Tucson, Arizona in February 1963:

◆◆ To the chiefs and Spiritual Leaders of the Indians of the North and South American Continents:
This is the day when the Great Spirit calls to all men.
This is the day when only the Great Spirit shall be glorified. This is the day all our great Chiefs spoke of. This is the day wherein all the Indian prophecies are fulfilled. This is the day of the Great Council Fire.
This is the day when you shall hear the Great Spirit speak through man again. This is the day when all the tribes shall come together and be one nation. This is the day when all the nations shall come together and be one world. This is the day when a new race of men shall be raised up by the power of the Great Spirit. This is the day of the Great Justice. . . .
You shall hear the voice of the Owl, the Fox, the Bear, the Coyote and the Eagle.
You shall hear one great voice coming from the east. This is the day when the Great Spirit shall be called by One Name.[24] ◆◆

The Native American Movement, 1963

The text of a 1963 Native American Movement pamphlet reads:

◆◆ The Native American Movement represents the reawakening of the Native American people and the revival of Americanist principles. It is the spiritual descendant of the earlier movements for unity organized by Tecumseh, Cuauhtemoc, Tupac Amaru, Po-pe, Cajeme, Wovoka and other great leaders.
The movement seeks to realize justice for Native Americans and all other peoples who suffer from discrimination. It does not draw any color line or exclude anyone. All persons who seek to advance the cause of true Americanism and of American unity are welcome. . . . All who struggle for justice and freedom are brothers! . . . Every person in the United States and in the Americas who has a drop of Native American ancestry is a member of the Movement if he stands for freedom and justice. . . .[25] ◆◆

Notes

1. A. Irving Hallowell, "The Backwash of the Frontier: The Impact of the Indian on American Culture," *Smithsonian Report for 1958*, p. 449.
2. Thomas Jefferson to John Adams, March 1812, in Foley, ed., *The Jefferson Cyclopedia*, pp. 422-3.
3. *Lives of Celebrated American Indians* (Boston: Bradbury, Soden and Co., 1843) pp. 179-180.
4. Verner W. Crane, *The Southern Frontier 1670-1732* (Ann Arbor: University of Michigan Press, 1959) pp. 300-301. Reprinted by permission of the University of Michigan Press.
5. *Lives of Celebrated American Indians*, p. 231.
6. *Lives of Celebrated American Indians*, pp. 283-7.
7. Grinnell, *Pawnee Hero Stories and Folk Tales*, pp. 258-9.
8. Samuel G. Drake, *The Book of the Indians of North America* (Boston: Antiquarian, 1836) Book V, Chap. vii, pp. 121-122.
9. *Lives of Celebrated American Indians*, pp. 274-275.
10. "Testimonio de Jatiñil," in Manuel C. Rojo, "Apuntes Historicos de la Baja California," M-M 295, Bancroft Library, Berkeley, California, pp. 41, 45-51. Used by permission of the Bancroft Library.
11. *Ibid.*, pp. 9-11. Used by permission of the Bancroft Library.
12. *Lives of Celebrated American Indians*, pp. 310-312.
13. Neihardt, *Black Elk Speaks*, pp. 5-9, 63, 217-218, 221. Reprinted by permission of the University of Nebraska Press and the author.
14. Grinnell, *Pawnee Hero Stories*, p. 81.
15. C. Daryll Forde, "Ethnography of the Yuma Indians," *University of California Publications in American Archaeology and Ethnology*, Vol. 28, No. 4, 1931, p. 213.
16. Neihardt, *op. cit.*, pp. ix, x, 1-3. Reprinted by permission of the University of Nebraska Press and the author.
17. *Ibid.*, pp. 5-6. Used by permission of the University of Nebraska Press and the author.
18. *Ibid.*, pp. 278-80. Used by permission of the University of Nebraska Press and the author.
19. Nipo Tach-num Strongheart, "The Winter Solstice and Christmas," *Talking Leaf*, December 1956.
20. Statement of George D. Heron to the House Subcommittee on Indian Affairs, reprinted in *The Kinzua Dam Controversy* (Philadelphia: Philadelphia Yearly Meeting of Friends, 1961) pp. 8-10.
21. Anonymous interview, in Karen Mendelson, "The Colonia Mexicana," unpublished manuscript, 1961, p. 18.
22. Reprinted from *Americas* (monthly magazine published by the Pan American Union in English, Spanish, and Portuguese) Vol. 14, No. 9, September 1962, pp. 7, 9.
23. *Ibid.*, pp. 9-10.
24. Francis Le Quier, "A Copy of the Proclamation posted on Indian Reservation, Tucson, Arizona, Feb. 22, 23, 24, 1963" (mimeographed sheet).
25. "Who are the Native Americans?" Native American Movement pamphlet, 1963.

FIVE

THE CONQUERED

Scholars and laymen have ordinarily given attention to the Native American only during the periods when he represented a military obstacle to the European. This is understandable since the "fighting Indians" were colorful, brave, and romantic, while conquered natives often became depressed, dirty, and disease-ridden. The latter phenomena, however, is reason enough for a thorough study of what takes place when a people suffer from military conquest. The accompanying impoverishment, sudden culture change, and mental shock may lead to a state of group depression from which a people arise only slowly and with great difficulty. This indeed is one of the central problems of the Americas today—how to awaken the indigenous and mixed-blood masses from their lethargy and withdrawal and bring them into full participation in modern life.

Thus it is important that we attempt to understand, even if only partially, what took place as the natives of the United States were conquered. The subject of the conquered native is, however, significant not merely for its relevance to broader problems of depressed populations. It also forms a meaningful part of the history of American labor and economic development. Natives in many areas were not simply killed or herded into seminary-like missions or onto reservations. Great numbers were put to work as laborers, craftsmen, cowboys, and even miners. The following selections are designed to illustrate the role of the defeated native as mission neophyte, *peón* or serf-style laborer, and as an independent miner, and, in addition, to provide some insight into the general effects of conquest.

ENFORCED ACCULTURATION (THE MISSIONS OF CALIFORNIA)

A vast amount of literature exists on the missions of the Southwest; much of it, however, is propagandistic or romantic in nature. The *reduciones* (*congregaciones* or missions) of the Spaniards were royal institutions designed to control native populations and transform them into Catholic subjects of the Crown. The salvation of souls was important to the more devout of the missionaries; however, the government was most interested in producing docile taxpayers and laborers—and the government established most of the missions (the Spanish Catholic Church did not exist as an institution independent of the Crown).

The missions of California were absolutely totalitarian institutions in which almost every phase of native life was regulated by the friars and soldiers. It was often difficult to secure voluntary converts to this kind of institution, and various devices, ranging from enticement with food and trinkets to the outright use of force, were utilized. In the latter part of the eighteenth century José Dario Argüello, an officer, commented upon the motives that led the Quechan of the Colorado River to ask for missionaries:

> . . . when the Indian Palma [a Quechan leader] came back [from a visit to Mexico City] . . . he brought a trunk full of decent clothing such as long shirts, decorated military coats, . . . a hat with three peaks, a baton, and other dressy finery, . . . [and] he made them [the Quechans] understand the great things he saw in Mexico and that most of the Christians went about as he presented himself to them . . . [and that he was Christianized and regaled] in order to persuade all his countrymen to become Christians, and he made a thousand promises in his speech that the same thing [being regaled] would happen to them. With this motive the [Quechan] Nation began to ask for priests to go to their land . . .[1]

No matter what means were used to entice Indians into a mission, however, force had to be used to keep them there and to coerce them into abandoning their native customs. In 1792 a Franciscan, Juan Domingo Arricivita, noted that Fray Francisco Garcés "asked for the protection of troops in order to propagate the faith; inasmuch as it is a well-known experience in all the Indies [Americas], that it is not possible to conserve or expand it without them." [2]

Converts frequently attempted to run away from the missions. Vassali Tarakanoff, a Russian captive in California, describes one such occurrence about 1816:

> The indios were away several days when a great number of soldiers came to the mission and they and some of the priests went out and stayed away many days, and when they came back, they brought most of the natives. They were all bound with rawhide ropes, and some were bleeding from wounds, and some children were tied to their mothers. The next day we saw some terrible things. Some of the run-away men were tied to sticks and beaten with straps. One chief was taken out to the open field and a young calf which had just died was skinned and the chief was sewed into the skin while it was yet warm. He was kept tied to a stake all day, but he died soon and they kept his corpse tied up.[3]

The effects of missionization varied from region to region. In general, however, the natives frequently became psychologically depressed and lethargic, giving the impression of dull-wittedness or stupidity. After examining several missions in the San Francisco Bay area in 1786, Jean de la Perouse remarked:

> These men [Indians of the Monterey region of California] have very few ideas, still less stability, and if they be not continually treated like children, they escape from those [missionaries] who have been at the trouble of instructing them. . . . reasoning has no effect upon them, so that their senses must be forcibly appealed to. . . . We saw men and women [in the missions] loaded with irons, others in the stocks, and at length the noise of the strokes of a whip struck our ears. . . . Corporeal punishments are inflicted on the Indians of both sexes who neglect pious exercises, and several sins . . . are punished with chains or the stocks. [De la Perous saw much similarity between the missions of California and the slave system of Haiti, although he admired the Franciscan friars' zeal and intentions].[4]

De la Perouse saw the San Francisco Bay natives as stupid *by nature;* however, the diarists who described them prior to their missionization were rather impressed by their appearance and behavior.

A great variety of punishments were common in the missions. At Santa Barbara, for example, lashing, shackles, stocks, imprisonment, and chaining in irons were used for men. Women were punished in the same manner; and in addition all unmarried females from the age of seven or eight were locked up each night in a fifty-one by twenty-one foot room called a *monjeria* (nunnery). Unmarried men were in some instances locked in at night as well.[5] The various punishments described above were for relatively minor crimes, such as running away, robbery, or breaking the sexual rules of the missionaries. More serious crimes resulted in extensive lashing, exile, and many years at hard labor. Occasionally rebels were executed.

The death rate in the California missions was extremely high—by 1800 deaths exceeded births by two to one, and eventually deaths exceeded both births and new conversions. Whereas in 1769 coastal California from San Francisco to San Diego had a population of 70,000 or more, in 1833-1835, when the missions were secularized, only 15,000 natives remained.

The high death rate and low birth rate (the latter caused in part by abortions) in the missions may have been stimulated partially by psychosomatic factors. Not only were the natives conquered and subjected to a coercive system very different from their traditional way of life, but systematic efforts were made to suppress native religion. In 1828, for example, a soldier at Santa Inés reported that three neophytes:

> . . . made a practice of dancing in one of the houses of the rancheria, and of bringing thither those of their comrades who were dangerously sick; the

latter being informed that each one who danced should contribute beads or some other offering, in order that the dance might find favor in the eyes of the devil, and they in consequence be healed.

The three were apprehended, admitted "sorcery" and were sentenced to be whipped and imprisoned by their priest.

The dancing took place on two several [sic] occasions, and . . . [it] . . . consisted in touching the sick with feathers as our priests touch persons with holy water, the medicine men meanwhile dancing. On the second occasion, some of the bystanders ridiculed the proceedings and one of the prisoners threatened to bring about the death of the skeptics by means of a composition of herbs.[6]

Rebellions sometimes occurred; however, the garrisons of soldiers at each mission were usually sufficient to control them. In 1824-1825, though, the Chumash of Santa Barbara succeeded in escaping to the San Joaquin Valley. Ten years later some of them were visited there by Anglo-Americans:

After we halted here we found that these people could talk the Spanish language, which we thought might be of great advantage to the company, and on inquiry ascertained that they were a tribe called the Concoas, which tribe some eight or ten years since resided in the Spanish settlements at the missionary station near St. Barbara, on the coast, where they rebelled against the authority of the country, robbed the church of all its golden images and candle-sticks, and one of the Priests of several thousand dollars in gold and silver, when they retreated to the spot where we found them—being at least 5 or 600 miles distant from the nearest Spanish settlement. This tribe is well acquainted with the rules of bartering for goods or anything they wish to buy—much more so than any other tribe we met with. They make regular visits to such posts where they are unknown, and also make appointments with ship traders to meet at some designated time and place; thus they are enabled to carry on a considerable degree of commerce. They still retain several of the images which they pilfered from the church—the greater part of which is the property of the chiefs. . . . These people are 7 or 800 strong, their houses are constructed of poles and covered with grass, and are tolerably well supplied with house-hold furniture which they brought with them at the time they robbed the church. They follow agricultural pursuits to some extent, raising very good crops of corn, pumpkins, melons, etc. All the out-door labor is done by the females. They are also in the habit of making regular visits to the settlements for the purpose of stealing horses, which they kill and eat.[7]

The Chumash who remained in the missions declined in numbers steadily (from perhaps 10,000 to 2,200); however, conditions were not altogether too severe at Santa Barbara in 1834:

The habitations of the neophytes are of adobe with roofs of tile and they form streets from south to north; they [the Chumash] are of very good disposition, subordinated to a particular comprehension for that which has been taught them and is being taught; they are now forming an orchestra of music for the church of ten or more instruments of string and wind, well regulated for harmony; and the same in singing with elegance; and they are industrious at work; both sexes are of good appearance, with an affable manner, which qualities distinguish them from the others of their caste.

The natives of nearby Purisima mission were quite different from those of Santa Barbara, although they were also Chumash.

The condition of these [neophytes] is vicious, they are naturally arrogant, proud and indocile, their manner is rough and the countenance or configuration of both sexes is ugly and disagreeable.[8]

The effects of missionization, therefore, varied considerably from region to region, except that the death rate was high everywhere.

THE EFFECTS OF CONQUEST (THE RESERVATIONS)

In a preceding selection George Catlin commented upon the visible cultural, and moral degeneration which often accompanied the native's conquest by Anglo-Americans. Rare indeed was the tribe which did not suffer seriously from the economic, political, cultural, and psychological effects of defeat and enforced impoverishment and concentration. Evidence relating to this phenomenon is interspersed throughout this work, however, three specific examples are given below.

E. A. Stevenson, an Indian agent, 1857

◆◆ I ascertained the number of [Shasta] Inds. at the Fort [Jones] to be about two hundred. They are a fine looking lot of Indians but have become like all other Inds. that have been long among the Whites in this country, addicted to drinking and prostitution with their attendant evils. [A short time later Achomawi Indians were met living on the Pit River who had had little contact with Whites.] They were the finest looking Inds. I have ever seen on the Pacific Coast.[9] ◆◆

Charles Granville Johnson, 1868

◆◆ This once powerful, numerous, and haughty tribe, the Yumas, are now reduced to a comparative fraction, and are generally broken down in Spirit, demoralized, and indolent, but perfectly docile and harmless, depending mainly upon the charities of the white people in the river settlements, and upon the military headquarters at Fort Yuma.[10] ◆◆

Captain J. Lee Humfreville, 1897

◆◆ The remnants [of the western tribes] . . . are now kept on Indian reservations, and are literally cabined, cribbed, and confined. . . . Today they . . . subsist on rations doled out to them with niggardly hand by government agents. They have become what they are in all portions of the country where they have been partly civilized, or an effort made to civilize them, namely, miserable specimans of humanity. . . .[11] ◆◆

THE INTRODUCTION OF VICES

According to two priests stationed at Santa Barbara, the most that the soldiers of that community had done to "advance" the Christian and non-Christian Indians of the nearby village of Siujtu was to show them how to be dexterous in card games. The priests could not allow female neophytes to go to the military establishment because

At Santa Barbara, 1800

◆◆ . . . there are many examples of these women, who for a watermelon or for a tortilla de maiz, will prostitute themselves. Some of the soldiers can say that they have carried them on horseback, and that they and other Spanish-speaking persons have had illicit relations with them.[12] ◆◆

Indian prostitution in Southern California, 1849

◆◆ . . . some of the Indians presented us with some women, offering them for a small fee. The prostitution among these savages is such that one of them offered herself to a traveler for a handkerchief, and he being repelled by the fear of syphilis, she responded that yes she was [infected]; but after these expressions she presented a young girl of her neighborhood, saying that [the young girl] was good; but she was worth one horse. Many other similar cases were noted, and I confirmed that . . . the various groups of California Indians have the custom of delivering women for whatever payment [is available].[13] ◆◆

THE NATIVE AS A LABORER

Many natives became laborers either as a result of conquest or because of a desire to obtain articles of value. In the seventeenth century free Indian labor was common during certain periods in both Massachusetts and Virginia. In California and in the Southwest, the Spanish-speaking population was more inclined to utilize native workers than were the Anglo-Europeans. Most of the Hispano-Mexican newcomers were prejudiced against certain kinds of labor—they wished to be men on horseback, supervising, but not actually working. As early as 1796 it was asserted that in the pueblos of California the Spanish-speaking settlers did nothing but sing and play the guitar. All labor was performed by non-Christian Indians who served as cowboys, laborers, and farmers.[14] And in the missions, of course, the neophytes performed every task involving physical labor.

In 1835 R. H. Dana noted that the Mexican officers at Monterey wore "the deerskin shoe, which is of a dark-brown color, and (being made by Indians) usually a good deal ornamented." Dana also noticed that

> the Indians . . . do all the hard work, two or three being attached to each house; and the poorest persons are able to keep one, at least, for they have only to feed them and give them a small piece of course cloth and a belt, for the males; and a course gown, without shoes or stockings, for the females.[15]

Labor in Los Angeles, 1841

♦♦ All labor in [Los Angeles] is done by the Indians recruited from a small rancheria [village] on the banks of the river on the outskirts of the pueblo. These poor wretches are often mistreated and do not always receive in full their daily pay, which is fixed at one *real* in money and one *real* in merchandise, in other words, one-fourth piaster.[16] ♦♦

Labor in Northern California, 1851

♦♦ Mr. S——— employed a host of Indians upon his ranch. . . . Nineteen years' salutary training had, in a measure, eradicated the indolent propensities inherent to the digger race. . . . Mrs. B——— [the daughter] performed no household duties herself. She had five or six well-trained Indian women for house servants, who labored hard for no other renumeration than their food and raiment. [At the home of General John Sutter near Marysville] The Indians in the immediate vicinity are devoted to the general's service; while the only renumeration they ask or expect is their food. His house servants are all the female diggers.[17] ♦♦

Indian workers in Southern California, 1852

♦♦ They [Luiseños and Diegueños] are a large majority of the laborers, mechanics, and servants of San Diego and Los Angeles

counties. . . . Nearly all speak the Spanish language, and some of the
chiefs read and write it. . . .

The Indian laborers and servants are domesticated; mix with us daily
and hourly. . . . They are almost the only house or farm servants we
have. . . .

No white man here, whether American, Sonoranian, or Californian,
will work for such wages, nor anything like it. . . . [These Indians]
built all the houses in the country, and planted all the fields and vineyards. . . . [They] are the only farmers living here, besides the Americans who have come into the country since the war, and a very few who
were here before. The California "Spaniard," (so to speak) loves his
fiery steed–not the plough. Many such a *ranchero,* rich in cattle and
"goodly acres" by the ten thousand, must go to his Indian neighbor
hard by on the rancho, if he would dine today on his maize or
frijole! [18]   ♦♦

Working conditions, Los Angeles, 1855

♦♦ A few days hence I saw an Indian girl lying in a
dying state by the wall. . . . An old man and woman, apparently her
parents, were with her. I learn today that a man (Spaniard) who had
her as a servant, when he found her dying or [believing] that she would
dye, to avoid the expense of her burial put her in a cart and took her
down there and unloaded her by the side of the road.[19]   ♦♦

Mexicans and Indians as farm laborers, 1862-1870

♦♦ All . . . labor on the ranch . . . was done for the
first few years by a dozen or fifteen Mexicans and domesticated Indians,
who with their families lived at the Rancheria, near La Presa [east of
San Marino, Calif.]. In speaking of Mexicans and Indians the distinction
is with practically no difference in appearance or temperament. The
Indians had much coarser hair, which was never wavy. Their complexions were invariably dark and cheekbones more prominent than those
of the Mexicans, whereas some of the Mexicans were fair. . . . Their
modes of living were the same. They fraternized readily and frequently
intermarried. . . . Both were bibulously inclined but rarely indulged in
drink other than Saturday nights. Their small huts were made of tule,
which grew in the swamp nearby. . . . Many of the happiest hours of
my young life were those I spent playing with the children of these
people. . . . I learned to speak Spanish as a native, in fact the first word
I ever uttered was agua, Spanish for water.[20]   ♦♦

Native American forty-niners, 1848-49

Many natives, both from California and elsewhere, participated in the
various gold rushes of the far west, some as employees of whitemen and
others as independent, though casual, miners. In 1848 E. Gould Buffum
noted that "a portion of the tribe go daily to the Yuba River [Cali-
fornia], and wash out a sufficient amount of gold to purchase a few
pounds of flour, or some sweetmeats, and return to their rancheria at
night to share it with their neighbours." [21]
During the following year Bayard Taylor learned that "many of the
Americans employed Sonorians and Indians to work for them, giving
them half the gold and finding them in provisions. . . . These people
could be kept for a dollar daily." [22]

SPANISH-SPEAKING CALIFORNIANS AND DISCRIMINATION, 1849-1850's

Participants in the gold rushes of California (and the West in
general) also included many persons of Mexican ancestry, some of whom
were pure native and others of mixed background. The following illustrates one of the reasons why these people (called "Spanish" in this instance) met with discrimination in the mines.

♦♦ The native Spanish inhabitants have suffered a cer-
tain check in their remarkable productivity from their irregular position.
The Spanish possessed an admixture of Indian blood, for which the
Americans entertained an undisguised and irritating contempt, that was
inconsiderately extended to almost any sunburned complexion. They
were thus exposed to the hostility of a discriminating mining [industry],
with the result of checking their influx [into the gold regions].[23] ♦♦

MEXICANS IN TEXAS, 1857

With the conquest of the Southwest by the United States, Anglo-
Americans came into increasing contact with large numbers of Mexicans
of native and part-native ancestry. In many regions, such as Texas, these
Mexicans were treated in part as a conquered people (as indeed they
were) and were subject to discrimination. Nevertheless, the Mexican's
labor was of great importance from the ranches of Texas to the developing vineyards and orchards of California; and furthermore, the proximity
of the Mexican border and the relatively great numbers possessed by
this group served to make their experiences somewhat different from
those of Tribal Americans.

◆◆ . . . we enter the square of the Alamo. This is all Mexican. Windowless cabins of stakes, plastered with mud and roofed with river-grass, or "tula"; or low, windowless, but better thatched houses of adobes (gray, unburnt bricks), with groups of brown idlers lounging at their doors. . . .

From the bridge we enter Commerce street, the narrow principal thoroughfare, and here are American houses, and the triple nationalities break out into the most amusing display, till we reach the main plaza. The sauntering Mexicans prevail on the pavements, but the bearded Germans and the sallow Yankees furnish their proportion. . . . The Mexican buildings are stronger than those we saw before but still of all sorts, and now put to all sorts of new uses. They are all low, of adobe or stone, washed blue and yellow, with flat roofs close down upon their single story. Windows have been knocked in their blank walls, letting the sun into their dismal vaults, and most of them are stored with dry goods and groceries, which overflow around the door. . . .

The doors of the cabins of the real natives stood open wide, if indeed they exist at all, and many were the family pictures of jollity or sleepy comfort they displayed to us as we sauntered curious about. The favorite dress appeared to be a dishabille, and a free-and-easy, lollopy sort of life generally seemed to have been adopted as possessing, on the whole, the greatest advantages for a reasonable being. The larger part of each family appeared to be made up of black-eyed, olive girls, full of animation of tongue and glance, but sunk in a soft embonpoint, which added a somewhat extreme good nature to their charms. Their dresses seemed lazily reluctant to cover their plump persons, and their attitudes were always expressive of the influences of a Southern sun upon national manners. The matrons, dark and wrinkled, formed a strong contrast to their daughters, though, here and there, a fine cast of feature and a figure erect with dignity, attracted the eye. The men lounged in roundabouts and cigaritos, as was to be expected, and in fact the whole picture lacked nothing that is Mexican. . . .

The town amusements of a less exciting character are not many. There is a permanent company of Mexican mountebanks, who give performances of agility and buffoonery two or three times a week, parading before night in their spangled tights with drum and trombone through the principal streets. They draw a crowd of whatever little Mexicans can get adrift, and this attracts a few sellers of whisky, tortillas and tamaules [sic] (corn, slap-jacks and hashed meat in cornshucks), all by the light of torches making a ruddily picturesque evening group. . . .

A day or two after our arrival, there was the hanging of a Mexican. The whole population left the town to see. Family parties, including the grandmother and the little negroes, came from all the plantations and farms within reach, and little ones were held up high to get their share of warning. The Mexicans looked on imperturbable.

San Antonio, excluding Galveston, is much the largest city of Texas. After the Revolution it was half deserted by its Mexican population, who did not care to come under Anglo-Saxon rule. Since then, its growth has been rapid and steady. At the census of 1850, it numbered 3,500; in 1853, its population was 6,000; and in 1856, it is estimated at 10,500. Of these about 4,000 are Mexicans, 3,000 Germans, and 3,500 Americans. The money-capital is in the hands of the Americans, as well as the officers and the Government. Most of the mechanics and the smaller shopkeepers are German. The Mexicans appear to have almost no other business than that of carting goods. Almost the entire transportation of the country is carried on by them, with oxen and two-wheeled carts. Some of them have small shops for the supply of their own countrymen, and some live upon the produce of farms and cattle-ranches owned in the neighborhood. Their livelihood is, for the most part, exceedingly meagre, made up chiefly of corn and beans.

We had before we left opportunities of visiting familiarly many of the Mexican dwellings. I have described their externals. Within, we found usually a single room, open to the roof and invariably having a floor of beaten clay a few inches below the level of the street. There was little furniture—huge beds being the universal piece de resistance. These were used by day as sofa and table. Sometimes there were chairs and a table besides; but frequently only a bench, with a few earthen utensils for cooking, which is carried on outside. A dog or a cat appears on or under the bed or on the clothes-chest, a saint on the wall, and frequently a gamecock fastened in a corner, supplied with dishes of corn and water.

We were invariably received with the most gracious and beaming politeness and dignity. Their manner towards one another is engaging and that of children and parents most affectionate. This we always noticed in evening walks and in the groups about the doors, which were often singing in chorus—the attitudes expressive of confident affection. In one house, we were introduced to an old lady who was supposed by her grandchildren to be over one hundred years old. She had come from Mexico, in a rough cart, to make them a visit. Her face was strikingly Indian in feature, her hair, snow white, flowing thick over the shoulders, contrasting strongly with the olive skin. The complexion of the girls is clear and sometimes fair, usually a blushing olive. The variety of feature and color is very striking, and is naturally referred to three sources—the old Spanish, the Creole Mexican and the Indian, with sometimes a suspicion of Anglo-Saxon or Teuton. The hair is coarse but glossy, and very luxuriant; the eye, deep, dark, liquid and well set. Their modesty, though real, we heard, was not proof against a long courtship of flattering attentions and rich presents. The constancy of the married women was made very light of, not that their favors were purchasable, but that they are sometimes seized by a strong penchant for some other than their lord. There was testimony of this in the various shades and features of their children; in fact we thought the number of babies of European hair and feature exceeded the native olive in number. . . . Their constitutions, in general, are feeble, and very many of both sexes, we were informed, suffered from scrofulous disease. Nevertheless, with good stimulus, the men make admirable laborers.

The common dress was loose and slight, not to say slatternly. It was frequently but a chemise, as low as possible in the neck, sometimes even lower, with a calico petticoat. On holidays they dress in expensive finery, paying special attention to the shoes, of white satin, made by a native artist.

The houses of the rich differ little from those of the poor, and the difference in their style of living must be small, owing to the want of education and of all ambition. The majority are classed as laborers. Their wages are small, usually, upon farms near San Antonio, $6 or $8 a month, with corn and beans. That of the teamsters is in proportion to their energy. On being paid off, they hurry to their family and all come out in their best to spend the earnings, frequently quite at a loss for what to exchange them. They make excellent drovers and shepherds, and in work like this, with which they are acquainted, are reliable and adroit. A horse-drover just from the Rio Grande with whom we conversed called them untiring and faithful at their work, but untrustworthy in character. To his guide he paid $24 a month, to his right bower $15, and to his left bower $12 a month.

Their tools are of the rudest sort. The old Mexican wheel of hewn blocks of wood is still constantly in use, though supplanted to some extent by Yankee wheels sent in pairs from New York. The carts are always hewn of heavy wood, and are covered with white cotton stretched over hoops. In these they live on the road as independently as in their own house. The cattle are yoked by the horns with raw-hide throngs, of which they make a great use.

They consort freely with the negroes, making no distinction from pride of race. A few, of old Spanish blood, have purchased negro servants, but most of them regard slavery with abhorrence.

The Mexicans were treated for a while after annexation like a conquered people. Ignorant of their rights, and of the new language, they allowed themselves to be imposed upon by the new comers, who seized their lands and property without shadow of claim, and drove hundreds of them homeless across the Rio Grande. They now, as they get gradually better informed, come straggling back, and often their claims give rise to litigation, usually settled by a compromise. . . .

Most adult Mexicans are voters by the organic law; but few take measures to make use of the right. Should they do so, they might probably, in San Antonio, have elected a government of their own. Such a step would be followed, however, by a summary revolution. They are regarded by slaveholders with great contempt and suspicion for their intimacy with slaves and their competition with plantation labor.

Americans, in speaking of them, constantly distinguish themselves as "white folks." I once heard a new comer informing another American that he had seen a Mexican with a revolver. "I shouldn't think they ought to be allowed to carry fire-arms. It might be dangerous." "It would be difficult to prevent it," the other replied; "Oh, they think themselves just as good as white men."

From several counties they have been driven out altogether. At Austin, in the spring of 1853, a meeting was held, at which the citizens resolved, on the plea that Mexicans were horse-thieves, that they must quit the county. About twenty families were thus driven from their homes, and dispersed over the western counties. Deprived of their means of livelihood, and rendered furious by such wholesale injustice, it is no wonder if they should take to the very crimes with which they are charged.

A similar occurrence took place at Seguin, in 1854; and in 1855, a few families, who had returned to Austin, were again driven out.

Even at San Antonio, there had been talk of such a razzia. A Mexican, caught in an attempt to steal a horse, had been hung by a lynching party, on the spot, for an example. His friends happened to be numerous and were much excited, threatening violence in return. Under pretext of subduing an intended riot the sheriff issued a call for an armed posse of 500 men, with the idea of dispersing and driving from the neighborhood a large part of the Mexican population. But the Germans, who include among them the great majority of young men suitable for such duty, did not volunteer as had been expected, and the scheme was abandoned. They were of the opinion, one of them said to me, that this was not the right and republican way. If the laws were justly and energetically administered, no other remedy would be needed. One of them, who lived on the Medina in the vicinity of the place of the occurrence, told us he had no complaint to make of the Mexicans; they never stole his property or troubled him in any way." [24] ◆◆

Notes

1. José Dario Argüello, Informe, 1797, C-A 217, Bancroft Library, Berkeley, California. Used by permission of the Bancroft Library.
2. Juan Domingo Arricivita, *Crónica Serafica y Apostolica* (Mexico: Zúñiga y Ontiveros, 1792) p. 499.
3. Vassali Tarakanoff, *Statement of my Captivity Among the Californians*, translated by Ivan Petroff (Los Angeles: Glen Dawson, 1953) p. 14. Reprinted by permission of Glen Dawson.

4. Jean de la Perouse, *A Voyage Round the World* (London: J. Johnson, 1789) pp. 205, 212.
5. Fray Esteban Tapis and Fray Juan Cortés, 1800, C-C8, Bancroft Library, Berkeley, California, pp. 99, 124.
6. Bancroft, *California Pastoral*, Vol. I, pp. 624-5.
7. W. F. Wagner, *The Adventures of Zenas Leonard* (Cleveland: Burrows, 1904) pp. 229-230.
8. C-A 20, Bancroft Library, Berkeley, California, pp. 160, 165. Used by permission of Bancroft Library.
9. Letter of E. A. Stevenson, September 30, 1857, ed. by Erminie Wheeler-Voegelin, *Ethnohistory*, Vol. IV, No. 1, Winter 1957, pp. 73-74.
10. Charles Granville Johnson, *History of the Territory of Arizona* (San Francisco: Ryan & Co., 1868) p. 17.
11. Humfreville, *Twenty Years Among Our Savage Indians*, p. 51.
12. Fray Esteban Tapis and Fray Juan Cortés, 1800, C-C8, Bancroft Library, Berkeley, California, p. 122. Used by permission of the Bancroft Library.
13. Diary of José Elias, in José Francisco Velasco, *Noticias Estadisticas del Estado de Sonora* (Mexico: Cumplido, 1850) p. 325.
14. Fray Isidro Salazar, "Informe," C-C8, Bancroft Library, Berkeley, California, p. 73.
15. R. H. Dana, *Two Years Before the Mast* (New York: A. L. Burt Company, n. d.) pp. 70, 76.
16. Eugene Duflot de Mofras, *Travels on the Pacific Coast,* translated and edited by Marguerite E. Wilbur (Santa Ana: Fine Arts Press, 1937) Vol. I, p. 186.
17. Bates, *op. cit.,* pp. 166, 168, 206.
18. John W. Caughey, *The Indians of Southern California in 1852* (San Marino: Huntington Library, 1952) pp. 16, 21-2, 60. Reprinted by permission of the Huntington Library.
19. Lyndley Bynum, ed., "Los Angeles in 1854-5: The Diary of Rev. James Woods," *Publications of the Historical Society of Southern California,* Vol. XXIII, No. 2, (1949) p. 81.
20. L. J. Rose, Jr., *L. J. Rose of Sunny Slope* (San Marino: The Huntington Library, 1959) pp. 54-5. Reprinted by permission of the Huntington Library.
21. Buffum, *Six Months in the Gold Mines* from *A Journal of Three Years in Upper and Lower California,* p. 46.
22. Bayard Taylor, *Eldorado or Adventures in the Path of Empire* (New York: G. P. Putnam's Sons, 1894) p. 85.
23. Bancroft, *History of California,* Vol. VII, p. 702.
24. Olmsted, *A Journey Through Texas,* pp. 149-165.

SIX

RED SLAVERY

When most people think of slavery in the United States they think only of the Negro. However, at various times in the history of North America people of Native American, Afro-Indian, Afro-Eurindian, and Eurafrican ancestry were also enslaved, and during certain periods there were slaves or servants of European and North African Caucasian background.

Christopher Columbus initiated the enslavement of Native Americans by Europeans in 1494 by sending more than 500 of them to Spain to be sold. Others followed, but in 1500 the practice was halted by the Crown. In the West Indies, however, Native Americans continued to be enslaved in great numbers. By 1500-1510 slave-raiders were depopulating the Bahamas and visiting Florida. Thereafter Florida and the southern United States served as a source of slaves for over half a century. Portuguese, English, French, and other ships occasionally carried off Native Americans from the Atlantic seaboard as well. For example, in 1500 the Portuguese navigator Gaspar Corte Real took Labrador natives as slaves to Portugal, and Jacques Cartier, in the 1530's, seized natives along the St. Lawrence River.

The great demand for slaves in the West Indies led to the enslavement of thousands of Mexican natives. From 1523 to 1528 Nuño de Guzmán used Pánuco, on the east coast of Mexico, as a center for the exportation of slaves, and from 1528 through the 1530's he extended his slave-hunting into Jalisco and Sinaloa. During 1537-1539 the Spaniards of Culiacán raided northward toward Sonora for slaves—Núñez Cabeza de Vaca found the Indians living "in great alarm and fear" of the slavers.

The mining boom in north-central Mexico in the 1540's led to a new need for slave labor, and the seminomadic tribes of the region were the victims of exploitation. By 1563-1572 Spaniards from southern Chihuahua were raiding for slaves as far north as the La Junta–Big Bend region of Texas. In 1581 Gaspar de Luxán led an expedition to La Junta to take captives, and this slave raid extended into Texas. The La Junta Indians were afraid of the Spaniards as a result of the previous slave raids. The inhabitants said that the invaders had taken their kinsmen, wives, and children captive and carried them away in chains.

The Espejo-Beltrán expedition to New Mexico in 1582 acquired female slaves and also at least one slave from La Junta. Slave-raiding was also carried on in northeastern Mexico, and in the 1590's bands of ex-soldiers were active there. This slave-hunting may also have extended into south Texas.[1]

Slave-raiding along the New England coast, 1614

♦♦ He [Squanto] was a native of this place [Plymouth], and scarce any left alive besids him selfe. He was carried away with diverce others by one *Hunt,* a [master] of a ship [in 1614], who thought to sell them for slaves in Spaine [and he, along with twenty-six other Indians, were sold at Malaga]; but he got away for England, and was entertained by a marchante in London, & imployed to New-foundland & other parts, & lastly brought hither into these parts. . . . [but only to find his people destroyed by disease].[2] ♦♦

Slave-raiding in New Mexico, 1627-1638

In 1627-1628 a group of Plains Apaches came into central New Mexico and became attracted to the Catholic faith; however

♦♦ . . . the demon had recourse to one of the wiles he is accustomed to employ in his defense, choosing as his instrument the greed of our Spanish governor [Phelipe Sotelo Ossorio]. In order to obtain slaves to sell in New Spain, the governor sent a brave Indian captain, who was an enemy of [the Apaches], to bring back as many captives as he could. [The raid was successful, the village of the friendly Apaches was destroyed, and many Indians were carried off. In *ca.* 1638 Spaniards, under orders of Governor Luis de Rosas] . . . killed a great number of the said friendly Apaches, and these killings were done in company with many infidel enemies of the said Apaches, an action prohibited by cédula of His Majesty . . . and they captured them in this unjust way, and they took them to sell in [Nueva Vizcaya].[3] ♦♦

Indian slavery in New England, 17th century

♦♦ With regard to enslaving the Indians, New England had early taken the lead and throughout the colonial period held more Indians in slavery than any of the other colonies except South Carolina, where in 1708 there were fourteen hundred Indian slaves against forty-one hundred Negroes.[4] ♦♦

♦♦ [In 1637] one hundred and eighty (Pequots) were taken prisoners. Most of the property . . . fell into the hands of the

English. . . . The captives and the booty were divided between Massa-chusetts and Connecticut. Some were sent by Massachusetts to the West Indies, and there, as slaves, dragged out a wretched but brief existence. . . . Those who fell to the colony of Connecticut found their condition more tolerable. Some of them, it is true, spent their days in servitude; yet its rigors softened as the horrors of war faded from the recollections of the English.[5] ◆◆

Slavery in New Mexico, 1680-1696

In 1680, when the Spaniards were expelled from New Mexico, they held at least 700 slaves and servants. Subsequently hundreds of Pueblo Indians were carried off as captives to El Paso, and some were sold farther south in Mexico. In 1696, after the Spaniards had reentered New Mexico Governor Diego de Vargas and Captain Antonio Valverde made a campaign against Pueblo Indians and Apaches and the captives were divided up among the soldiers as slaves.

◆◆ It is true that in the last campaign which was made to the plains, among the Apache children that he took to sell in Vizcaya [Mexico] the said Antonio Balverde carried two little Christian Indians and he sold them as slaves as [he did] with the rest that he carried.[6] ◆◆

Indian slavery in South Carolina, 1708

◆◆ In 1708, when the total population of South Carolina was 9,580, including 2,900 Negroes, there were 1,400 Indian slaves held in the province. Probably the number of Indians employed by the Carolina planters did not greatly increase thereafter. . . . From an early time the exportation of captured Indian slaves was favored. . . . Indian slaves were constantly escaping . . . and . . . their presence . . . raised the danger of conspiracies with enemy Indians. . . . On all accounts it was better to ship off the Indians to New England or the West Indies, and to import Blacks. . . . In the early eighteenth century (1706-1717) the *Boston News Letter* printed frequent advertisements of runaway Carolina Indians.[7] ◆◆

Captain Thomas Nairne, Carolinian leader, 1708

◆◆ Some men think that it [Indian slavery] both serves to Lessen their numbers before the French can arm them, and it is a more Effectuall way of Civilising and Instructing (them) than all the Efforts used by French Missionaries.[8] ◆◆

Reverend Francis Le Jau, Episcopal clergyman, 1712

◆◆ [The Yamasee Indians desire missionaries but] the Indian traders have always discouraged me. . . . It appears they do not care to have Clergymen so near them who doubtless would never approve those perpetual warrs they promote amongst the Indians for the onely reason of making slaves to pay for their trading goods; and what slaves! poor women and children; for the men taken prisoners are burnt most barbarously.[9] ◆◆

John Norris, advice to prospective slave-owners, 1712

◆◆ An Indian Man or Woman may cost 18 or 20 Pound, but a good Negro is worth more than twice that sum.
To set up a plantation for £1500:

Imprimus:	Fifteen good Negro Men at 45£ each	£675
Item,	Fifteen Indian Women to work in the Field, at 18£. each	270
Item,	Three Indian Women as Cooks for the Slaves, and other Household Business	55

For a small plantation of 100 to 200 acres
Two Slaves: a good Negro man and a good Indian Woman at £45 and £18 respectively.[10] ◆◆

French enslavement of the Natchez, 1729

◆◆ The French army . . . carried the Natchez as slaves to New Orleans, where they were put in prison; but afterwards, to avoid an infection, the women and children were disposed of in the King's plantation, and elsewhere. . . . Some Time after, these slaves were embarked for St. Domingo, in order to root out that nation [the Natchez] in [Louisiana]. . . . And thus that nation, the most conspicuous in the colony, and most useful to the French, was destroyed.[11] ◆◆

Advertisements for runaway Indian slaves in South Carolina, 1732-1753

◆◆ Sarah, "brought up to Household Work" [1732]; Deborah, "handy at Women's Work" [1732]; Peter, "both a Carpenter and Cooper" [1736]; Jack, "by trade a Tanner" [1738]; "a young Indian House Wench" [1746]; James, "a Cooper by trade" [1747]; and Jack, "seems to understand something of the shoemaker's trade." [12] ◆◆

Decline of Indian slavery along the Atlantic Seaboard

In 1782 Thomas Jefferson wrote that "an inhuman practice once pre-vailed in this country, of making slaves of the Indians." [13] This state-ment indicates Jefferson's belief that the enslavement of Redmen had ceased. This was not, however, entirely correct, for the descendants of Indian slaves were apparently still slaves, but by 1782 they were inter-bred with African Negroes. Furthermore, as late as 1748 Richard Ran-dolph of Virginia, in his will, left a slave named "Indian John" to his son Ryland Randolph. In 1831, as a result of the Nat Turner rebellion in Virginia, many eastern shore Afro-Indians were enslaved and sold.[14]

The slave trade of Sonora and Arizona, 1746-1776

After the seventeenth century the Hispano-Mexicans did not make raids for slaves nearly as frequently as before. However, they did pur-chase captives from friendly native groups and thus encouraged the latter to acquire prisoners. Extensive damage was done to tribes that were the principal victims of the search for slaves (such as the Piutes of southern Utah and the Halchidhoma of the Colorado River). After purchase by the Hispano-Mexicans, the captives became servants with-out liberty (although they were not property as were slaves in the south-ern United States). In 1746 Father Jacobo Sedelmayr wrote that the Nijoras (Yavapais), Maricopas, and Quechans fought with each other "and sold boys and girls [captives] for things of little value to the Pimas, and these [sold them] to the Spanish for ten items. . . . All of these captives are called Nijores [in Sonora]." [15]

In 1775 Father Tomás Eixarch purchased an Apache child in exchange for a horse and commented that along the frontier of Sonora it was common to barter for captives, although it was against Spanish law.

♦♦ There are many half-breed gentlemen who pride themselves on having Indian captives in practical slavery, ignoring in their pride of the fact that the Indians were born free, and that doubt-less they have better and purer blood than their half-breed Spanish lordships, themselves.[16] ♦♦

In the same year Father Pedro Font noted that the wars of the Colorado River tribes lasted only a few days.

♦♦ Many of them assemble with the captain or someone who commands them; they go to a village of their enemies; they give the yell or war-cry, in order that their oponents may flee or become terrified if taken by surprise. They usually kill some woman, or someone who has been careless, and try to capture a few children in order to take them out to sell in the lands of the Spaniards. These captives are called *Nixoras* by us in Sonora, no matter where they come from, and this commerce in *Nixoras,* so unjust, is the reason why they have been so bloody in their wars.[17] ◆◆

Slavery in Alaska, 1762

The Pushkareff expedition to Alaska returned to Asia, taking with them "thirty natives, mostly women, as prisoners and slaves; but on the voyage home they wantonly murdered them all except two." Thereafter many Alaska natives were enslaved by the Russians.[18]

Slavery among the Oakinacken (Okanagan) Indians of Washington, 1811

◆◆ . . . they are kind and indulgent to their slaves. War not being their trade, there are but few slaves among them, and these few are adopted as children, and treated in all respects as members of the family. . . . The property of each individual, even of the slave, is held sacred.[19] ◆◆

The "liberated" mission Indians of California, 1835-1836

R. H. Dana wrote:

◆◆ At last, a law was passed . . . . declaring all the Indians free and independent Rancheros [*i.e.,* secularization of the missions occurred]. The change in the condition of the Indians was, as may be supposed, only nominal: they are virtually slaves, as much as they ever were. But in the missions, the change was complete. The priests have now no power . . . and the great possessions of the missions are given over to be preyed upon by the harpies of the civil power, who are sent there in the capacity of *administradores,* to settle up concerns; and who usually end, in a few years, by making themselves fortunes . . .[20] ◆◆

Francisco M. Alvarado, an Hispano-Californian, wrote in 1836: "The Indians cannot be controlled except by flogging." [21] This indeed was the extent to which the missionized natives were liberated in 1833-1835; they could now be flogged by civilians instead of by clerics! The investigations carried out by William Hartnell in 1839-1840 confirmed Dana's opinions. The natives had simply been transferred from religious to secular control, with the difference that economic exploitation of them had increased.

The slave trade in Sonora-Arizona, 1840's

In 1849 José Agustín de Escudero wrote that the Pima Indians held an annual fair along the Gila River at which they sold, among other things, Yuma (Quechan) and Apache slaves to the Mexicans of Tucson. These slaves were then taken farther south and "they form a large proportion of the servants in the Sonoras." [22]

Indian debt slavery in Southern California, 1849

♦♦ The Indians and Mexicans, or rather the natives of California, are here [Southern California] as they were in Mexico, mere peons, knowing nothing but the life of a slave. . . . Wages are higher here, . . . but this is balanced again by the price of goods and necessaries furnished by the master to his peon; and both ends seldom meet at the end of the year, but the slave finds himself deeper in debt. . . .[23] ♦♦

Natives as expendable property in California, 1853

E. F. Beale, Superintendent of Indian Affairs for California, visited Rancho San Pablo in Contra Costa County and found ninety sick and starving Indians, eighteen of whom had already died. The natives were "survivors of a band who were worked all last summer and fall and as the winter set in, when broken down by hunger and labor and without food or clothes they were turned adrift to shift for themselves. . . ." These and other natives had been enslaved in the Clear Lake region by Californianos who made a regular practice of raiding for slaves.[24]

Slave raids in Northern California, 1857

In northeastern California E. A. Stevenson, an Indian Agent, and his men

♦♦ . . . strike a trail of a large number of Indians and horses, and find that a large lot of Klamath Indians under the command of the great Northern Chief *Laylake* have [been] down to the Pitt River country to steal squaws and children which they take into Oregon and sell as slaves. These Indians have been at war for some time.[25] ♦♦

Indian slavery in California, 1850-1869

In 1850 the Pueblo of Los Angeles adopted an ordinance making it possible to auction Indian prisoners (usually charged with drunkenness)

to the highest bidder ". . . and in that manner they shall be disposed of for a sum which shall not be less than the amount of their fine for double the time which they were to serve at hard labor." The Indians were sold in the plaza each Monday morning. This practice continued until at least 1869, with the Indians being kept in perpetual slavery, as they were usually paid with, or were furnished, alcoholic beverages so that they would become intoxicated and could be arrested over again.[26]

◆◆ Los Angeles had its slave mart . . . only the [Indian] slave at Los Angeles was sold fifty-two times a year as long as he lived, which generally did not exceed one, two or three years. . . . [He was] invariably . . . paid in aguardiente [alcohol]. . . . Those thousands of honest, useful people were absolutely destroyed in this way.[27] ◆◆

◆◆ The habits of the Indians [of Los Angeles County] are such that decay and extermination has long since marked them for their certain victims. . . . Their scanty earnings at the end of the week are spent for rum. . . . For years past it has been the practice of [our farmers] . . . to hang around the Mayor's court on Monday morning and advance the degraded Indian a few dollars with which to pay his nominal fine. . . . and on Saturday night, after deducting the sum advanced, pay him a couple of dollars, which insures him a place in the station house on the following Monday . . . and thus the process goes on.[28] ◆◆

Scalps and slaves in Sonora and Arizona, 1863

◆◆ Governor Pesquiera of Sonora has offered a bounty of $100 per scalp for Apaches, and a proportionate sum for animals retaken from them. This should be imitated by the Authorities of Arizona. The Pimos (Pimas) and Papago Indians would be most valuable auxiliaries in the pursuit of these "human wolves." They lately killed about sixty Apaches and took several prisoners in a single campaign. The children of the Apaches when taken young, make good servants and are sold by the Pimos in the Territory [Arizona] and in Sonora.

There is only one way to wage war against the Apaches. . . . They must be surrounded, starved into coming in, surprised or inveigled— by white flags or any other method, human or divine—and then put to death.

If these ideas shock any weak-minded individual, who thinks himself a philanthropist, I can only say that I pity, without respecting, his sympathy. A man might as well have sympathy for a rattlesnake or a tiger.[29] ◆◆

Indian slavery in New Mexico, 1866

◆◆ On the subject of peonage, the qualified slavery still prevalent in New Mexico, authorized by its laws, and encouraged and practiced by its people, . . . and natives of the United States . . . , Mr. Graves's [J. R. Graves's] statements, with the evidence presented therewith, are such as to leave no doubt of the duty of Congress to take the matter in hand. . . . This office has done all that lay in its power, by promulgating the order of the President forbidding the practice . . . , but in spite of all this, it is clear that the practice still continues to a greater or lesser extent.[30] ◆◆

Apache Slaves for sale in Arizona, 1868

◆◆ At Maricopa Wells I saw Apache captives who had been offered by the Pimos at forty dollars a head, while no American rebuked them. . . . But they did not sell them. Why? The Americans wanted them for twenty-five dollars! [31] ◆◆

Slavery among the Chilkat Indians of Alaska, 1891

◆◆ There were a few slaves among my numerous Indian packers, slavery having once flourished extensively among the Chilkats, but having diminished both in vigor and extent, in direct ratio to their contact with the whites. . . . Entering a Chilkat house nowadays, one can hardly distinguish a slave from the master . . . and while the slaves are supposed to do all the work, the enforcement of the rule appears to be very lax. Still it is interesting to know that the fourteenth amendment to the United States constitution is not held inviolable in all parts of that vast country.[32] ◆◆

Notes

1. Jack D. Forbes, *Apache, Navaho and Spaniard* (Norman: University of Oklahoma Press, 1960) pp. 7, 34, 47-49, 62-63, 66.
2. Bradford, *History of Plimoth Plantation*, p. 116.
3. Alonso de Benavides, *Memorial of 1630*, translated by Peter P. Forrestal (Washington: Academy of American Franciscan History, 1954), pp. 55-56; and *Patronato 244, Ramo VII* (Seville: Archivo General de Indias). Benavides's selection is reprinted by permission of the Academy of American Franciscan History.
4. James Truslow Adams, *Provincial Society 1690-1763* (New York: Macmillan, 1927) p. 101. Reprinted by permission of the Macmillan Company.
5. G. H. Hollister, "The Pequot War," in Morris and Leigh, eds., *The Great Republic*, Vol. I, pp. 170-171.

6. Archivo General de Indias, Seville, Spain, Guadalajara 142. See also Forbes, *op. cit.*, pp. 179, 271-2.
7. Crane, *The Southern Frontier 1670-1732*, pp. 113-114. Reprinted by permission of the University of Michigan Press.
8. Captain Thomas Nairne's Memorial of 1708, quoted in *Ibid.*, p. 114. Reprinted by permission of the University of Michigan Press.
9. Quoted in *Ibid.*, p. 152. Reprinted by permission of the University of Michigan Press.
10. Quoted in *Ibid.*, p. 113, 113n. Reprinted by permission of the University of Michigan Press.
11. Le Page du Pratz, "Louisiana and the Natchez," in *The Great Republic*, Vol. I, p. 216.
12. From *South Carolina Gazette*, quoted in Crane, *op. cit.*, p. 113n. Reprinted by permission of the University of Michigan Press.
13. Foley, ed., *The Jefferson Cyclopedia*, p. 813.
14. William Cabell Bruce, *John Randolph of Roanoke 1773-1833* (New York: G. P. Putnam's Sons, 1922), Vol. I, p. 18.
15. Jacobo Sedelmayr, "Relación de 1746," Biblioteca del Ministerio de Hacienda 969, Madrid, Spain.
16. Bolton, *Anza's California Expeditions*, Vol. III, p. 322. Reprinted by permission of the University of California Press.
17. *Ibid.*, Vol. IV, p. 102. Reprinted by permission of the University of California Press.
18. Schwatka, *A Summer in Alaska*, p. 354.
19. Ross, *Adventures of the First Settlers on the Oregon or Columbia River*, pp. 320, 323.
20. Dana, *Two Years Before the Mast*, p. 158.
21. Bancroft, *History of California*, Vol. IV, p. 53.
22. José Agustín de Escudero, *Noticias Estadisticas de Sonora y Sinaloa* (Mexico: Rafael, 1849) pp. 142-3.
23. George W. B. Evans, *Mexican Gold Trail* (San Marino: The Huntington Library, 1945) p. 182. Reprinted by permission of the Huntington Library.
24. Stephen Bonsal, *Edward Fitzgerald Beale* (New York: G. P. Putnam's Sons, 1912) pp. 177-8. Reprinted by permission of G. P. Putnam's Sons.
25. Letter of E. A. Stevenson, Sept. 30, 1857, ed. by Erminie Wheeler-Voegelin, *Ethnohistory*, Vol. IV, No. 1, Winter 1957, pp. 76-77.
26. J. M. Guinn, "The Passing of the Old Pueblo," *Publications of the Historical Society of Southern California*, Vol. V, 1901, p. 117.
27. Horace Bell, *Reminiscences of a Ranger* (Los Angeles: n. d., 1881) pp. 35-36.
28. *Los Angeles Semi-weekly News*, February 11, 1869.
29. Sylvester Mowry, *The Geography and Resources of Arizona and Sonora*, as quoted by Arthur Woodward, "Side Lights on Fifty Years of Apache Warfare, 1836-1886," *Arizoniana*, Vol. II, No. 3, Fall 1961, p. 9.
30. *Annual Report, U.S. Department of the Interior, 1865-66* (Washington: U.S. Government Printing Office, 1867) p. 33.
31. Stephen Powers, *Afoot and Alone* (Hartford: Columbian Book Co., 1872) p. 234.
32. Schwatka, *op. cit.*, pp. 38-39.

SEVEN

UNITED STATES POLICY 1789-1870

Upon achieving independence the United States became the possessor of several native policies inherited from the colonial period. On the one hand stood the "Imperial" policy which had sought to conciliate native groups in order to provide stability and encourage commerce, and on the other was the "European settler's" policy which had sought the removal of the natives and the acquisition of land. These two policies were contradictory and the enforcement, by the British government, of the Imperial policy had contributed in no small measure to the rebellion of the European colonials. The new United States, representing the White settlers as it did, could be expected to pursue an expansionist, anti-Indian policy; but for a few years the triumph of the latter approach was delayed by the relative weakness of the United States government.

During this initial period of weakness the United States admitted, in effect, that it had not acquired complete ownership (or even control) over the regions quit-claimed by the British in 1783, and that it was necessary to negotiate with the tribes. Nevertheless, this *de facto* recognition of tribal quasi-independence was not based upon any desire to uphold the principle of self-determination for small nations. On the contrary, it was but an initial concession to military realities. As rapidly as the balance of power in any given region tipped in favor of the Federal government, the United States crushed the respective native groups and broke treaties as it saw fit.

The reader should not be surprised, therefore, if he finds in the following selections contradictory statements made by Federal officials. They refer not merely to different viewpoints or phases of policy development but often to two different levels of policy: one being the verbal "legalistic" level, and the other being the basic underlying policy of conquest.

The United States Constitution

◆◆ The Congress shall have power. . . . To regulate commerce with foreign nations, and among the several states, and with the Indian tribes. . . . ◆◆

United States Congress, 1789

♦♦ The utmost good faith shall always be observed towards the Indians; their land and property shall never be taken from them without their consent; and in their property, rights and liberty, they shall never be invaded or disturbed, unless in just and lawful wars. . . .[1] ♦♦

Secretary of War Henry Knox, 1789

♦♦ It would appear, that Congress were of the opinion that the Treaty of Peace of 1783, absolutely invested them with the fee of all the Indian lands within the limits of the United States; that they had the right to assign, or retain such portions as they should judge proper. [However, the Indians said that] they were the only rightful proprietors of the soil, and it appears by the resolve of July 2, 1788 that Congress so far conformed to the idea, as to appropriate a sum of money solely to the purpose of extinguishing the Indian claims. . . . The principle of the Indian right to the lands they possess being thus conceded, the dignity and the interest of the nation will be advanced by making it the basis of the future administration of justice towards the Indian tribes. . . . the Indians being the prior occupants, possess the right of the soil. It cannot be taken from them unless by their free consent, or by right of conquest in case of a just war. . . . [The Indian tribes] ought to be considered as foreign nations, not as subjects of any particular state. ♦♦

From the United States to the Delaware Nation, 1792

♦♦ Brothers: The President of the United States entertains the opinion, that the war which exists is founded in error and mistake on your parts. That you believe the United States want to deprive you of your lands and drive you out of the country. Be assured that this is not so; on the contrary, that we should be greatly gratified with the opportunity of imparting to you all the blessings of civilized life; . . . so as ever to dwell upon the land. . . . make a peace, founded upon the principles of justice and humanity. Remember that no additional lands will be required of you, or any other tribe, to those that have been ceded by former treaties.[2] ♦♦

Thomas Jefferson and the Native Americans

The Indian policy of the United States during the early period, as has been pointed out, was somewhat ambiguous and contradictory. On the one hand, the United States sought to conciliate the more powerful of the native states while, on the other, her citizens were pressing for the acquisition of more land. No better illustration of the disparity that existed between pronouncements and deeds can be found than in the writings and policy of Thomas Jefferson, the greatest liberal leader of the early United States. Jefferson was certainly not anti-Native American, at least not in the same sense as were his contemporaries; however, as the following letter (1776) illustrates, he was capable of favoring strong measures whenever the natives did not cooperate with a cause that he approved.

♦♦ I am sorry to hear that the Indians have commenced war, but greatly pleased you have been so decisive on that head. Nothing will reduce those wretches so soon as pushing the war into the heart of their country. But I would not stop there. I would never cease pursuing them while one of them remained on this side of the Mississippi. . . . [The Indians] are a useless, expensive, ungovernable ally.[3] ♦♦

In writing to a European, ten years later, Jefferson expressed a very different point of view:

♦♦ It may be regarded as certain, that not a foot of land will ever be taken from the Indians, without their own consent. The sacredness of their rights is felt by all thinking persons in America as much as in Europe.[4] ♦♦

In 1792 Jefferson analysed the rights of native states as opposed to European states:

♦♦ We consider it as established by the usage of different nations into a kind of *jus gentium* for America, that a white nation settling down and declaring that such and such are their limits, makes an invasion of those by any other white nation an act of war, but gives no right of soil against the native possessors. . . . [It is] an established principle of public law among the white nations of America, that while the Indians included within their limits retain all other natural rights, no other white nation can become their patrons, protectors or mediators, nor in any shape intermeddle between them and those within whose limits they are.[5] ♦♦

Jefferson wrote to William H. Harrison in 1803:

♦♦ Our system is to live in perpetual peace with the Indians, to cultivate an affectionate attachment from them, by everything

just and liberal which we can do for them within the bounds of reason. . . .[6] ◆◆

And he wrote to Andrew Jackson in the same year:

◆◆ I am myself alive to the obtaining of lands from the
Indians by all *honest* and *peaceable means,* and I believe that the honest
and peaceable means adopted by us will obtain them as fast as the expansion of our settlements with due regard to compactness, will require. . . .
The Indian Tribes . . . have for a considerable time been growing
more and more uneasy at the constant diminution of the territory they
occupy, although effected by their own voluntary sales, and the policy
has long been gaining strength with them of refusing absolutely all
further sale on any conditions. . . . In order peaceably to counteract this
policy of theirs and to provide an extension of territory which the rapid
increase of our numbers will call for [they should be led to an agricultural way of life, thus lessening their need for land]. In leading them
thus to . . . civilization . . . I trust and believe we are acting for their
greatest good.[7] ◆◆

Jefferson's Second Inaugural Address, March, 1805

◆◆ The aboriginal inhabitants . . . I have regarded with
the commiseration their history inspires. Endowed with the faculties
and the rights of men, breathing an ardent love of liberty and independence, . . . the stream of overflowing population from other regions directed itself on these shores . . . [and] they have been overwhelmed . . . ;
now reduced within limits too narrow for the hunter's state, humanity
enjoins us to teach them agriculture and the domestic arts. . . . We have
therefore liberally furnished them with [implements and instrucors] . . .
and they are covered with the aegis of the law against aggressors from
among ourselves. But the endeavors to enlighten them . . . have powerful obstacles to encounter; they are combated. . . . [by the Indians'
ignorance, pride, and habits and by leaders who] inculcate a sanctimoni-
ous reverence for the customs of their ancestors. . . . they too have their
antiphilosophists . . . who dread reformation. . . .[8] ◆◆

Jefferson to the Senate, 1805-1808

While the natives of the Ohio country were becoming more and more
restless as a result of extensive land cessions, Jefferson's annual reports to
Congress were full of phrases such as: "We continue to receive proofs of
the growing attachment of our Indian neighbors. . . . These dispositions
are inspired by their confidence in our justice and in the sincere concern
we feel for their welfare [December, 1805]."[9] Two years later he had to

report, however, that "among our Indian neighbors . . . some fermenta-
tion was observed . . . threatening the continuance of our peace. . . .
instructions were given to require explanations . . . to admonish the
tribes to remain quiet at home, taking no part in quarrels not belonging
to them." [10]
In January 1808 he reported:

♦♦   Although it is deemed very desirable that the United
States obtain from the native proprietors the whole left bank of the
Mississippi . . . yet to obliterate from the Indian mind an impression
deeply made in it that we are constantly forming designs on their lands
I have thought it best . . . to leave to themselves and to the pressure of
their own convenience only to come forward with offers of sale to the
United States. [However, Jefferson submits a 5,000,000 acre cession by
the Choctaws and a 5,000,000 acre cession by various northern tribes to
the Senate].[11]   ♦♦

In spite of Jefferson's pious pronouncements he was dependent upon
the political support of frontier whites who were solely interested in acquiring Indian land as rapidly as possible. In theory, Jefferson favored
the amalgamation of the whites and Indians by intermarriage, but this
utopian solution was abandoned, practically, in 1802. Frightened by the
expected French acquisition of Louisiana, Jefferson ordered his lieuten-
ants (especially Governor William Henry Harrison of Indiana Territory)
to begin acquiring, as rapidly as possible, all Indian lands east of the
Mississippi. By 1809 more than 100 million acres were acquired by in-
timidation, bribery, questionable treaties, and dubious procedures. Jefferson's policy did not change with the acquisition of Louisiana in
1803; instead, he favored removal of the tribes west of the Mississippi. In
1808 some Upper Cherokees told Jefferson that they wished to own their
lands in severalty and become citizens of the United States, but the
president, in direct opposition to his pre-1802 philosophy, urged them to
move west of the Mississippi instead. Thus, for all of Thomas Jefferson's
well-known liberalism and humanitarianism, his administration saw the
beginning of what might be termed a "harsh" Indian policy. The so-
called War of 1812 was in great part an outgrowth of this ruthless policy
toward the aborigines.[12]
By 1812 Jefferson could write: "the Indians backward [in civilization]
will yield, and be thrown further back. They will relapse into barbarism
and misery . . . and we shall be obliged to drive them with the beasts
of the forest into the stony [Rocky] mountains." [13]

*President James Monroe's view of the rights of Native Americans,
1817*

♦♦   The hunter state can exist only in the vast uncul-tivated desert. It yields to the . . . greater force of civilized population; and, of right, it ought to yield, for the earth was given to mankind to support the greater number of which it is capable; and no tribe or people have a right to withhold from the wants of others, more than is neces-sary for their support and comfort.[14]   ♦♦.

This statement deserves comment because it is similar to the justifica-tions used in the conquest of territory not merely from tribal Americans but also from Mexicans and other non-English-speaking groups. Needless to state, it is also similar to the arguments used to support Hitler's con-quest in eastern Europe: A superior people have the right to take over land being used in an unsatisfactory manner by inferior or backward populations. Monroe's assertion that no people have a right to withhold from the wants of others "more than is necessary for their support and comfort" is also interesting to read in an age in which the people of the United States have great wealth while other peoples live in poverty and under overcrowded conditions. But of course the arguments once ap-plied to one group by another to justify aggression are not intended to be applied to the aggressor group at a later date!

John C. Calhoun, 1820

♦♦   [The Indians] must be brought gradually under our authority and laws. . . . It is impossible, with their customs, that they should exist as independent communities in the midst of civilized society. They are not, in fact, an independent people, . . . nor ought they to be so considered. They should be taken under our guardianship; and our opinions, and not theirs, ought to prevail, in measures intended for their civilization and happiness.[15]   ♦♦

Who owns the land? 1823

In *Johnson and Graham's Lessee* vs. *McIntosh* the Supreme Court, in John Marshall's words, held that "discovery" gave the exclusive title to the land of the United States, while the Indians were admitted

♦♦   to be the rightful occupants of the soil, with a legal as well as just claim to retain possession of it, and to use it according to their own discretion; but their rights to complete sovereignty, as inde-pendent nations, were necessarily diminished, and their power to dispose of the soil at their own will . . . was denied by the original fundamen-tal principle, that discovery gave exclusive title to those who made it. [European nations claimed ultimate dominion for themselves and the power to grant the soil even while it was in the native's possession. But the title granted is] "subject to the Indian right of occupancy." [The United States holds] that discovery gave exclusive right to extinguish the Indian title of occupancy either by purchase or by conquest; and gave also a right to such a degree of sovereignty as the circumstances of the people would allow them to exercise. However extravagant the pretension of converting the discovery of an inhabited country into conquest may appear, if the principle has been asserted in the first instance, and afterwards sustained; if a country has been acquired and held under it; if the property of the great mass of the community originates in it, it becomes the law of the land, and cannot be questioned. So, too, with the concomitant principle that the Indian inhabitants are . . . to be protected, indeed, while in peace, in the possession of their lands, but to be deemed incapable of transferring the absolute title to others.[16]   ◆◆

Treaty with the Choctaw Nation, 1830

◆◆ . . . no territory or state shall ever have a right to pass laws for the government of the Choctaw Nation . . . and their descendants; and that no part of the land granted them shall ever be embraced in any territory or state; but the United States shall forever secure said Choctaw Nation, from, and against, all laws except such as from time to time may be enacted in their own National Councils, not inconsistent with the Constitution, Treaties, and Laws of the United States.[17]   ◆◆

Thomas Forsyth on the benefits of a coercive policy, 1831

◆◆ I have no doubt, that in most of the misunderstandings which take place between the whites and Indians in the interior of the Indian country, the fault is with the white people, except among the Commanches. . . . In my intercourse with the Indians for the last forty years I never found that coercive measures ever had any good effect with Indians, but that conciliatory measures always tended to produce every purpose required. . . . Several persons in this place [St. Louis] say that there is much room for improvement in our relations with the different Indian nations.[18]   ◆◆

Westward movement at gun point, United States policy, 1830-1854

From 1802-1809 President Jefferson had advocated the removal of all Indians from their lands east of the Mississippi. In 1824-1825 President Monroe and Secretary of War Calhoun attempted to implement this policy but with only partial success. Then in May, 1830 President Jackson persuaded Congress to pass appropriate legislation.

♦♦   The act of [May 28, 1830] authorized the President to exchange the public domain in the West for Indian lands in the East, [and] to give perpetual title to the country thus exchanged. . . . The law . . . designated the region west of Missouri and Arkansas for the red men. . . . In the early forties the "Indian Territory" extended from the Red River on the south to the Platte. The Sioux and their neighbors further north were not disturbed at this time. . . .[19]

In 1846 Congress considered setting up an Indian confederacy in the area, but this idea was soon abandoned. In 1854 the Kansas-Nebraska Act doomed the Indian Territory concept, with all of its pledges of "perpetual title." ♦♦

Worcester vs. Georgia (Supreme Court decision), 1832

♦♦   [The Indian tribes] . . . had always been considered as distinct, independent, political communities, retaining their original natural rights . . . and the settled doctrine of the law of nations is, that a weaker power does not surrender its independence—its right to self-government—by association with a stronger, and taking its protection. . . . The Cherokee Nation, then, is a distinct community . . . in which the laws of Georgia can have no force, and which the citizens of Georgia have no right to enter, but with the assent of the Cherokees . . . or in conformity with treaties, and with the Acts of Congress.[20] ♦♦

Force prevails

In spite of the Supreme Court, in spite of solemn treaties, in spite of the Constitution, and in spite of a professed belief in the right of self-government for all peoples, the native groups east of the Mississippi were relentlessly driven westward and despoiled by avaricious whites. Referring to the opening up and sale of Creek lands from 1834 to 1837 George Dewey Harmon wrote: "It is . . . safe to conclude that no greater frauds were ever perpetrated upon mankind than these inflicted upon the innocent Creeks of Alabama." [21]

Commissioner of Indian Affairs Luke Lea, 1851

♦♦   . . . on the general subject of the civilization of the Indians, many and diversified opinions have been put forth; but, unfortunately, like the race to which they relate, they are too wild to be of much utility. . . . [a proper program should provide for] their concentration, their domestication and their ultimate incorporation into the great body of our citizen population.[22] ♦♦

Commissioner Lea herein expresses a viewpoint that was to become dominant after 1870. The native groups are to be concentrated on small reserves, they are to be "domesticated," and incorporated. "Domestication" meant, in effect, a policy of enforced acculturation in violation of the principles laid down in *Worcester* vs. *Georgia,* in violation of treaties, and in violation of the Constitution's guarantees of personal liberty.

A bill to create Indian Territories, 1854

Lea's approach was not immediately successful, and in 1854 there was a last attempt at allowing native groups to incorporate themselves gradually, through their own institutions, into the United States. Under the leadership of Senator R. W. Johnson, the Senate Committee on Territories recommended a bill to erect three territories for the Indians in what is now Oklahoma:

◆◆ The Bill, as amended, provides for the erection (with the assent of these several nations) into Territories of the country which they own and occupy, and certain other country to be annexed thereto. The Territory of Chah-ta is to consist entirely of the lands owned by absolute grant from the United States by the Choctaws and Chickasaws. That of Muscogee, of these owned by the Creeks and Seminoles, and that of Chelokee, of those owned by the Cherokee . . . [and of the Osages, Quapaws, Senecas and Shawnees].

It vests the executive power in a governor for each Territory, to be elected by the people, serve for four years, be commissioned by the President, and supercede the principal or highest chief of each nation; [and it] gives each Territory . . . a delegate to the House of Representatives. It provides that nothing contained in it shall be so construed as to abrogate, change, alter, or impair the constitution or laws, or the customs . . . of either of said nations of Indians. . . . The legislative authority is to continue to be vested, as at present, in the national council of the Cherokees . . . , in the general council of the Choctaws and Chickasaws . . . , and in the general council of the Creeks. . . .

By section 35, it is enacted that all of the free citizens of the said several nations, to wit: the Cherokees, Creeks, Seminoles, Choctaws, and Chickasaws resident, or hereafter moving into and settling in said Territories, being of Indian or Indian and white blood, shall, when this act takes effect as to each nation . . . become and be, citizens of the United States; and the Constitution of the United States shall have the same force and effect . . . as elsewhere within the United States. . . . Provision is made that the Senecas, Senecas and Shawnees, and Quapaws may be incorporated in the Territory, and become an integral part of the Cherokee people, and citizens of the United States. . . .

Each legislature is required to enact laws regulating marriage, making it a contract for life, not dissolvable at the pleasure of the parties, prohibiting polygamy. . . .

This bill has no political, party, or sectional features, but is intended solely as a measure of justice to a brave and intelligent, but oppressed and unfortunate, race. It is meant to place something to the credit of this government against the long array of injuries done the red man with which our annals are running over. . . .

Over and over again . . . we have guaranteed to [Indian] nation after nation such of its lands as remained to it, after we had cajoled or forced it into a cession; and, as often, after a lapse of a few short years, has the wave of white population . . . [forced] it ever westward, and by new negotiations, new appliances of money and presents to corrupt greedy chiefs, and new threats of leaving them to the tender mercies of State sovereignty, another and another cession of land has been extorted. . . .

The leading principle of the bill is, that nothing is proposed to be done in reference to these Indians without their own consent. The question of authority and power over them is waived. . . . We cannot civilize a people by giving them good laws, no matter how wisely enacted; but to be effectual, those laws must be the result and product of their own civilization. . . .

We imagine that no one can mistake the duty of the government of the United States to these Indian tribes. . . . While our sympathies are profusely poured forth for every people that writhes under the iron heel of the oppressor. . . . while we cheer on the Hungarian and the Italian . . . we ought not to forget that we have in our midst organized communities of men, born as free and independent as ourselves . . . and whom we hold in vassalage; to whom we deny the protection of the Constitution. . . . Why should the Hungarian, the Italian, the Cuban, receive more of our sympathy than those who were the original owners of this broad continent. . . .

No one who has any regard for the faith and honor of the nation . . . can have failed to note with alarm and concern, that it has already been announced by those holding high places in the councils of the nation, that the most solemn treaties . . . , the most formal promises that the Indians west of the Mississippi shall never be included in any State or Territory . . . are to be but like threads of flax in the fire, before the irresistable onward rush of natives and foreign emigration. . . .

This clearly indicates that it is absolutely indispensable for some new system to be adopted in regard to those of our Indian tribes that have made some advance in Civilization. That these tribes cannot long exist as isolated and independent communities has become obvious. . . . The object, therefore, now to be attained, is to persuade these Indians to open their land to emigration and settlement—to cease to hold their lands in common—to divide them out in severalty . . . to intermingle with, and become an integral part of, the people of the United States—to look

forward with confidence to the time when they will constitute a portion
of the Union, and add another star to its flag.[23] ◆◆

Commissioner of Indian Affairs Denver, 1857

Johnson's proposals came too late, however. During the 1850's and
1860's tens of thousands of Anglo-Americans and European newcomers
sought lands in the Far West, and pressure increased in favor of Lea's
approach. In 1857 Commissioner of Indian Affairs Denver wrote:

◆◆ Reservations should be restricted so as to contain only
sufficient land to afford them a comfortable support by actual cultivation,
and should be properly divided and assigned to them, with the obliga-
tion to remain upon and cultivate the same [in order to put into effect
an enforced acculturation policy].[24] ◆◆

Secretary of the Interior Caleb B. Smith, 1862

◆◆ The rapid progress of civilization upon this continent
will not permit the lands which are required for cultivation to be surrendered to savage tribes for hunting. . . . Indeed, whatever may be the
theory, the Government has always demanded the removal of the Indians when their lands were required for agricultural purposes. . . .
although the consent of the Indians has been obtained in the form of
treaties, it is well known that they have yielded to a necessity to which
they could not resist. . . . Instead of being treated as independent nations [as in the past] they should be regarded as wards of the Government. . . .[25] ◆◆

How does one reduce a free people to the status of "wards"? Where
in the Constitution or in the several treaties with Indian tribes is the
status of "wardship" provided for? During the 1860's there was very
little concern with the niceties of law and justice. The natives were being
militarily conquered, their lands were being taken from them, and they
were becoming involuntary recipients of a Federal "dole." This dole developed as a way of feeding natives whose ordinary means of subsistence
had been destroyed or impaired—it also helped to break their spirit of independence and eventually led to the establishment of a bureaucracy to
administer the dole.

The federal handout, 1863

In December, 1863 Superintendent Charles Poston took government
supplies to the starving Quechan (Yuma) Indians.

◆◆   Great were the rejoicings when we opened the boxes and bales of merchandise. . . . Red, white, green, and gray blankets; military suits, glittering with tinsel; old swords, four feet long, sunglasses for lighting cigars; . . . There were axes of the best Collins brand, that flew to pieces like glass . . . and hats made by steam, and flaming red vests stitched by magic . . . and tin kettles that might be opened, but never upon earth shut again. . . . We gave them damaged hominy and hoes, and spades and shovels, and sashes and military buttons, charms, amulets, . . . and beads; shook them by the hand collectively and in detail, and pow-wowed generally in the approved style.[26]   ◆◆

The first Territory of Oklahoma, 1866

The United States negotiated a new treaty with the Choctaws and Chickasaws of Indian Territory (an unorganized territory).

◆◆   The provisions in regard to a general council are agreed to with more detail than in the other treaties, and its powers clearly defined, so as to establish, for many purposes not inconsistent with the tribal laws, a territorial government, with the Superintendent as governor, the Territory being named "*Oklahoma.*"[27]   ◆◆

The Thirteenth Amendment, 1868

◆◆   Neither slavery nor involuntary servitude, except as a punishment for crime, whereof the party shall have been duly convicted, shall exist within the United States, or any place subject to their jurisdiction.   ◆◆

It seems quite obvious that, while Negroes were expected primarily to benefit from this amendment, its provisions were applicable to Native Americans also. Nevertheless, Native Americans were forced into "involuntary servitude" by the government on innumerable occasions after 1868, without recourse to judicial procedures.

The Fourteenth Amendment, 1870

◆◆   All persons born or naturalized in the United States, and subject to the jurisdiction thereof, are citizens of the United States and of the States wherein they reside. . . . The right of citizens of the United States to vote shall not be denied or abridged by the United States, or by any State, on account of race, color, or previous condition of servitude.   ◆◆

This amendment, while designed to benefit Negroes, would seem to have covered Native Americans born in the United States as well, since they were subject to the jurisdiction of the United States. Thus it would appear that the rights of citizenship were bestowed upon most Native Americans in 1870; however, the federal and state governments disregarded this interpretation and denied Native Americans basic civil rights, even going so far as to forcibly suppress their religion, customs, social organization, and languages. It cannot be argued that Native Americans, as members of tribes or "nations," were outside the jurisdiction of the United States since Congress chose to legislate for the natives, thus denying that they were independent. Of course, the government considered most Native Americans "wards" of the United States. However, the Constitution does not extend to the government the authority to declare residents of the United States "wards," nor did the original treaties with the several tribes, or the Treaty of Guadalupe Hidalgo with Mexico, give the government any such authority. Furthermore, the fourteenth amendment does not make any exceptions to its provisions, nor does it mention the existence of "wards."

It would appear, then, that all of the coercive policies adopted by the federal government from 1870 to 1928 were strictly illegal, since they were in violation of the fourteenth amendment as well as of the first, second, fifth, tenth, and thirteenth amendments. Thus, much of United States native policy since 1870 has been erected upon a nonexistent legal base.

Notes

1. "A Sketch of the Development of the Bureau of Indian Affairs and of Indian Policy," (Washington: Bureau of Indian Affairs, December 1956) p. 2. Hereinafter cited as "A Sketch of the Bureau of Indian Affairs."

2. *American State Papers, Indian Affairs*, Vol. I, No. 2, p. 13; Vol. I, No. 29, p. 230; Vol. II, No. 4, p. 53.

3. Foley, ed., *The Jefferson Cyclopedia*, p. 422.

4. *Ibid.*, p. 423.

5. *Ibid.*, pp. 420-421.

6. *Ibid.*, p. 423.

7. Richardson, Vol. 1, p. 340; Foley, p. 423.

8. James D. Richardson, ed., *Messages and Papers of the Presidents* (Washington: Bureau of National Literature, 1913) Vol. I, p. 368.

9. *Ibid.*, Vol. 1, pp. 395-6.

10. *Ibid.*, Vol. 1, pp. 415-416.

11. *Ibid.*, Vol. 1, pp. 422-3.

12. See George Dewey Harmon, *Sixty Years of Indian Affairs* (Chapel Hill: University of North Carolina Press, 1941), pp. 59-93, for a discussion of Jefferson's policies.

13. Letter of Jefferson to John Adams, March 1812, in Foley, ed., *op. cit.*, pp. 422-3.

14. *American State Papers, Indian Affairs*, Vol. II, No. 207, p. 496.

15. *American State Papers, Indian Affairs*, Vol. II, No. 162, pp. 200-201.

16. *Johnson and Graham's Lessee* vs. *McIntosh*, 21, U.S., 543.
17. C. J. Kappler, ed., *Indian Affairs, Laws and Treaties* (Washington, 1892-1913), Vol. II, p. 311.
18. Letter of Thomas Forsyth, Oct. 24, 1831, in *Ethnohistory*, Vol. IV, No. 2, Spring 1957, pp. 207, 209.
19. Harmon, *op. cit.*, p. 175. Reprinted by permission of the University of North Carolina Press.
20. *Worcester* vs. *Georgia.*
21. Harmon, *op. cit.*, pp. 224-5. Reprinted by permission of the University of North Carolina Press.
22. "A Sketch of the Bureau of Indian Affairs," p. 5.
23. R. W. Johnson, Committee on Territories, in *U.S. Senate, Reports of Committees, 33rd Congress, 1st Session*, Serial 707, Document No. 379, pp. 1-8.
24. "A Sketch of the Bureau of Indian Affairs," p. 6.
25. "A Sketch of the Bureau of Indian Affairs," p. 6.
26. J. Ross Browne, *Adventures in the Apache Country* (New York: Harpers, 1869) pp. 51-60.
27. Report of the Commissioner of Indian Affairs, in *Annual Report, U.S. Department of the Interior, 1865-66* (Washington: U.S. Government Printing Office, 1867) p. 9.

EIGHT

UNITED STATES POLICY SINCE 1870

A new era in federal policy toward the Native Americans commenced in 1870-1871. John Collier refers to one facet of this policy when he writes that:

> Beginning about 1870, a leading aim, of the United States was to destroy the Plains Indians' societies through destroying their religions; and it may be that the world has never witnessed a religious persecution so implacable and so variously implemented.[1]

While this judgment may be a trifle stong, it is nonetheless true that in spite of constitutional provisions relating to religious freedom, the federal government conducted a sixty-year program of enforced acculturation that bears comparison with some of the most notorious eras of religious and social totalitarianism in modern history. Native groups were placed in concentration camps, shifted about at the whim of bureaucrats, starved, intimidated, and persecuted. Their religious ceremonials were forcibly suppressed, and every effort was made to destroy their secular cultural heritage as well. And as if this official policy were not enough, the administrators of the program were often corrupt and supplies intended for the impoverished natives ended up in the hands of whites.

In 1871 the United States Congress decided that henceforth

> no Indian Nation or Tribe within the territory of the United States shall be acknowledged or recognized as an independent nation, tribe or power with whom the United States may contract by treaty: Provided further that nothing herein contained shall be construed to invalidate or impair the obligations of any treaty heretofore lawfully made and ratified with any such Indian Nation or Tribe.[2]

Thus the United States was not going to sign any more treaties, perhaps because the process of continually breaking existing ones had become so burdensome. This decision was, however, not without its problems, since there were still several independent tribes, and a number of previously subdued groups possessed no treaty protections. These tribes without treaties especially were to suffer after 1871, being deprived of their land without compensation and being offered only minimal and belated federal assistance.

In 1872 General Francis C. Walker, Commissioner of Indian Affairs, expressed the government's native policy as follows:

> There is no question of national dignity, be it remembered, involved in the treatment of savages by civilized powers. With wild men, as with wild beasts, the question of whether in a given situation one shall fight, coax, or run, is a question merely of what is easiest and safest. . . . the Indians should be made as comfortable on and as uncomfortable off, their reservation [as possible]. . . .[3]

General Walker set out to carry out the second part of his policy, but failed miserably at the first.

TOTALITARIAN AMERICA: THE UNKNOWN LAND

Almost completely unknown to most Americans, or of little interest to them, was the totalitarian state within a state that existed for over half a century—the Bureau of Indian Affairs and its empire of "wards." In the twentieth century many Americans have come to think of Nazi Germany and the Soviet Union of Stalin as prototypes of the all-embracing state, but Hitler and the Stalinists might well have been imitating the system of coercive culture change used earlier by the United States.

Nothing was too insignificant to escape the attention of the Bureau of Indian Affairs bureaucrats (as the following selections illustrate); no constitutional guarantees, treaties, or principles of freedom proved to be obstacles in the path of their carrying out what many of them thought was "for the Indians' own good." The rights of parents ceased to exist; with the founding of Carlisle Indian School in 1879 by Captain R. H. Pratt, native children were removed as far from their parents as possible and frequently were not even allowed to return home on vacation. The theory behind this treatment was: "to civilize the Indian, put him in the midst of civilization. To keep him civilized, keep him there." [4] Of course, to become "civilized" was simply to become a brown-skinned Anglo-American. Everything native had to be destroyed—even if the process sometimes meant destroying the native himself.

In 1887 the Commissioner of Indian Affairs issued the following order:

> It is believed that if any Indian vernacular is allowed to be taught by missionaries in schools on Indian reservations it will prejudice the pupil as well as his parents against the English language. . . . This language which is good enough for a white man or a black man ought to be good enough for the red man. It is also believed that teaching an Indian youth in his

own barbarous dialect is a positive detriment to him. The impractability, if not impossibility, of civilizing the Indians of this country in any other tongue than our own would seem obvious.[5]

The Indian is to be "individualized," 1889

Commissioner of Indian Affairs Morgan asserted that reservations should be eliminated. The Indian was to be absorbed, not as an Indian, but as an "American," and he was to be "individualized," i.e., the tribes and traditions were to be destroyed. The Indian would have to ". . . conform to the White man's ways, peaceably if they will, forceably if they must. . . ."

This policy, expressed most fully in the Dawes Allotment Act, sought to break up tribally owned holdings and divide them up among individual families, the "surpluses" going to Whites. In destroying tribal cooperatives, the government not only violated many treaties but also sought to accomplish an economic purpose unprecedented in American history—forcibly altering the manner in which a group has voluntarily arranged its wealth. Needless to state, no White corporate entity has ever been so treated, with "surpluses" after division being taken from the group and redistributed by the government.

As a result of the allotment system, "in the year 1890 alone, more than 17,400,000 acres, or about one-seventh of all remaining Indian land, was acquired by the Federal government." [6]

Cultural change: haircuts at gun point, 1896

◆◆ As with Samson of old, the Indians' wildness lay in their long hair, which the returned educated Indians wore because, as they boasted, "It made them wild." All energies were bent to compel the adult males to cut their hair and adopt civilized attire in vain. . . . I directed the (Indian) police to cut theirs or leave the force. They reluctantly complied, but once accomplished they were only too eager to compel the rest, and they cheerfully, under orders, arrested and brought to me every educated Indian on the [Mescalero Apache] Reservation. There were twenty of these, gorgeous in paint, feathers, long hair, breechclouts and blankets. . . . The Indian Office, at my request, issued a preemptory order for all to cut their hair and adopt civilized attire; and in six weeks from the start every male Indian had been changed into the semblance of a decent man, with the warning that confinement at hard labor awaited any backsliders. [The philosophy behind this action was that] the United States has for years footed the bills that maintained them in idleness, filth, immorality, and barbarism, and where a policy for their good has been adopted, they will not be consulted.[7] ◆◆

Not all culture change was accompanied by as rigid a system of coer-
on, as witness this statement of the condition of the Alaska natives,
91:

◆◆ . . . [The Hydahs, Thingits, and Tsimpseans] have
come partly civilized by contact with the whites and through the in-
ence of schools and missions, and there is a large number of those who
n speak English and have become excellent citizens. The Aleuts
e also partly civilized, but . . . conforming more nearly to that of the
ussian than our own. The Tinnehs [Athapaskans]. . . . may properly
designated as Indians. The other natives of Alaska are not true Indians
d have not generally been treated as such by the government. . . .
he progress of the natives of Southeastern Alaska toward civilization
steady and certain, though it must not be supposed that these people
t take high rank in learning, intelligence or morality. . . . They have
Asiatic cast and the coast people are generally thought to have origi-
ated from Japanese stock. . . . These people are all self-supporting.
. . [Sitka] contains a large industrial school, attended by 200 native
ys and girls. . . . [Wrangell] has a flourishing industrial school for
e Indian girls.[8] ◆◆

he qualitative aspects of native administration, 1892

◆◆ The most shameful chapter of American history is
at in which is recorded the account of our dealings with the Indians.
he story of our government's intercourse with this race is an unbroken
arrative of injustice, fraud, and robbery. Our people have disregarded
onesty and truth whenever they have come in contact with the Indian,
d he has had no rights because he never had the power to enforce any.
Protests against governmental swindling of these savages have been
ade again and again, but such remonstrances attract no general atten-
on. Almost everyone is ready to acknowledge that in the past the In-
ans have been shamefully robbed, but it appears to be believed that
is no longer takes place. This is a great mistake. We treat them now
uch as we have always treated them. Within two years, I have been
esent on a reservation where government commissioners, by means of
reats, by bribes given to chiefs, and by casting fraudulently the votes
absentees, succeeded after months of effort in securing votes enough
warrant them in asserting that a tribe of Indians, entirely wild and
tally ignorant of farming, had consented to sell their lands, and to set-
e down each upon 160 acres of the most utterly arid and barren land
be found on the North American continent. The fraud perpetrated
this tribe was as gross as could be practised by one set of men upon
other. In a similar way the Southern Utes were recently induced to
onsent to give up their reservation for another.

Americans are a conscientious people, yet they take no interest in thes
frauds. They have the Anglo-Saxon spirit of fair play, which sympathize
with weakness, yet no protest is made against the oppression which th
Indian suffers. They are generous; a famine in Ireland, Japan or Russi
arouses the sympathy and calls forth the bounty of the nation, yet the
give no heed to the distress of the Indians, who are in the very mid:
of them. They do not realize that Indians are human beings like then
selves.

For this state of things there must be a reason, and this reason is to b
found, I believe, in the fact that practically no one has any person;
knowledge of the Indian race. The few who are acquainted with the
are neither writers nor public speakers, and for the most part would fin
it easier to break a horse than to write a letter. If the general publi
knows little of this race, those who legislate about them are equall
ignorant. From the congressional page who distributes the copies of
pending bill, up through the representatives and senators who vote fc
it, to the president whose signature makes the measure a law, all are er
tirely unacquainted with this people or their needs.[9] ◆◆

Legal recognition of an accomplished fact, 1902

In *Lone Wolf* vs. *Hitchcock* the Supreme Court held that:

◆◆ The power exists to abrogate the provisions of an I»
dian treaty. . . . When, therefore, treaties were entered into betwee
the United States and a tribe of Indians it was never doubted that th
power to abrogate existed in Congress. [The court went on to state, hov
ever, that] presumably such power will be exercised only when circun
stances arise which will not only justify the government in disregardin
stipulations of the treaty, but may demand, in the interest of the countr
and the Indians themselves, that it should be so.[10] ◆◆

Citizens can still be wards, 1916

In *U.S.* vs. *Nice* the Supreme Court held that

◆◆ . . . Citizenship is not incompatible with tribal exis
ence or continued guardianship, and so may be conferred without con
pletely emancipating the Indians or placing them beyond the reach c
congressional regulations adopted for their protection.[11] ◆◆

A last fling at religious persecution, 1922-1929

In the 1920's the Bureau of Indian Affairs

♦♦ . . . set in motion an open drive, aimed principally at the Pueblo tribes, for the suppression of all the native Indian religions still existing. . . . The campaign followed these lines: The Pueblos and their friends were . . . anti-American, and subversive. In fact, they were "agents of Moscow." They were cultists of Indian paganism, and the pagan cults were horrible, sadistic and obscene. They were seeking to discredit and weaken the United States Government . . . Then in 1926, the Indian Bureau moved from defamation to action. Commissioner Charles H. Burke visited the Taos Pueblo, and notified the old men in council assembled that they were "half animals," through their pagan religion. . . . Then the whole governing body of Taos Pueblo was thrown into prison for violating the Bureau's religious crimes code. Nevertheless, in 1929, the Pueblo Indians emerged victorious with the help of white friends and thanks to their own all-Pueblo Council.[12] ♦♦

THE RED MAN'S NEW DEAL

During the 1920's the position of Tribal Americans gradually improved. John Collier, former Commissioner of Indian Affairs, has summarized this period as follows:

♦♦ Moving rapidly up the years from 1920, we witness first the defeat, in 1922-23, of the official attempt to disperse the Pueblos. We witness the enactment of legislation to reinvest the Pueblos with land. That legislation was passed in 1924. We witness the enactment, in 1926, of legislation placing executive order reservations upon a parity with treaty reservations, thus vetoing the official plan of 1923 to transfer more than half of the then Indian estates to whites. We witness, in 1926, the invoking of the help of the United States Public Health Service in an effort to check the rising death rates of the tribes. We see the Indians organizing the Council of All the New Mexico Pueblos, a still-continuing active organization, the first example of this Indian political renaissance. In 1924, expressly in recognition of their World War services, full citizenship was voted to all Indians by Congress. In 1927, for the first time, we see an action by the Department of the Interior to bring the light of social science to bear upon the Indian need and upon its Indian Bureau's operations. The monumental study by the Institute for Government Research, known as the Meriam Survey, resulted from the initiative of the then Secretary of the Interior. In 1928 the Senate moved into action, and the hearings and documents of the special committe upon Indian investigations of that body totaled thirty-six printed volumes by 1939.

With the year 1929, an intellectual revolution was in full swing within the official Indian Bureau. The schooling policies of the Indian Office were fundamentally modified starting with that year. The movement was from uniformity of curriculum to diversity, and from mere classroom activity to community schools.

In 1929, the Secretary of the Interior and the Commissioner of Indian Affairs joined in memorials to Congress, asking for legislation to re-establish the local democracy of Indians, to curtail the absolutism of the government's Indian system, to apply the concept of constitutional right to Indian economic affairs, and to settle decently and promptly the host of Indian tribal claims growing out of breached treaties and compacts of the past years. . . .

Public opinion could not move all at once; neither could Indian opinion, nor administrative or congressional thinking. Active, continuous attention by the chief executive was needed; and in 1933, at last, the needed assembled data and administrative trends were made available to President Roosevelt. And in 1933, by secretarial order, the sale of Indian lands was stopped. Without public shock, the Indian cultures and religions were put in possession of the full constitutional guarantees. Without public shock, the institutionalized boarding schools for Indians were cut by one-third and the children were moved to community day schools, and thousands of children never schooled before were brought into the classroom.

Then the Indian Reorganization Act was formulated. The administrators took this proposed reform legislation to the Indians in great regional meetings, and through the Indians assembled there, back to all of the Indian communities. For the first time in history, all Indians were drawn into a discussion of universal problems of the Indians, and these universal problems focused upon the most ancient and most central Indian institution, local democracy integrated with the land.

Congress passed the Indian Reorganization Act in 1934, and it incorporated in this act a feature new in federal legislation, the referendum. The act, as passed by the Congress and signed by the President, was by its own terms merely permissive. Every Indian tribe might adopt it or reject it by majority vote by secret ballot.

The Indian Reorganization Act, under which today 74 percent of the Indians are living and functioning, does not contain the whole of the present Indian program. There are tribes not under the act which are realizing a creative self-determination not less than tribes that are under the act. And there are many tribes, under the act by their own choice, which have chosen to go forward with their ancient and never extinguished types of local democracy, rather than to adopt the parliamentary type of self-government. . . .[13] ◆◆

The 1934 reforms represented a revolution in United States native policy. Whereas the previous goal had been to destroy the tribal organizations, now native societies were to be utilized as vehicles for progress.[14]

◆◆   Indian societies must and can be discovered in their continuing existence, or regenerated, or set into being de novo and made use of. . . . the Indian societies . . . must be given status, responsibility and power. . . . the land, held, used and cherished in the way the particular Indian group desires, is fundamental in any lifesaving program. . . . each and all of the freedoms should be extended to Indians. . . . Organization is necessary to freedom: help toward organizing must be extended by the government.[15]   ◆◆

Some of the specific benefits of the Indian Reorganization Act were as follows:

◆◆   . . . Indian tribes gained the power of approval or veto over the disposition of all tribal assets; they were authorized to take over control of their own resources as rapidly as they could . . . ; they were given the right to employ legal counsel, the right to negotiate with federal, state and local governments. . . . they were also assisted and encouraged in the development of representative tribal governments under tribal constitutions. . . .[16]   ◆◆

Perhaps the most interesting aspect of the legislation is the extent to which it reveals what native organizations could *not* do prior to 1934. One pauses to wonder how the tribes could possibly not have previously possessed the powers granted to them, especially when one considers the freedom of operation enjoyed by White-owned corporate entities during the nineteenth and early twentieth centuries.

The Collier reforms also had a great effect upon the educational techniques utilized by Indian Bureau teachers. Some effort was made to adjust to the use of indigenous languages in instruction, although generally only as a prelude to learning English.

◆◆   For more than fifty years a conscientious attempt was made to ignore Indian cultures and to impose our ways and the English language. . . . Yet on most reservations the Indian language is the language of all social intercourse, and English is used only in dealing with whites. . . . Traders and missionaries generally use the native language in relations with Indians. . . . the purposes of the [Bureau of Indian Affairs] bilingual education program are multiple. . . . Realizing the need for an effective means of communication with the Navajo, Oliver La Farge and Dr. John Harrington developed a popular alphabet. . . . This is the system employed by the Indian Service. . . . Our aim is to promote bilingualism, but we are compelled to deal with the majority of the tribe in Navajo. . . . Today not more than 10 per cent of the Navajo people speak English at all. . . . There is

also in press a series of books in Sioux and English. . . . Here in
America the outstanding example [of a written Indian language] is the
Cherokee . . . which was written in a relatively difficult syllabic system
invented by Sequoyah. . . . A newspaper was published regularly, and
it was the written language as long as the Cherokee maintained their
identity as Indians. It is still used and known to a few of the Cherokee
in Oklahoma today. . . . Is it Utopian to hope that, in the future
[by using native languages] . . . a significant written literature might
grow? [17] ◆◆

THE REACTION, 1950-1960

The "New Deal" may be said to have come to an end soon after
1950, and especially during 1952-1953. A series of laws and directives
were enacted and implemented which were opposed by many native
groups.

◆◆ The Indians of the United States and Alaska are
undergoing a deadly and sustained attack. . . . The onset is both
administrative and Congressional. . . . This crisis dates from 1950,
when Dillon S. Myer was made Commissioner of Indian Affairs under
President Truman. Myer's crystallizing experience had been that of
Director of the War Relocation Authority—of the prison camps where
100,000 Japanese-Americans were kept behind barb-wire. . . . To Myer,
the Indian communities and land-reservations appeared as prison camps
from which their inmates needed to be set free. . . . The health services of the Government, its schooling and land-restoration and conservation services, and its protection of Indian assets from white predators
were discriminative over-privileges; the Indian communities were the
foes of Indian individuality; and the guarantees against local, state in-
terferences with Indian life-ways and against local property taxation
. . . were gratuitously extended over-privileges. All these conditions
must be annihilated. . . . Myer was removed by President Eisenhower
but . . . the newly manned Interior Department moved swiftly, on
many fronts, to translate the Myer fantasy into lethal reality. The first
accomplishment of the new administration was Public Law 280. . . .
This enactment empowers any State (no exceptions) to impose on any
and all tribes its own civil and criminal codes and enforcement machin-
ery and thus to annihilate the tribal codes and tribal authorities of
self-protection. Then the present congress assembled; and the Interior
Department presented a flood of bills, each aimed at Indian destruction. . . .

What is the identical pattern of these many bills? It is to lift the
Federal trust from the Indian properties and cast the properties onto
the local tax-rolls; to repeal the Indian Reorganization Act and outlaw
the 100 Tribal constitutions and 200 Tribal Corporations; to resume

the forced individualization of the Indian properties; and to make the Government-Indian treaties forgotten scraps of paper. In brief, to renew in all its essential the "Century of Dishonor." [18]   ◆◆

Relocation and termination ·

Two of the most controversial of the Bureau of Indian Affairs' new programs were (1) termination of the traditional federal-tribal relationship and incorporation of the tribal regions into the states, and (2) the resettlement of rural Native Americans in urban regions as a means both of easing reservation population pressure and fostering rapid assimilation. A study made by Quakers discusses the effect of these and other policies during 1953-1956:

◆◆ But the era of good feeling [initiated by the reforms of 1934] ended abruptly in 1953 with passage of House Concurrent Resolution 108. This measure states, in part: "It is the policy of Congress, as rapidly as possible to make the Indians within the United States subject to the same laws and entitled to the same privileges and responsibilities as are applicable to other citizens of the United States, to end their status as wards of the United States, and to grant them all of the rights and prerogatives pertaining to American citizenship. . . ."

Passage of this resolution, and proposal of the "Termination" bills which followed it, did much to confuse the already complex Indian situation and to divert attention from the real needs of Indians.

During the past three years, the energies of thousands of elected officials and government employees have been devoted to implementing the new Indian policy. The Senate and House have held scores of hearings and new branches have been set up with the Bureau of Indian Affairs to plan and program the government's withdrawal from Indian administrative responsibility.

Forced concentration on termination has given Indian Bureau personnel little time to find ways of helping Indians solve the basic problems which confront them. True, the Bureau has devoted increasing time and funds to its relocation program, the resettlement of reservation Indians in urban areas, but this program has won acceptance as a new technique for encouraging rapid "assimilation."

Tribal resistance to hasty termination, coupled with aroused public concern, resulted in the defeat of half the termination bills introduced for specific tribes in the 83rd Congress, and apparently gave pause to those who would have abruptly changed the Indian-government relationship.

Still, it can be said that little is being accomplished today. Termination remains the official Federal policy and opposition to premature change continues as the prime objective of most Indians and groups concerned with their welfare. In a sense, both positions are negative, for they prevent concentration on the essential task of finding ways to meet the needs of Indians, both as individuals and as members of communities.[19] ◆◆

Termination has always been implicit in federal native policy, or at least since the period when the government saw fit to deny the native groups self-government and substituted instead the wardship system. Having assumed the burden of being a trustee in order to "civilize" the aborigine, the government could be expected to end trusteeship when the process of assimilation was complete or nearly so. In 1940 Assistant Commissioner Joseph C. McCaskell stated that

◆◆ . . . we see the Indian Office divesting its authority into three directions; first among other agencies of the Federal government . . . ; second among the local, state and county governments . . . ; and finally among the tribal governments which have organized governing bodies; and which expect eventually to take over and manage all of the affairs of Indians.[20] ◆◆

The termination of special federal services and trusteeship is dependent upon certain other programs, among which is relocation. The present reservations are insufficient to support the Tribal American population, in part because inferior lands were generally set aside for them. Furthermore, the lands reserved for native use were periodically diminished prior to 1933 by various means (and no allowance was made for future population increase). Now the federal government is faced with two alternatives: relocating surplus population away from the reservations or attempting to enlarge the tribal domains and to develop economic opportunities nearby. Current efforts are aimed in both directions, although during the late 1950's relocation seemed to have been emphasized. Between 1952 and 1957 relocation service and assistance

◆◆ . . . have been provided to over 17,000 persons. Of this number, more than 12,000 persons are still relocated and are self-supporting and are enjoying the advantages of self-dependence. They are steadily employed, better housed, better fed and better clothed than ever before.[21] ◆◆

Relocatees in Chicago and Los Angeles

From 1952 through 1955 some 3,000 reservation Indians, many from the Southwest, were relocated in Chicago. Of these, six hundred had returned to their reservations by 1955.

◆◆ There is no doubt of the success of the Chicago experiment. True, the present generation of relocated Indians, handicapped by lack of education and unfamiliarity with urban culture, fill the lesser jobs, live in the lesser neighborhoods. But the overwhelming majority are doubtlessly better off from every angle. Their children, of course, will make the great gains and flow most easily into their rightful place in the mainstream of American Life.[22] ◆◆

Whether or not the relocatees are "better off from every angle" is perhaps debatable. A study of the operations of the program in Los Angeles seems to indicate that serious problems still remain.

◆◆ A summary of [Indian] . . . responses . . . shows one problem standing clearly above all the rest—that is the problem of alcoholism. . . . every person interviewed mentioned this problem. . . . However, alcoholism, it was pointed out, is of itself simply the result of other stresses. For the present generation of relocated Indians in this area, these stresses include a lack of education, an unfamiliarity with urban culture, insufficient incomes, unemployment, substandard housing, and economic and social discrimination. . . . On the basis of the information . . . the condition of the relocated peoples in the city would seem to be a major blot on the national conscience, for instead of helping the Indians to solve their problems, we seem simply to have allowed them to bring the problems . . . with them to the city.[23] ◆◆

Alchoholism is symptomatic of a number of basic problems faced by Native Americans whenever they have been forced to adjust to a profound change in their relationships with the world beyond the tribe. To move from a rural to a highly urban environment creates tension enough—to move from a tribal society into the center of a great city must be, for many, a traumatic experience. The trauma is deepened by the fact that the federal government seems concerned only with acquiring initial housing and employment for the relocatee. His social-psychological adjustment is of little moment, and if a meaningful life is to be discovered in the city, the Indians themselves must discover it. Perhaps to be truly "assimilated" every minority group must become urban slum-dwellers, sinking into the whirlpool of a great city and becoming absorbed in the mass of humanity around them. But how many private tragedies occur in the whirlpool, and how many useful lives are lost along the way?

United States Congress, the principles of termination, 1953

◆◆ It is the policy of Congress, as rapidly as possible, to make the Indians within the territorial limits of the United States

subject to the same laws and entitled to the same privileges and responsibilities as are applicable to other citizens . . . to end their status as
wards . . . and to grant them all the rights and prerogatives pertaining
to American citizenship.[24] ◆◆

*Commissioner of Indian Affairs Glenn L. Emmons (speaking to
various tribal groups), 1953*

◆◆ What we are trying to achieve essentially, as I see
it, is a condition of parity or equality for the Indian people as compared
with the rest of the population. This does not mean that we are expect-
ing Indians to give up their own culture and be just like everyone else.
. . . I know that there are some Tribes which are ready and anxious
to take over full responsibility for their own affairs . . . and that others
will have to move . . . much more slowly and gradually. [For these
latter, "trusteeship" may have to continue for several years.] [25] ◆◆

As a part of the termination philosophy there was a shifting of emphasis from tribal development toward the integration of the individual
native into the life of the dominant society.

Bureau of Indian Affairs, policy on termination, 1956

◆◆ It is apparent that some people feel that the interests of the tribal groups should be given priority over the rights and
interests of the individual Indian. . . . We believe, on the other hand,
in the primacy of the individual Indian and his right to choose his own
way of life without pressure or coercion. . . . But we are not seeking
a solution by trying to break up Indian communities.[26] ◆◆

One might well wonder, however, whether the concept of the tribe
versus the individual is valid. Tribes are in fact composed of individuals
and their governing bodies are democratically chosen. Thus this is in
reality a question of the interests of a majority of persons in a community as opposed to the interests of a minority. Another fundamental
problem created by this policy is: how can the individual Native
American protect himself if his organizations are weakened? How can
he advance economically if the only organs capable of financing entre-
preneurial development, the tribes, are bypassed?
    The inconsistency of the Bureau of Indian Affairs' position can be
seen if we substitute the following: "it is apparent that some people feel
that the interests of the corporations should be given priority over the
rights and interests of the individual stockholder. . . . We believe, on
the other hand, in the primacy of the individual stockholder." Such a
position would, of course, be unacceptable in the United States, and

yet it is even more absurd when applied to tribal societies. Whereas White corporations are generally nondemocratic (with votes being distributed according to how much wealth a stockholder has invested), native tribes are democratic societies and thus better represent the individual member. Perhaps, therefore, the Bureau of Indian Affairs' desire to develop the individual was really a disguised effort to weaken and destroy the tribes as such.

Commissioner Glenn L. Emmons, "consultation" and termination, 1956

◆◆   The principle of consultation with Indians was enunciated by President Eisenhower and lies at the heart of our actions. . . . We are not proceeding [with termination] arbitrarily. [Consultation involves learning] what the Indian people have on their minds, [giving the latter a chance to express their views, and giving] the fullest possible consideration [to] the clear consensus [of] . . . a majority segment of the tribal population. Finally, in those cases where there are good and compelling reasons for not complying with the tribal requests or recommendations, it means . . . [offering explanations to them. Indian "consent" would not have to be obtained] before Congress can enact legislation affecting Indians. . . . No group should have the power to thwart the will of the Congress. . . . The Federal government became trustee of the Indians' property on the basis that Indians were sometimes unable to manage their own property. It is unusual to assume this and then also assume that Indians are capable of making decisions for the Government—If the Indians' consent is necessary, the question might well be raised if Federal trusteeship is needed.[27]   ◆◆

The above statement ignores the legal/moral question of whether a treaty (contractural) relationship can be severed simply by means of "consultation." In addition, the statement that "no group should have the power to thwart the will of Congress" contradicts the fact that our constitutional system is specifically designed to allow the courts and the states to "thwart" Congress. During this period the Bureau of Indian Affairs wished to extend to the federal government powers over native affairs that Whites would not tolerate having applied to them.

Termination and socialism, 1960

Since World War II a major attack has been made upon the Bureau of Indian Affairs and its policies by groups opposed to the "welfare state" in general and to welfare programs for Native Americans in particular. These groups have favored termination; they oppose tribes as "socialistic" entities. To some extent they echo advocates of the allotment plan of the 1880's who sought to substitute "rugged individualism" for native communalism. The following selection illustrates this view. It appeared in *The Arizona Republic* and was reprinted as a brochure entitled "Box Canyon for the Navajo."

◆◆ Frustrated by years of fumbling guidance . . . [the Navajo Tribe] is following a wily scout who knows all the twists and turns of the path to success in our modern world. Sadly enough, say many, the trail leads to a fatal dead end, to a box canyon of this age's popular but false "isms," of socialism, of a growing totalitarianism, of tribal and federal paternalism, of tribal nationalism. . . . an assistant to a prominent Democratic senator asserts flatly, "The Navajos are building a socialistic empire and the federal government's helping them do it." A republican congressman tells you over a cup of coffee in the House cafeteria: "We've made some awful bad Indian law, and now we have a socialistic state on the Navajo Reservation. . . ."

Congressmen who have tried to untangle U.S. Indian problems and help the Indians . . . have discovered with shock that such projects offer little to gain and a great deal to lose. . . . The Association of American Indian Affairs (led by "Chief Troublemaker," Oliver La Farge), the Indian Rights Association and the National Congress of American Indians will attack anyone who proposes changes for Indians or hints that Indian problems are not "working themselves out" through greater and greater federal paternalism. . . . Big brother is watching over the Navajo. . . .

"I don't know why these Indian groups resist any changes," said Governor Fannin [of Arizona] with a shake of his head, "Everything else in our country is changing. Why not the Indians too?" . . . It is perhaps one of the economic lessons of the century that government management of resources and production is almost automatically wasteful. . . . Application of state law to the reservation . . . would be a first step toward making Indians . . . full fledged participants in American Society. . . .

White man's whiskey and white man's socialism, both have proved popular with some Navajos. Neither is doing the Navajo much good. . . . "Termination" is a hated word among the professional Indian groups and Indian politicians who would rather keep the status quo . . . [but] termination [would not] mean destruction of "Indianhood," another bugaboo used by well-meaning persons, most of whom live on the East Coast, most of whom have never seen an Indian. . . . If the state does act to bring total integration to the Navajo, the people of Arizona must be ready to resist the din and clamor of local and national Indian groups who will surely besiege the public. . . . If the state does not act, it can stand by and observe . . . the less-able Navajos isolated in a decreasingly valuable tourist trap, objects of curiosity frozen in a vast anthropological museum. . . .[28] ◆◆

The Arizona Republic may indeed see wisdom in destroying "Navajo Socialism"; however, how does the latter differ from the "socialism" of our large corporations? What makes the Navajo Tribe, Inc., different from a White joint-stock corporation? The answer is, of course, that the Navajo corporate entity is democratically controlled and not wealth-controlled. What can be gained by weakening the Navajo tribe with its tribally developed economic enterprises? Perhaps the answer is that land and resources in northern Arizona can be acquired for exploitation by White entrepreneurs without supervision by the federal government. And as regards federal "paternalism," have the White politicians and businessmen of Arizona opposed federal handouts in the form of reclamation, water projects, defense contracts, military installations, agricultural subsidies, et cetera? Is paternalism good for Whites and bad for Native Americans?

Political promises, 1960

In the 1960 presidential campaign both political parties and their candidates made many promises to Native Americans. The Democratic platform stated that

◆◆ We recognize the unique legal and moral responsibility of the Federal government for Indians in restitution for the injustice that has sometimes been done them. . . . Free consent of the Indian tribes concerned shall be required before the Federal government makes any change in any Federal-Indian treaty or other contractual relationship. ◆◆

Presidential candidate John F. Kennedy stated in a letter to Oliver La Farge, President of the Association on American Indian Affairs:

◆◆ There would be no change in treaty or contractual relationships without the consent of the tribes concerned. No steps would be taken by the Federal government to impair the cultural heritage of any group. There would be protection of the Indian land base. . . .[29] ◆◆

THE NEW FRONTIER AND THE NATIVE

President Kennedy's "Task Force on Indian Affairs" was organized early in 1961 under the chairmanship of W. W. Keeler, Executive Vice President of the Phillips Petroleum Company and Principal Chief of the Cherokee Nation. By July it had the following to report:

◆◆   The Task Force feels that recent Bureau policy has placed more emphasis on [termination] than on [development]. As a result, Indians, fearful that termination will take place before they are ready for it, have become deeply concerned. Their preoccupation was reflected in vigorous denunciation of the so-called "termination policy" during the many hearings which the Task Force conducted with Indian leaders. No other topic was accorded similar attention. It is apparent that Indian morale generally has been lowered and resistance to transition programs heightened as a result of the fear of premature Federal withdrawal. Now, many Indians see termination written into every new bill and administrative decision and sometimes are reluctant to accept help which they need and want for fear that it will carry with it a termination requirement. During the Task Force hearings in Oklahoma City, Acting Commissioner Crow pointed out to those present that a few years ago it was possible for Bureau employees to sit down with Indians and talk constructively about the time when special Federal services for Indians would no longer be provided. "Now," said the Commissioner, "we have reached a point where we can't talk about it to each other; we don't want to talk about it, and if we do talk about it, we have rather harsh words on the subject."

The experience of the past few years demonstrates that placing greater emphasis on termination than on development impairs Indian morale and produces a hostile or apathetic response which greatly limits the effectiveness of the Federal Indian program. The Task Force believes it is wiser to assist the Indians to advance socially, economically and politically to the point where special services to this group of Americans are no longer justified. Then, termination can be achieved with maximum benefit for all concerned. Furthermore, if development, rather than termination, is emphasized during the transitional period, Indian cooperation—an essential ingredient of a successful program—can be expected. . . .

In the opinion of the Task Force, the Bureau of Indian Affairs should seek attainment of the following related Objectives:

1. Maximum Indian economic self-sufficiency.
2. Full participation of Indians in American life.
3. Equal citizenship privileges and responsibilities for Indians.

The Task Force strongly emphasizes that the aid of the tribe—or, more properly, the Indian community—is crucial to the achievement of these objectives and this support should be secured before projects are commenced. The Indians can retain their tribal identities and much of their culture while working toward a greater adjustment, and, for the further enrichment of our society, it is in our best interests to encourage them to do so.[30]   ◆◆

"New trail" for Indians endorsed by Secretary Udall, July 12, 1961

◆◆   A "new trail" for Indians leading to equal citizenship, maximum self-sufficiency, and full participation in American life
was endorsed today by Secretary of the Interior Stewart L. Udall.

Secretary Udall endorsed the "new trail" approach in announcing the
completion of a 77-page report by a Task Force on Indian Affairs which
he appointed earlier in February.

"Preparing the new trail will require the collaboration of the Indians,
State and Local governments, and the American people," Secretary
Udall said.

"We plan to place emphasis on Indian development rather than on
termination in the belief that this approach will win the cooperative
response from our Indian Citizens which is the keystone of a successful
program," he said. . . .

Calling attention to the serious shortage of employment opportunities
for Indians, the report recommends development of Indian-owned resources, more vigorous efforts to attract industries to reservation areas,
and an expanded program of vocation training and placement. It also
calls for the creation of a special Reservation Development Loan Fund
and expansion of the present Revolving Loan Fund maintained by the
Bureau of Indian Affairs.

The Task Force notes that in some areas, reservation development is
complicated by the fact that Indian land allotments have many owners
who either cannot be located or will not agree on how the property is
to be used. In cases where such lands can produce income through
timber leasing, the Task Force recommends that the Secretary of the
Interior seek authority from Congress to negotiate leases and distribute
the proceeds among the Indian owners, without having first to obtain
their consent.

The report emphasizes the need for securing the aid of Indian communities in connection with reservation development and comments
that "Indians can retain their tribal identities and much of their culture
while working toward a greater adjustment."

"It is in our best interest to encourage them to do so," the report adds.

The Task Force asks the Federal Government to accelerate its negotiations with States and counties, and resort to the courts where necessary, to make certain that off-reservation Indians are accorded the same
rights and privileges as other citizens of their areas.

With respect to the complex problem of legal jurisdiction over reservation Indians, the Task Force recommends negotiation among the
States, the Indians and Federal Government to make certain that the
interests of all are protected. It advocates piecemeal, rather than total,
transfer of jurisdiction to the States and comments that such transfer

might be effected immediately in such areas as juvenile affairs, institutional commitments and domestic relations.

The report urges the Bureau to work with the States and the Tribes toward the end of bringing tribal law and order codes into conformity with those of the various States and counties in which reservations are located. However, it calls attention to the serious differences which exist between Indians and a number of States over such matters as water rights and hunting and fishing rights. These, the report says, must be adjudicated before a complete transfer of law and order responsibility is feasible.

Citing the continuing need for more classroom space for Indian children, the Task Force recommends that consideration be given to keeping schools in operation the year round. Also suggested is the use of school facilities for summertime programs which will help Indian youngsters make constructive use of their leisure time. . . .[31] ◆◆

*Address of Philleo Nash, Commissioner of Indian Affairs,
December 6, 1962*

◆◆ During the present century we have been moving steadily away from the all pervasive paternalism of the 1880's and '90's toward a more wholesome respect for the human dignity of individual Indians as well as for the values of age-old tribal cultures. In 1924 our Congress enacted a law declaring that all Indians born in the United States are citizens of the United States without giving up their tribal affiliations. Ten years later Congress passed the Indian Reorganization Act, another milestone piece of legislation, which explicitly recognized the right of Indian tribes and bands to self-government and established basic principles to be followed by the Bureau of Indian Affairs in dealing with tribal governments and helping to strengthen their operations.

These two statutes are both important planks in the platform on which we are now conducting our operations in the Bureau of Indian Affairs. They have set the stage, so to speak, and provided much of the legal underpinning. But there is also a third Congressional plank which is equally significant. This is the marked tendency which Congress has shown over the past dozen years or so to appropriate liberally for activities aimed at the ultimate objective of bringing Indians up to a state of general parity with the rest of the population in terms of health, education, occupational skills and economic opportunity. Even a cursory review of Congressional appropriations for Indian affairs since 1950 will clearly reveal both the scope and the depth of Congressional intention along these markedly progressive lines. . . .

According to the 1960 Census, we have in the United States today about 550,000 people who are identifiable as Indians plus an additional 25,000 or so Eskimos and Aleuts in the State of Alaska—who are also a concern of the Bureau of Indian Affairs. But only about two-thirds of these people—roughly 380,000—come within the scope of the programs conducted by our Bureau. The balance of the Indian population— around 179,000—consists of people who live away from Indian country and are, for all practical purposes, indistinguishable from their non-Indian neighbors. So it is the 380,000 who directly concern us and there can be no doubt that they constitute one of the most seriously disadvantaged groups we have in the United States. One way of summing it up is to point out that adult Indians living on reservations today are, as a group, only about half as well educated as other citizens, have approximately two-thirds the life expectancy, and are receiving somewhere between one-third and one-fourth as much income. . . .

Although the Bureau no longer exercises a comprehensive guardianship over the persons of individual Indians, as it did 75 or 80 years ago, it still functions in a very meaningful way as the trustee for much of the Indians' property. Included in the scope of this trusteeship are about 50.5 million acres of land, located mainly on Indian reservations. Roughly two-thirds of this acreage is tribally owned and the balance consists of tracts that were allotted, for the most part many years ago, to individual tribal members. As the administrators of the Federal Government's trust responsibility, we in the Bureau have on our hands one of the biggest and most complex real estate operations that has ever come to my attention. The mere job of record keeping is almost staggering and all I can say is thank the Lord for automatic data processing. But the job goes far beyond the keeping of records; it involves the actual supervision of all types of realty transactions such as sales, exchanges, rights-of-way, and leases both for surface use and mineral development. It involves the exercise of technically informed judgment to protect the best long-range interests of the Indian owners—tribal or individual—in all of these transactions.

Furthermore, the job is not merely a negative one of protecting the Indians against unwise use or disposition of their assets; it also carries a positive or constructive responsibility to help the Indians in realizing the best possible income from their lands and other resources consistent with sound conservation principles. Thus we are engaged in far-reaching and highly technical programs of forest management, construction and operation of irrigation projects, range management, soil and moisture conservation, and practical guidance in farming and home making practices.

All of these functions are directly related to the basic trust responsibility and they constitute one important phase of our total operation. A second phase, which also embraces several of our older programs, finds us providing Indians with several types of public services which have traditionally in the United States been furnished to non-Indian citizens by State and local units of government. Included in this category are education for the young, welfare aid, law and order activities and the construction and maintenance of local roads. The Bureau's involvement in these fields was an inevitable outgrowth of the fact that Indian trust lands have always been, with a few rare exceptions, exempt from local real estate taxes and outside the sphere of State criminal and civil jurisdiction. So the Bureau has been compelled over the years to develop its own school system, its own welfare organization, its own law enforcement staff, its own program of road construction and maintenance.

Let me quickly add, however, that the picture today on Indian reservations is by no means one of pure Federal activity in these various fields. Over the past 25 years or so, largely as a result of Federal subsidies made possible by the Johnson-O'Malley Act of 1936, many of the States have taken over a substantial share of the responsibilities for educating Indian children on reservations and several of them are now educating all Indian children without financial help from the Bureau of Indian Affairs. To a lesser extent, similar progress has been made in welfare, law enforcement and road operations.

Despite this recent trend, however, the Bureau still remains highly active in all four of these fields, and, actually, the scope of our operations today is bigger than ever on most fronts because of the steady increase in reservation populations.

Education is by far the biggest single function of our Bureau both in terms of manpower and in terms of dollars. If you include construction of schools and directly related facilities in addition to the operation and maintenance of existing schools, then education today accounts for just about three out of every five dollars that we spend in the Bureau. During the fiscal year that ended last June we operated a total of 263 schools ranging in size from single classrooms in trailers or quonset huts at remote locations on the Navajo Reservation to the Intermountain School at Brigham, Utah, which has an enrollment of over 2,100 students. About 75 of these schools are boarding institutions and in them we have the responsibility not merely for providing instruction but also for feeding the students three meals a day and for maintaining and staffing dormitories. All in all, it adds up to quite a sizeable operation and it requires a very substantial number of personnel. . . .

In approaching the subject of law enforcement on Indian reservations in the United States, I feel almost as if I were opening up Pandora's box. It is a subject of tremendous complexity and full exploration of its many ramifications could undoubtedly keep us occupied for the next several hours. To spare you this ordeal, let me just say that most Indian reservations, but not all, are still outside the sphere of State criminal and civil jurisdiction, and are subject to Federal jurisdiction for the major types of felonies and to some form of tribal jurisdiction for the lesser crimes and misdemeanors. The Bureau maintains law and order personnel on most reservations and they work quite closely with the tribes in providing police protection.

The road program of the Bureau differs from the other functions I have just been mentioning since it has been administered for many years in the same division of our organization as the various resource activities I spoke of earlier. Yet I bring it in here because road construction and maintenance is—like education, welfare and law-enforcement—essentially a local governmental function in the United States apart from the major Federal highway system and, of course, the Indian reservations. The Bureau's system now includes about 16,000 miles of road altogether and it is being improved at an encouraging rate and expanded somewhat thanks to substantially increased appropriations in recent years. Especially on the 25,000 square mile Navajo Reservation in our Southwest, we are now bringing all-weather roads into remote localities that have been virtually isolated for generations. I realize, of course, that some of my fellow anthropologists may view this development with mixed emotions. But certainly there can be no argument about the desirability of putting in bus routes so that children can attend school regularly for the first time in their lives or of giving isolated settlements quick and easy access to hospitals and other medical services.

And this brings up another phase of Federal activity in the field of Indian affairs which I want to mention briefly even though it is no longer a function of the Bureau of Indian Affairs. Up until 1955 the Bureau administered a rather far-reaching health program for Indians which included both curative and preventive medical activities. It involved the operation of about 60 hospitals and a large number of health centers and clinics as well as a wide range of activities to promote better environmental sanitation in Indian communities. Since 1955 this program has been administered by the United States Public Health Service and its scope has been substantially enlarged as a result of increased appropriations. Today all qualified observers agree that health conditions across the Indian country generally are markedly better than they were seven years ago and are steadily improving. We in the Bureau of Indian Affairs have a working relationship with our Public Health Service colleagues which is on the whole excellent and we maintain a continuing active interest in effective health protection for Indians. . . .

In 1956 Congress enacted a statute, designated as Public Law 959, which enabled us to broaden the scope of our employment assistance work along lines which have already proved highly beneficial. This law authorized us to provide Indians, principally between the ages of 18 and 35, with three kinds of occupational training. One is vocational training in regularly established schools which equips the trainee with a skill which he or she can use in a wide variety of job situations. The second is on-the-job training which involves orientation of the trainee to the requirements of a particular job in a particular plant. And the third is training for apprentices.

The program came along at just about the right time since one of our major difficulties under the earlier operation was that we were relocating a large number of wholly unskilled workers who presented an increasingly challenging problem of placement. Today we are placing the unskilled workers in schools both in the States where the reservations are located and in the cities where we maintain our urban offices. We are providing on-the-job training for others in plants situated on or near the reservations. And we have recently started to move actively on an apprentice training program.

Through this operation we are turning out skilled machinists, welders, barbers, beauticians, and people trained in just about every other occupation you can think of that does not require the achievement of a college or university degree. The program has been tremendously popular with the Indians and one of our major problems has been to keep abreast of the constantly growing number of applicants. Fortunately the program has also won widespread Congressional approval and just last year Congress increased the authorization for annual appropriations to finance this program from $3.5 million to $7.5 million. During the present fiscal year we have nearly $5.5 million available for training activities, and this enables us to keep about 1,400 Indians, as a general average, in training status. The average cost per trainee is about $250 per month.

Admittedly, this is a rather expensive operation since it includes not just the costs of tuition but also the living expenses for the trainee plus family dependents, if any, during the course of instruction. But there is no doubt in my mind that the benefits amply justify the expense. Acquisition of a salable skill makes an almost night-and-day difference in the economic prospects of the individual Indian. It greatly enhances his chances of being hired, boosts his earning capacity, provides him with additional job security, and broadens his chances for steady advancement.

In addition to the training made possible by our funds in the Bureau of Indian Affairs, Indians are also benefiting nowadays from training grants made by the Area Redevelopment Administration of the Department of Commerce and this promises to be a resource of continuing importance in the future. Furthermore, a third resource for training of Indians is now shaping up in the United States Department of Labor under provisions of the Manpower Development Training Act enacted by Congress earlier this year. So the outlook for moving substantial numbers of Indians out of the unskilled category and giving them new status as skilled workers is today much more promising than it was as recently as 1960.

Another one of the Bureau's recent programs that has special relevance in this context is our work in the field of industrial development. This program was started about six or seven years ago and is designed to help tribal organizations in attracting new manufacturing plants—usually of the light industry type—to the areas on and around the reservations as a means of making additional jobs available for Indian workers. This is not easy to accomplish since the local competition for industrial plants in our country is exceptionally keen—as it is also in Canada, I suspect—and many of the reservations are, unfortunately, located in sections of the Nation which have never been especially attractive to American private industry. Nevertheless it seems clear to me that we should by all means continue this activity since any progress we make is better than nothing at all. One of the big problems we have faced for many years on a large number of the reservations is the fact that steady, year-round jobs are simply not available. And so the Indian families have had to depend to a large extent on seasonal work on nearby farms and ranches supplemented by relief checks during the off-season.

Establishment of new plants with more or less dependable payrolls provides an opportunity to break away from this age-old pattern and move in the direction of greater economic and social stability. . . .

Today we have a total of 26 plants operating in predominantly Indian localities, including eight that have been established in the calendar year 1962. Altogether these plants are providing jobs for some 1,300 Indian workers and the prospects are that they will eventually hire about twice this number. This, of course, is not a staggeringly impressive total out of the 380,000 Indian men, women and children who come within the purview of Indian Bureau responsibilities. But on several reservations the industrial payrolls have already helped perceptibly to brighten the local economic and social atmosphere. And I am optimistic that further important alleviations of chronic Indian poverty can be made through this avenue of approach.

In addition, we are giving greatly increased attention to the encouragement of tribally sponsored and tribally financed business enterprises that will create more jobs for tribal members. Earlier I mentioned that I was deferring discussion of one of the Bureau's "old line" programs and it seems logically appropriate to go into it here. This is the revolving credit program which was originally authorized by the Indian Reorganiation Act of 1934. A total appropriation of $10 million was made possible by the 1934 enactment and this was increased by subsequent statutes of more limited geographic scope to $17 million. Over the years the Bureau has used these funds to good advantage to finance many Indian enterprises, both tribal and individual, which have produced significant and durable economic benefits. The record of repayment has been excellent and the loan collections have been used to make additional lendings in accordance with the revolving principle.

Meanwhile Indian tribes, with help and guidance from the Bureau's credit specialists, have been receiving an increasing amount of financing from banks and other sources that serve the non-Indian citizen. In fact, the total amount of financing obtained by Indians and Indian tribes from such sources has for years far exceeded that made available by the Bureau. In recent years, however, it has become increasingly apparent that if we are to make a truly significant break-through against Indian poverty—and the whole gamut of human ills that accompany it—there will be a need for financing of Indian agricultural and business enterprises, on repayment terms that only the Bureau can provide, far beyond the dimensions that were contemplated when the revolving loan fund was first set up in the middle 1930's.

In partial recognition of this, Congress in 1961 increased the authorization from $17 million to $27 million and appropriated an additional $4 million for the fiscal year that ended last June 30. For the current fiscal period another $4 million was provided. With these funds we have been able to make a number of important loans that will finance tribal developments of outstanding potentiality. The backlog of tribal requests and applications for loans that we have not been able to act upon, however, is both voluminous and impressive. So we are making plans and hoping for a really sizeable increase in our loan fund authorization; I personally believe it is crucially important to our whole effort. . . .

There is one final activity of the Bureau which I want to mention before I close. This is the work that we have very recently undertaken in the field of Indian housing. Because the United States Government has a wide array of housing programs designed to meet a great variety of citizen needs, we have not felt that it would be wise or justifiable for the Bureau to become directly engaged in such activity on Indian reservations. We have, however, recruited a small staff of specialists who devote full time to the housing needs of Indians—which, incidentally, are tremendous—and to serving as our liaison with the existing housing agencies of the Federal Government. . . .

We are now exploring the possibilities of self-help housing along lines that have already proved successful in Puerto Rico and other areas. The method of approach here would be for the Bureau to provide the Indians with some building materials and technical guidance and for them to supply the labor, working as teams in most cases, for the construction of new and better homes. On their own initiative, the Indians of the Fort Apache Reservation in Arizona have made a small but encouraging start along this line and we look forward hopefully to launching a substantial number of such enterprises in other tribal areas. . . .

Although I could not prove it like a mathematical theorem, I feel deeply that the Indians of the United States are further along toward those three goals I mentioned earlier than they were just two or three years ago. And I believe also that the pace of advance can and will be additionally accelerated as some of our recently initiated programs come to full fruition.[32] ◆◆

Do actions speak louder than words? the Kinzua Dam controversy

During the Eisenhower administration plans were developed to build the Kinzua Dam in the midst of the Seneca's treaty-protected lands. These plans were approved by various agencies without seeking any new negotiation of the treaty of 1794, thus ignoring the moral and legal problems involved. The Seneca then advanced their own alternative proposal, which would have saved their lands and, according to their supporters, produced a better project for less money. In February 1961 Basil G. Williams, President of the Seneca Nation, called upon newly elected President Kennedy to fulfill his campaign promises by refusing to allow a violation of the treaty of 1794, and he said further,

◆◆   The Seneca Nation asks you . . . to make an independent investigation . . . and that in the interim you direct that work be halted on the authorized project. Only in this way, Mr. President, will you uphold the sacred honor of the United States and, we are confident, also save our sacred homeland.[33]   ◆◆

The Senecas were supported by many groups, newspapers, and writers; however, Congress and the President refused to accept any changes in the Kinzua project. In April 1963 columnist Brooks Atkinson had this to say in *The New York Times:*

◆◆   Sometime in May the council of the Seneca Nation of Indians, Salamanca, N.Y., must petition Congress for money enough to re-establish community life on lands not flooded by the Kinzua Dam.

Everything is behind schedule except the dam, which is ahead of schedule. The dam in the Allegheny River is a massive engineering project composed of amenable materials like earth, sand and cement. But the Seneca Nation is composed of human beings. Six or eight hundred of them will be driven out of their homes by the time the dam is finished in January 1965, if not before.

Despite a crushing schedule of committee meetings for more than a year, the Senecas are not sure what to do or what precise actions to take. Since 1794, when their forebears signed a treaty with the United States, the nation has lived on its reservation with the assumption that it would never be "disturbed," as the treaty promised. Having never been abrogated, the treaty is still technically in force and remains the oldest in the national archives. But the inexorable rise of a $114,000,000 dam illustrates the value the United States places on the treaty today.

Having lost their attempt to keep the treaty inviolate, the individual Senecas have a simple attitude: "If they are taking away my home, why don't they give me a new one?" A new one, in fact, that will not require a mortgage and living expenses higher than they can afford. But communities are more intricate than engineering projects. Planning for resettling the Senecas is alarmingly behind schedule because no one Government agency has the authority and resources to make definite commitments.

Until the Army Corps of Engineers appropriated $50,000 a few weeks ago to hire the services of a firm of consultants, the Senecas had no government money with which to meet their emergency—although the Pennsylvania Railroad was paid $20,500,000 last summer for, among other things, a right-of-way that it is abandoning. Various Government agencies have been willing to help and have sent representatives to Salamanca to study the problem. But it took the Department of the Interior nine months—from last June to last March—to deliver a legal opinion that authorized agencies to go ahead.

About 150 Seneca families will have to be resettled in new houses by October 1964. The houses cannot be built until new roads are constructed. The roads cannot be built until the ground plans become final. The ground plans cannot be final until the Senecas know what Congress will do for them. Congress cannot decide what to do until the Senecas ask for appropriations. The Senecas do not know how much money they will need until the planning engineers submit their plan and government agencies reconcile their differences or coordinate their services. In effect, the United States says: "Why don't you repair the damage we have done to you?"

For the first time since 1794 some land that belonged to the Senecas has been removed from treaty protection. A lot of organizations would like pieces of it or of lands that the Government might buy in lieu of those that will be flooded. New York State is taking some to build a limited access highway down one side of the reservation. The Allegheny State Park could use a little. The Cattaraugus County Planning Board is staking out claims for a comprehensive public recreation program in the area before the Senecas can organize their own. Newly available land stimulates indecent rapacities.

Everything about the situation is complex except the moral problem. For no one disputes the fact that the United States is breaking a treaty. But people are tired of the moral problem, which seems to them petty and obsolete. "Well, now, really, in this day and age," they say in effect, "why all this fuss over some Indians?" In the Salamanca Republican-Press of Feb. 9th, an anonymous Salamanca resident said: "They have had the land well over 100 years and what have they done with it? Nothing, absolutely nothing."

They have lived on it. But what they have or have not done is beside the point. Our first President added his personal assurance to the treaty of 1794 that the land would be the Senecas' forever. It is not the Senecas but the United States that has broken faith.[34] ◆◆

The settlement of Indian claims, 1963

◆◆   The Department of the Interior has asked Congress
for legislation to authorize disposition of funds arising from a $567,000
judgment in favor of the Snake or Paiute Indians (in this case, the names
are synonymous) of the former Malheur Reservation in Oregon. . . .
The requested legislation would authorize and direct the Secretary of
the Interior to prepare a roll of persons of Snake or Paiute Indian blood
living on the date the bill becomes law, who were members or who are
lineal descendants of members of the bands as they existed in 1879 and
whose chiefs or headmen were parties to an unratified treaty of December
10, 1868. . . .

The Federal Government . . . [1866] had extended its authority without formal purchase over the territory of the "Western Shoshoni" and
included within it the northern part of the lands occupied by the Northern Paiute tribes, assuming "the right of satisfying their claims by as-
signing them such reservations as might seem essential for their occupancy and supplying them in such degree as might seem proper with
necessaries of life."

From 1864 to 1874 the President, by Executive Order, created several
reservations to accommodate the Northern Paiute, including, in 1872, the
Malheur Reservation for the Snake Indians. The lands were taken into
possession by the Government "without formal relinquishment by the
Indians," who did not, by any means, confine themselves to the reservations established for them.

In December 1868, the chiefs and headmen of the Snake—We-
you-wa-wa, Caha-nee, E-hi-gast, Po-nee, Chaw-wat-na-nee, Ow-its, and
Yash-a-go signed a treaty with the Federal Government. The treaty was
never ratified by the United States Senate. Thereafter, and for diverse
reasons, the Snake and Paiute Indians became increasingly hostile to the
changes that were taking place around them and reluctant to accept the
reservation environment that was eventually thrust upon them. The
Bannock, a detached branch of the Northern Paiute, enlisted the sympathy and support of the Snake in an uprising in 1878 occasioned by the
loss of Bannock lands, failure of the buffalo herds, and the lack of
prompt relief on the part of the government.

The uprising was suppressed in 1879 by Gen. O. O. Howard and the
Snake were removed by the military to the Yakima Reservation in the
State of Washington. Soon after their arrival on the Yakima Reservation,
the Snake or Paiute began drifting away. Many went back to their old
home country in Harney Valley and settled in what is now the town of
Burns, Oregon, where some still reside. Some affiliated with other bands
of Paiute. Others settled on the Warm Springs Reservation in Oregon.
The Malheur Reservation, upon which they were originally settled, was

abandoned and later restored to the public domain without compensation to the Indians.

As a result of the scattering of the Snake following settlement on the Yakima Reservation, and their continued affiliation with the Bannock, efforts to locate a record of the members of the respective bands of Snake or Paiute Indians whose chiefs were parties to the unratified treaty of December 10, 1868, have been unsuccessful. An 1877 census roll and an 1875 subsistence list appear to be the best records available to establish eligibility of living Snake or Paiute Indians to share in the distribution of the judgment funds.

The judgment fund constitutes payment for the lands which were set aside by Executive Order in 1872 for use and occupancy of the individual bands of Snake or Paiute Indians and were, by Executive Orders issued in 1882 and 1883, restored to the public domain without payment of any compensation to the Indians. Legal fees and other expenses reduced the amount [to?] $468,395.50, but this, drawing interest at 4 percent per year, had grown to the substantial sum of $519,827.49 by June 5, 1963.[35] ◆◆

It is interesting to note that while this payment represents a step forward, the natives are *not* being paid for the balance of the lands taken from them, nor are they being paid interest on the value of the land since the 1870's, nor are they being paid for losses and damages suffered during the period of unjust military action. Thus, as with most (if not all) "settlements," the natives can still be said to possess a "lien" upon the land.

Notes

1. Collier, *Indians of the Americas*, p. 133. Reprinted by permission of the author.
2. "A Sketch of the Bureau of Indian Affairs," p. 7.
3. "A Sketch of the Bureau of Indian Affairs," p. 8.
4. Edward E. Dale, *The Indians of the Southwest* (Norman: University of Oklahoma Press, 1949) p. 178. Reprinted by permission of the University of Oklahoma Press.
5. Commissioner of Indian Affairs, quoted in *Ibid.*, pp. 185-186.
6. "A Sketch of the Bureau of Indian Affairs," p. 8.
7. Lt. V. E. Stottler, as quoted in C. L. Sonnrichsen, *The Mescalero Apaches* (Norman: University of Oklahoma Press, 1958) pp. 223-4. Reprinted by permission of the University of Oklahoma Press.
8. Schwatka, *A Summer in Alaska*, pp. 364-70.
9. George Bird Grinnell, *Blackfoot Lodge Tales, the Story of a Prairie People* (Lincoln: University of Nebraska Press, 1962) pp. xi, xii.
10. *Lone Wolf* vs. *Hitchcock*, 187, U.S., 553, 565-566 (1903).
11. *U.S.* vs. *Nice*, 241, U.S., 591.
12. Collier, *Indians of the Americas*, pp. 146-52. Reprinted by permission of the author.

13. John Collier, "Introduction," in Oliver La Farge, ed., *The Changing Indian* (Norman: University of Oklahoma Press, 1942) pp. 3-10. Reprinted by permission of the University of Oklahoma Press.
14. *Ibid.*
15. Collier, *Indians of the Americas,* pp. 154-5. Reprinted by permission of the author.
16. "A Sketch of the Bureau of Indian Affairs," p. 19.
17. Edward A. Kennard, "The Use of Native Languages and Cultures in Indian Education," in *The Changing Indian,* pp. 109-115. Reprinted by permission of the University of Oklahoma Press.
18. John Collier, "Return to Dishonor," *Frontier,* June 1954, pp. 8-9. Reprinted by permission of *Frontier Magazine.*
19. *The Spirit They Live In* (Philadelphia: American Friends Service Committee, 1956) pp. 12-13.
20. "A Sketch of the Bureau of Indian Affairs," p. 13.
21. Bureau of Indian Affairs, "Relocation Services," 1957, p. 1.
22. Madelon Golden and Lucia Carter, "New Deal for America's Indians," *Coronet,* October 1955. Reprinted by permission of Esquire, Inc.
23. Joanna V. McKenzie, "The Relocation Program and the Problems of the Relocated Indian in the Los Angeles Area," unpublished manuscript, 1961, pp. 15-16. Reprinted by permission of the author.
24. *Ibid.*, p. 16.
25. "A Sketch of the Bureau of Indian Affairs," pp. 16-17.
26. Bureau of Indian Affairs, "Statement on Current Issues in Indian Affairs," April, 1956, pp. 1-3.
27. *Ibid.*
28. Bob Piser, "Box Canyon for the Navajo," from a reprint of *The Arizona Republic,* 1960.
29. *The Kinzua Dam Controversy* (Philadelphia: Philadelphia Yearly Meeting of Friends, 1961) pp. 14-15.
30. *Report to the Secretary of the Interior by the Task Force on Indian Affairs, July 10, 1961,* pp. 5, 6, 8.
31. Department of the Interior, Information Service press release, July 12, 1961.
32. Department of the Interior news release, December 7, 1962, pp. 3-11.
33. *The Kinzua Dam Controversy,* p. 20.
34. Brooks Atkinson, "Critic at Large," *The New York Times,* April 19, 1963. Copyright by *The New York Times.* Reprinted by permission of *The New York Times.*
35. Department of the Interior news release, August 6, 1963.

NINE

RACE MIXTURE

> We are not Europeans, we are not
> Indians, but a type intermediate be-
> tween aborigines and Spaniards.
>
> —Simón Bolivar, 1819

One of the most interesting and significant aspects of American history since 1492 has been the creation of a new American race (or races), called by some the "cosmic race" because its components stem from the entire world. In some regions the New American is of predominantly native ancestry (as in Mexico, where 80 percent of the "genetic pool" is thought to be Native American, 10 percent European, and 10 percent African). In other areas he is more akin to the European (as in Argentina and Uruguay, where the once dominant mestio (Eurindian) class has been diluted with twentieth century European immigration). In many regions he is a mestizo, with perhaps a varying admixture of African ancestry. In still other areas he is an African–Native American or African–Native American–European hybrid. And finally, he may be predominantly African in appearance, with the native strain, if present, completely obscured.

The United States and Canada superficially appear to be racially distinct from Ibero-America; however, the New American has also made his appearance here, and the difference is largely one of degree. The following selections should shed some light upon race mixture in the United States as it involves persons of indigenous ancestry.

Franz Boas, "The Half-blood Indian," 1894

◆◆ There are few countries in which the effects of intermixture of races and of change of environment upon the physical characteristics of man can be studied as advantageously as in America, where a process of slow amalgamation between three distinct races is taking place. Migration and intermarriage have been a fruitful source of intermixture in the Old World, and have had the effect of effacing strong contrasts in adjoining countries. While the contrasts between European, Negro, and

Mongol are striking, their territories are connected by broad stretches of land which are occupied by intermediate types. For this reason there are only a few places in the Old World in which the component elements of a mixed race can be traced to their sources by historical methods. In America, on the other hand, we have a native race which, although far from being uniform in itself, offers a marked contrast to all other races. Its affiliations are closest toward the races of Eastern Asia, remotest to the European and Negro races. Extensive intermixture with these foreign races has commenced in recent times. Furthermore, the European and African have been transferred to new surroundings on this continent and have produced a numerous hybrid race, the history of which can also be traced with considerable accuracy.

We find, therefore, two races in new surroundings and three hybrid races which offer a promising subject for investigation: the Indian-White, the Indian-Negro, and the Negro-White. The following study is devoted to a comparison of the Indian race with the Indian-White hybrid race.

It is generally supposed that hybrid races show a decrease in fertility, and are therefore not likely to survive. This view is not borne out by statistics of the number of children of Indian women and of half-blood women. The average number of children of five hundred and seventy-seven Indian women and of one hundred and forty-one half-blood women more than forty years old is 5.9 children for the former and 7.9 children for the latter. It is instructive to compare the number of children for each woman in the two groups. While about ten percent of the Indian women have no children, only 3.5 percent of the half-bloods are childless. The proportionate number of half-bloods who have one, two, three, four, or five children is smaller than the corresponding number of Indian women, while many more half-blood women than full-blood women have had from six to thirteen children. . . . The facts disclosed by this tabulation show that the mixed race is more fertile than the pure stock. This cannot be explained by a difference of social environment, as both groups live practically under the same conditions. It also appears that the small increase of the Indian population is almost entirely due to a high infant mortality, as under better hygenic surroundings an average of nearly six children would result in a rapid increase. It is true, however, that a decrease of infant mortality might result in a decreased birth rate.

Among the Indians of the Pacific Coast the infant mortality is also very great, but we find at the same time a still larger proportion of women who bear no children.

It is of some interest to note the average number of children of women of different ages as indication of the growth of families. Among the Indians there is an average interval of four years and a half as shown in the following table—which, however, must not be confounded with an average interval between births:

Indian women 20 years of age have on the average 1 child.
"   "   25 "   "   "   "   "   "   "   2   "
"   "   28 "   "   "   "   "   "   "   3   "
"   "   33 "   "   "   "   "   "   "   4   "
"   "   38 "   "   "   "   "   "   "   5   "

Among the half-bloods the interval is shorter, but the number of available observations is insufficient for carrying out the comparison in detail.

The stature of Indians and half-bloods show differences which are also in favor of the half-bloods. The latter are almost invariably taller than the former, the differences being more pronounced among men than women. The White parents of the mixed race are mostly of French extraction, and their statures are on an average shorter than those of the Indians. We find, therefore, the rather unexpected result that the offspring exceeds both parental forms in size. This curious phenomenon shows that size is not inherited in such a manner that the size of the descendant is intermediate between those of the parents, but that size is inherited according to more intricate laws.

From investigations carried on among Whites we know that stature increases under more favorable surroundings. As there is no appreciable difference between the social or geographical surrounding of the Indians and of the half-bloods, it seems to follow that the intermixture has a favorable effect upon the race. . . .

Another important phenomenon is revealed by a comparison of the growth of Indians and half-bloods. When the average statures of children of both races are compared, it appears that during the early years of childhood the Indian is taller than the half-blood, and that this relation is reversed later on. This is found in both the groups for tall tribes and for tribes of medium stature. It is to be regretted that this comparison cannot be carried on for Whites also. The social surroundings of the White child are, however, so entirely different from those of the Indian and of the half-blood children that no satisfactory conclusions can be drawn from a comparison. It is difficult to see why the laws of growth of the Indian and half-blood should differ in this manner; why the Indian child at the age of three years should be taller than the half-blood child, and then develop more slowly than the latter. This peculiarity is most striking in the growth of the tribes of medium stature, as in this case the difference in the statures of adults is so considerable. Unfortunately, we do not know if the same difference prevails at the time of birth; but even if this were the case the difference in the rate of growth would remain mysterious. The various phenomena described here merely emphasize the fact that the effect of intermixture is a most complicated one, and that it acts upon physiological and anatomical qualities alike. We observe in the mixed race that the fertility and laws of growth are affected, that the variability of the race is increased, and that the resultant stature of the mixed race exceeds that of both parents.

One of the most striking characteristics of the Indian face is its great breadth as compared with that of the Whites. It is therefore of peculiar interest to compare this measurement among the full-blood Indian, the half-bloods, and the Whites. . . . Among adult students of American colleges we find an average breadth of face (between the zygomatic arches) of 140 millimeters, while the average value among Indians is nearly 150 millimeters. The facial measurements of the half-bloods are intermediate, the average value being near the typical Indian measurement and remote from the White measurement. We find in these curves also the peculiarity observed before—that the half-blood is more variable than the pure race.

When comparing the average breadth of face for Indians, half-bloods and Whites, another interesting phenomena may be seen. The average breadth of face of the half-blood stands between that of the Indian and of the White, but nearer the former. When computing this average from year to year, it is found that the same relation prevails throughout from the fourth year to the adult stage, and in men as well as in women. The relation of the three groups remains unchanged throughout life. The amount of White and Indian blood in the mixed race is very nearly the same. We find, therefore, that the Indian type has a stronger influence upon the offspring than the White type. The same fact is expressed in the great frequency of dark hair and of dark eyes among half-bloods.

Two reasons may be assigned for this fact. It may be that the dark hair and the wide face are more primitive characteristics of man than the narrow face and light eyes of the Whites. Then it might be said that the characteristics of the Indian are inherited with greater strength because they are older. It must, however, also be considered that half-bloods are almost always descendants of Indian mothers and of White fathers, and this may have had an influence upon the race, although there is no proof that children resemble their mothers more than they resemble their fathers.

Another characteristic difference between Indians and halfbloods will be found by comparing the breadth of nose of both races. It is well known that the nostril of the Indian is round, and that it is bordered by thick alae, while the nostril of the White is elongated and has fine alae. Unfortunately, there are no measurements of the nose of the White available, but a comparison of the transversal breadths of the nose of Indian and half-bloods makes it clear at once that intermixture has the effect of making the nostril narrower and the alae thinner, thus producing a much narrower nose. It appears at once that the nose of the half-blood man is not wider than that of the full-blood woman. The three-quarter bloods of the Ojibwa are found to take an intermediate position between full-bloods and half-bloods.

We will finally consider the effect of intermixture upon the length of head from the point between the eyebrows (the glabella) to the occiput among a tribe with a head that is shorter than that of the American White. The Ojibwa has a head which measures about 191 millimeters, while that of the White measures about 195 millimeters. A comparison of the three classes shows a gradual increase in length from the full-blood, through the three-quarter blood, to the half-blood.

We find, therefore, that the laws of heredity in the forms of the head and face are uniform, in so far as intermediate forms are produced. I presume, however, that in all cases the middle forms are not found as frequently as forms resembling the two parental types.[1] ◆◆

Wilcomb E. Washburn, 1957

Boas's study was one of the first and last studies of the American-European hybrid in the United States. Other authors, however, do occasionally refer to the subject and the following, by Wilcomb E. Washburn, raises some interesting questions that demand further investigation.

◆◆   Do we need a poet to write of the effect of the Indian woman on the White man? In the early years of the Virginia settlement, John Rolfe wrote Governor Sir Thomas Dale about "an unbeleivinge Creature" named Pocahontas. Three hundred years later a man named Ernest Hemingway wrote in a similar spirit . . . about an Ojibwa girl named Trudy Gilby.

What was the effect of such liaisons both on the Indian girls and on White men? How were the White men's attitudes towards themselves and towards White women affected? What was the effect on the Indian tribes of which the girls were members? To what extent did the relationship influence what Perry Miller calls the "iconography of the blond and brunette" in American fiction: that is, the stereotyped representation in literature of the dark girl as wild, passionate, and alluring but somehow tainted in the blood, so that the hero must finally return to proper, cold, respectable blondness? What effect did such liaisons have on White attitudes towards the Church? Conversely, what effect did the Church's attitude have on such relationships? Why did the Spanish report in 1611 that 40 or 50 of the Virginia settlers had married Indian women, that English women were intermingling with the natives, and that a zealous minister had been wounded for reprehending it? Why were there, at this time in Virginia, such severe penalties for running away to join the Indians? Why, indeed, did so many Whites *want* to run away to join the Indians? [2] ◆◆

HISPANO-INDIAN-AFRICAN MIXTURE

The Spaniards who came to the Americas were mostly men and
hey readily formed liaisons with Native American women. Subsequently
Africans were introduced and they too mixed with the natives and with
Europeans. From this three-way mixture stems the modern Ibero-Ameri-
an with the variations indicated previously. Even in those areas of Ibero-
America now thought of as being predominantly European this amalgamation process took place, as witness this description of Argentina in
816:

> The *Criollos,* or descendants of Spaniards in the Americas, make up the
> dominant class (in the provinces of the River Plate), although they are more
> or less mixed with the Indian race or with Africans. In Buenos Aires . . .
> they still brag a great deal today that the blood of the inhabitants has re-
> mained tolerably pure or with little admixture of African blood. . . . In
> Cordoba the color of the inhabitants begins to darken visibly, and the num-
> ber of mulattoes and mestizos increases as one goes into the interior. In
> the province of Santiago, the inhabitants are almost more Indian than *criollo,*
> but at the same time lighter and more yellowish than the Cordobans.[3]

In those portions of the Spanish Empire specifically relevant to United
States history miscegenation was the general rule. Only mere handfuls
of Spanish women ever penetrated into the northern frontier regions and
their place was taken by mixed-bloods, Africans, and natives. Furthermore, after the sixteenth century a very high proportion of the Spanish-
peaking males were of mixed or non-European background.

The status of the mixed-blood varied greatly and depended to a con-
iderable measure on whether he was raised by his father or was turned
adrift at an early age. In 1621 Domingo Lázaro de Arregui describes the
Eurindians as follows: "and those persons who proceed from these two
bloods are called *mestizos* and they are of very good natural dispositions,
very agile and courageous and of much honor, a thing which ought to
much contradict the Indian blood." [4]

Miscegenation in New Mexico, 1600-1680

Numerous Eurindians, Eurafricans and Afro-Eurindians were among
the people who migrated into New Mexico after 1600. In 1640-1643, a
civil war broke out in that province and one of the factions, that of
Governor Luís de Rosas, was said to be made up of mestizos and mulattos.
Rosas' successor was allegedly backed by "a stranger and a Portuguese
and mestizos and sambahigos, sons of Indian men and Negroes, and mulat-
os." In 1661 New Mexico had only one hundred Spanish-speaking citi-

zens (males), including everyone who had any degree of European ancestry. The total population of Santa Fé, including mixed-bloods and Indians, between 1630 and 1680 seems to have been about 1,000. When the
natives of New Mexico successfully rebelled in 1680 they were aided by
many mixed-bloods. Alonso Catati, a mestizo, was one of the rebel leaders
and the Spaniards complained of the "confident coyotes, mestizos and
mulattoes" who were able to fight on horseback and with guns as well as
any Spaniard. (A "coyote" was the progeny of a mestizo and an Indian.)[5]

After several centuries of race mixture there were, of course, few pure-
blood Europeans in Mexico, aside from government officials and priests
sent over from Spain. Most soldiers along the northern frontiers were
mixed-bloods. In 1744 the Marquis de Altamira wrote that many garri-
son-troops along the frontier and especially in Texas "are not Spaniards,
but of other inferior qualities, and [are] ordinarily vicious. . . ." In 1760
Pedro de Labaquera asserted that most of them were mulattos of low
character and without ambition.[6] On the other hand, it should be noted
that many hybrids rose to positions of prominence, although when this
occurred they were usually reclassified as "Español." In the northern
portions of the empire those persons who were Spanish-speaking but of
mixed or non-European ancestry were referred to as *gente de razón,* that
is, reasonable or civilized people.

A royal official asserted in 1774 that the *gente de razón* were of Negro,
Indian and European ancestry and were so intermixed as to create great
confusion for anyone who wished to trace their background.[7] Extremely
elaborate systems of terminology had been developed in order to refer
to the various mixtures; however, these eventually gave way to more
general, and less precise, terms.

The founders of Los Angeles, 1781

California was settled after 1769 by Spanish-speaking persons who
largely belonged to the *de razón* class. In fact, there *gente de razón* came
to refer to all Spanish-speaking persons, including Europeans. The following list of settlers who founded Los Angeles in 1781 should provide
some insight into the racial character of the Hispano-California population.

(1) Felix Antonio Villavicencio, Español, 45, married to María
     de los Santos Sobernia, Indian, 30, one daughter.

(2) Antonio Mesa, Negro, 36, married to Ana Gertrudes López,
     Mulatto, 27, two daughters.

(3) José Lara, Español, 50, married to María Antonia Campos,
     Indian, 20, one son and two daughters.

(4) José Vanegas, Indian, 28, married to Mariana Agular, Indian,
     20, one son.

(5)   Pablo Rodríguez, Indian, 25, married to María Rosario Noriega, Indian, 26, one daughter.

(6)   Manuel Camero, Mulatto, 30, married to María Tomosa, Mulatto, 24.

(7)   José Navarro, Mestizo, 42, married to María Rufina Dorotea, Mulatto, 47, two sons and one daughter.

(8)   José Moreno, Mulatto, 22, married to María Guadalupe, Mulatto, 19.

(9)   Basilio Rosas, Indian, 67, married to María Manuela Calistra, Mulatto, 43, five sons and one daughter.

(10) Alejandro Rosas, Indian, 19, married to Juana Rodríguez, Coyote, 20.

(11) Antonio Rodríguez, Chinese, 50, a widower with one daughter.

(12) Luís Quintero, Negro, 65, married to Petra Rubio, Mulatto, 40, three daughters and two sons.[8]

Since the children of the founders intermarried among themselves and with California Natives, it can be seen how within a very few generations nearly everyone could trace his ancestry to three continents.

The creation of the Californians

In both Baja California and California, Spanish-speaking men commonly married and/or had relations with missionized native women. Several authors indicate that the Franciscan friars occasionally had affairs with neophytes: "in place of taking a wife, they [the friars] have to do with a great many women, both Spanish and native, and have many children running about the missions, which they call soldiers' orphans." [9] More common, of course, were liaisons involving soldiers and settlers and from the latter came the *Californiano* of the 1840's. Referring to this period, Manuel C. Rojo wrote:

◆◆ On the frontier [of Baja California] they call persons who are white or Mestizo or who are not pure Indian "Gente de Razón," in order to differentiate them [from the Indians] although they do not have any better understanding than do the aborigines of the country. The de razón men are generally sons of the soldiers that came to the conquest [of the region] and of Indian women of the missions who were distinguished for their pleasant appearance, docility towards learning white customs and good conduct [and] with whom the soldiers married and founded families.[10]   ◆◆

R. H. Dana, 1835

◆◆ Their complexions are various, depending—as well as their dress and manner—upon their rank; or, in other words, upon the amount of Spanish blood they can lay claim to.

Those who are of pure Spanish blood, having never intermarried with aborigines, have clear brunette complexions, and sometimes, even as fair as those of English-women. There are but few of these families in California, being mostly in official stations, or who, on the expiration of their offices, have settled here upon property, which they have acquired; and others who have been banished for state offenses. These form the aristocracy, intermarrying, keeping up an exclusive system in every respect. They can be told by their complexions, dress, manner and also by their speech; for calling themselves Castilians, they are very ambitious of speaking the pure Castilian language, which is spoken in a somewhat corrupted dialect by the lower classes. . . .

From this upper class [of pure Spaniards], they go down by regular shades, growing more and more dark and muddy, until you come to the pure Indian who runs about with nothing upon him but a small piece of cloth, kept up by a wide leather strap round his waist. Generally speaking, each person's caste is decided by the quality of the blood, which shows itself, too plainly to be concealed, at first sight. Yet the least drop of Spanish blood, if it be only of quadroon or octoroon, is sufficient to raise them from the rank of slaves and entitles them to a suit of clothes, boots, hats, cloak, spurs, long knife, all complete, and course and dirty as may be—and to call themselves Españoles, and to hold property, if they can get any. . . .

The soldiers [who came to California], for the most part, married civilized Indians—and thus in the vicinity of each presidio, sprung up, gradually, small towns.[11] ◆◆

The foregoing is confirmed by Thomas O. Larkin, who wrote in 1846 that the Californianos were "descendants of Spanish and Mexican fathers, and mostly from native mothers." [12]

Edwin Bryant, 1847

◆◆ The Californians do not differ materially from the Mexicans. . . . in other provinces of that country—Physically and intellectually, the men, probably, are superior to the same race farther south. . . . The intermixture of blood with the Indian and negro races has been less, although it is very perceptible.[13] ◆◆

Benjamin D. Wilson, 1852

◆◆ There are striking examples of Indian women married to foreigners and native Californians, exemplary wives and mothers. . . . the Indians of San Juan [Capistrano] . . . are now nearly extinct, from intermarriage with the Spaniards and other more usual causes of Indian decay.[14] ◆◆

Miscegenation in California after annexation

Miscegenation continued in California after United States acquisition. The dispersal of Indian and Negro genes into the incoming Anglo-American population greatly increased the extent of hybridization, although the quantity of non-European admixture in individual cases was more and more minute with each generation. On the other hand, more obvious race mixture also took place, as witness the following examples. In 1860, "the population of about one hundred and twenty-five [at San Gabriel, California] were practically all Mexican peons and half-breeds or domesticated Indians," and in the general area natives and Mexicans were intermarrying freely.[15] A high percentage of California Indians acquired an admixture of outside ancestry during this period. In 1909 an observer noted that the natives on the Saboba reservation possessed "a noticeable admixture of Mexican blood, pure breeds being in the minority." [16] In a similar vein the 1910 census reveals that of the identifiable Chumash Indians, 71 percent were of mixed ancestry.[17]

Initiated by the Spanish, miscegenation, either known or unknown, is a continuing process in the Southwest, and current marriages between Anglo-Americans and Mexican-Americans are contributing further to this process of hybridization.

FRANCO-INDIAN MIXTURE

Race mixture at Natchez, 1716-1728

◆◆ The French by their gallantry, pursued the destructive course said to have been in Sodom of olden times . . . they made free with the men and married their women. They were tolerated in their love to their women with seeming good will by the natives for they saw the advantage that would ultimately result through their [the Frenchmen's] blind devotion to love. . . . as was expected their lewd practices soon caused a relaxation in their vigilance and discipline, for they frequented the [Natchez] town at night in a careless manner and unguardedly admitted the women into the fortress at night and made them welcome visitants at all times, the Indians saw how remiss and negligent the French were getting in their manner of living . . . and they for revenge secretly and exultingly proceeded to put their scheme in execution. . . .[18] ◆◆

Fur trappers and their offspring, 1834

◆◆ [At the fur trappers' rendevous of 1834, in addition to Nez Percé, Bannock and Shoshoni Indians, there were] a great variety of personages amongst us; most of them calling themselves white men, French-Canadians, half-breeds, etc., their color nearly as dark, and their manner wholly as wild, as the Indians with whom they constantly associate. These people, with their obstreperous mirth, their whooping, and howling, and quarreling . . . render our camp a perfect bedlam. . . . Goddin's son [Goddin was a Canadian], a half-breed, is now with us as a trapper,—he is a fine sturdy fellow, and of such strength of limb and wind, that he is said to be able to run down a buffalo on foot, and kill him with arrows.

On the farm, in the vicinity of the fort [Fort Vancouver, Washington], are thirty or forty log huts, which are occupied by the Canadians, and others attached to the establishment. . . . The most fastidious cleanliness appears to be observed; the women may be seen sweeping the streets and scrubbing the doorsills. . . . [but] I had reason, subsequently, to change my opinion with regard to the scrupulous cleanliness of the Canadians' Indian wives, and particularly after inspecting the internal economy of the dwellings.[19] ◆◆

Willamette Valley, 1843

◆◆ The few Canadian-French who were located in the Willamette Valley were mostly, if not entirely, connected by marriage with the Indians, the Frenchmen having Indian wives, and were considered to some extent as a part of their [the Indian's] own people.[20] ◆◆

Fort Laramie, 1846

◆◆ Numerous squaws, gayly bedizened, sat grouped in front of the rooms they occupied; their mongrel offspring, restless and vociferous, rambled in every direction through the fort; and the trappers, traders, and engages of the establishment were busy at their labor or their amusements. . . . Beneath us was the square area surrounded by little rooms, or rather cells, which . . . served chiefly for the accommodation of the men . . . or of the equally numerous squaws whom they were allowed to maintain in it. . . . [There were Indians there who] were fathers, brothers, or other relatives of the squaws in the fort,

where they were permitted to remain, loitering about in perfect idleness.
. . . The [Anglo-Americans] emigrants felt a violent prejudice against
the French Indians, as they called the trappers and traders.²¹ ◆◆

Eurindians in Western Canada, 1869-1885

◆◆ Beyond the scattered posts of the great fur-trading
company [Northwest Territory] was occupied by roving Indians, and
by the twelve thousand inhabitants of the Red River settlement (Manitoba), nearly ten thousand of whom were half-breeds. . . . The half-
breeds were . . . divided, some being of Scottish origin . . . while others
were in speech and origin French. . . . The faction that came to the
front [in a rebellion against the Canadian government in 1869-1870] was
that of the Métis, or French half-breeds, under their fanatical leader,
Louis Riel. . . . [He] was the son of a full blooded white father and a
half-breed mother. He was educated at Montreal for the priest-hood, but
returned to Red River without taking orders. . . . [In 1870 Manitoba
was admitted as a province, the revolt was settled and] one million four
hundred thousand acres of land were reserved for the settlement of half-
breed claims. . . . [but] many of the half-breeds were unwilling to submit to the new authority. Sullenly they withdrew to . . . the Saskatch-
ewan [where Riel led a new rebellion in 1885].²² ◆◆

French-Cree mixed-bloods, 1897

◆◆ The French Canadians took many [Cree] women as
wives, and the half-breeds and their numerous descendants in that
region today are largely of Cree blood. . . . Some of the French Canadian half-breed trappers and hunters became more vicious and villainous
than the savages. . . . and as they were more intelligent than the latter
they soon combined the vices of barbarism and civilization, without the
virtues of either.²³ ◆◆

Eurindians in Manitoba, 1961

◆◆ There are close to 50,000 persons of Indian ancestry
in Manitoba whose identity is recognized as such. That group represents
more than thirty percent of the population who could claim some Indian ancestry. Over the years the majority have been completely assimilated. Once acculturation has progressed to a certain point, people with
some Indian ancestry prefer to identify themselves by their European
ancestry and are usually successful in passing as such. . . . By definition
a Métis or half-breed is a person of mixed Indian and European ancestry. . . . There are close to 25,000 persons who . . . are usually identified as Métis or half-breeds in Manitoba. It is estimated that this figure

represents no more than 25 percent of the total population who could claim some mixed Indian and European ancestry. Before the first large wave of migrants to Manitoba in the early 1870's, there were 10,000 Métis in the province compared to 1,500 whites.[24] ◆ ◆

ANGLO- AND DUTCH-INDIAN MIXTURE

It has often been maintained that the English and other North Europeans who settled in the Americas refrained from extensive intermixture with Native Americans and Africans, in contrast to the Spanish, Portuguese, and French, and this thesis is partially borne out by the evidence. However, this relative lack of intermixture does not seem to have been due to any widespread antagonism on the part of the English toward race mixture *per se*. Several factors tended to inhibit the amalgamation of Indians and Anglo-Europeans: (1) The English usually came to America in family units and thus tended to possess a sufficient number of females; (2) their orientation was toward transplanting small peasant and bourgeois traditions to America and not toward creating a feudal society with a conquered population. In the South, where a feudal society did develop, extensive miscegenation occurred, both with African and Indian servants; (3) Calvinism, with its antagonism toward all foreign cultures, tended to erect a wall between European and American. The native, representing Satan, would seduce the immigrants unless the ruling authority prohibited intercourse and intermarriage; and (4) the Atlantic seaboard native groups often retreated to the west rather than be incorporated into Anglo-European society.

For these and many other reasons, Indian-English intermixture tended to occur only outside of marriage and in certain regions (such as the frontier) where many Europeans were able to escape from the social controls established by the ruling authorities.

Nevertheless, amalgamation has been advocated from time to time by various Anglo-Americans as representing a solution to the "Indian problem." In 1705 Robert Beverly wrote that "intermarriage had been indeed the method proposed very often by the Indians [of Virginia] in the beginning, urging it frequently as a certain rule, that the English were not their friends if they refused it." Beverly seems to agree that the history of early Virginia would have been better if the English had pursued such a policy.[25] Thomas Jefferson was, on several occasions, an advocate of race mixture. In 1803 he wrote: "The ultimate point of rest and happiness for them [the Indians] is to let our settlements and theirs meet and blend together, to intermix, and become one people. . . . this is what the natural progress of things will of course bring on, and it will be better to promote than to retard it."[26] Six years later Jefferson asserted: "In time you [Indians] will be as we are, you will become one people with us. Your blood will mix with ours, and will spread with ours, over this great island." [27]

In 1904 the anthropologist Livingston Farrand wrote:

> The future of the Indians cannot be predicted with confidence. It has been shown that while decreasing in numbers, the diminution is not rapid— it is quite conceivable, even if not probable, that more thorough adaptation to a civilized environment might check the process of extinction. . . . Absorption by the whites is regarded by many as the natural and ultimate outcome, and the increasing number of mixed bloods on the reservations indicates such a possibility. The product of such mixture seems also to be well adapted to survive. There is no evidence that the often described undesirable qualities of the mixed blood are inherent in the crossing. . . . Virtually an outcast from both the higher and lower groups, it is not strange that the adult half-breed should exhibit questionable characteristics. . . . In the light of the processes now in operation, gradual absorption by the surrounding whites seems to be the Indian's most probable fate.[28]

Miscegenation in New England–New York, 1623-1644

There is some evidence that the Puritan religious leaders had difficulty in restraining their followers from occasionally intermixing with the natives. At Massachusetts Bay in 1623 it was charged that the leader of the English was wasting supplies among the natives because he was "keeping Indean women." [29] Seven years later Edward Ashley, an Englishman who traded with the natives, was charged with having "comited uncleannes with Indean women." [30] And the surviving Indian groups in New England (Narragansetts and others) are almost all mixed-bloods.

In New York the Dutch apparently sought Indian mates with great vigor and enthusiasm, as is attested to by a number of observers. In 1644 Johannes Megapolensis noted that the Mohawk women "are exceedingly addicted to whoring; they will lie with a man for the value of one, two or three schillings, and our Dutchmen run after them very much." The settlers of New Amsterdam did not, however, have to journey to Albany for pleasure, for the native women of Manhattan were frequently both attractive and promiscuous.[31]

Miscegenation in Virginia

It would appear that mixture between natives and Englishmen occurred early and frequently in Virginia. As noted previously, the Spanish learned in 1611 that in spite of clerical opposition forty or fifty Englishmen had married natives and that English women were "intermingling" with the natives. In 1613 Diego de Molina wrote that many Englishmen "have gone over to the Indians." [32] And then, of course, we know of the famous marriage between John Rolfe and Pocahontas, from whose liaison perhaps tens of thousands of Anglo-Americans share descent.

In spite of early mixtures, however, the government of Virginia by the late 1600's and early 1700's saw fit to relegate mixed-bloods to an inferior position and to prohibit marriage between natives and Whites (although not between Eurindians and Whites).

> By the Virginia Act of 1682 Christianity was held not to confer freedom upon Negroes, mulattoes and such Indians as were sold by others as slaves. . . . in 1705 the term "mulatto" was legally held to include not only the children of mixed unions between whites and Indians but also the great-great-grandchildren of such connections with Negroes. Miscegenation . . . was legislated against in all the [English] colonies, always with severer penalties for the Negro. . . . In 1705 in Virginia, Negroes, Mulattoes and Indians were forbidden to hold any civil, military or ecclesiastical office, and in 1723 even the suffrage was denied to free Negroes, mulattoes and Indians.[33]

It is certain, however, that intermarriage and extra-marital mixture continued. Many mixed-bloods and non-Europeans fled to the North Carolina border, where they were sheltered by Whites.[34] Marriages between White and native are known in the 1770's, and the remnant Indian groups in Virginia, as elsewhere, rapidly became mixed. In 1782, Jefferson wrote:

> There remain of the Mattaponies three or four men only, and [they] have more negro than Indian blood in them. They . . . have, from time to time, been joining the Pamunkies, from whom they are distant but ten miles. The Pamunkies are reduced to about ten or twelve men, tolerably pure from mixture with other colors.[35]

RACE MIXTURE IN THE WEST

Native attitudes, 1823

◆◆ The chiefs and influential men in some of the tribes, object to intermarriages with the whites, on account of the aberation [sic] from this standard colour ["coppery darkness] which is exhibited in the offspring; white being regarded [as] characteristic of effeminacy and cowardice, and all the shades between it and their own as naturally influenced by those qualities, in proportion as it preponderates. They nevertheless think these traits may be corrected by rigid discipline and strict attention to early education.[36] ◆◆

Half-breeds as desirable immigrants, 1831

◆◆ In the Hudson Bay establishments on Red River there are many half-breeds who are altogether brought up to hunting.

. . . Genl. [William] Ashley . . . has had the address to gain over many of those half-breeds to the American concern. . . .[37] ◆◆

Caucasian-African-Indian mixed-bloods, 1830's

◆◆ Where ever there is a cross of the blood with the European or African, which is frequently the case along the Frontier, a proportionate beard is the result. . . . There has been much speculation . . . as to the results of the intercourse between the European and African population with the Indians on the borders . . . [and] I cannot help but express my opinion . . . that generally speaking, these half-breed specimens are in both instances a decided deterioration from the two stocks, from which they have sprung; which I grant may be the consequence that generally flows from illicit intercourse, and from the inferior rank in which they are held by both (which is mostly confined to the lowest and most degraded portions of society), rather than from any constitutional objection, necessarily growing out of the amalgamation.

The finest built and most powerful men I have ever yet seen, have been some of the last-mentioned, the Negro and the North American Indian mixed, of equal blood. These instances are rare to be sure, yet are occasionally to be found amongst the Seminolees and Cherokees, and also amongst the Comanchees even, and the Chaddoes.[38] ◆◆

Shoshoni beauties, 1833

"[At the fur trappers' rendezvous] there were three rival camps near each other. The presence of the Shoshoni tribe contributed occasionally to temporary jealousies and feuds among the mountain men. The Shoshoni beauties became objects of rivalry among some of the amorous men. Happy was the trader who could muster up a red blanket, beads, or a paper of precious vermillion with which to win the smile of a Shoshoni fair one." [39]

A mountain man's companions, 1840's

"[Killbuck stated] for twenty year I packed a squaw along. Not one, but a many. First I had a Blackfoot—the darndest slut as ever cried for fofarrow [trinkets and finery]. I lodge-poled [disciplined] her on Colter's Creek and made her quit. My buffalo hos, and as good as four packs of beaver, I gave for ol' Bulltail's daughter. Thar wasn't enough scarlet cloth nor beads, nor vermillion in Subblette's packs for her. Traps wouldn't buy her all the fofarrow she wanted, and in two years I sold her to Cross-Eagle [a Swede] for one of Jake Hawkin's guns. Then I tried Sioux, the Shian, and a Digger from the other side, who made the best

moccasin as ever I wore. She was the best of all and was rubbed out by
the Yutas—Bad was the best; and after she was gone under I tried no
more." [40]

Sutter's Fort, California, a "hotbed" of miscegenation, 1841

John Sutter had thirty white employees at his fort—Germans, Swiss,
Canadians, Anglo-Americans, English, and French. "All these men live
with Indian or Californian women, and the colony contains not less
than two hundred souls." [41]

Mixed bloods in Kansas, 1850

♦♦ Our camp [west of Kansas City] was near the habitation of a half-breed Shawnee Indian who was born and raised in Ohio,
from whence he came twenty years ago. He was industrious, had a farm
of thirty acres, which was planted in corn. . . . he had cows and made
very good butter. . . .

We arrived at the "Potawotamie Manual Labor School [100 miles
west of Kansas City]. . . . It is a Baptist Mission. . . . This school was
established in 1848 by the Baptist denomination, assisted by the General
government. The buildings are very good. . . . There were fifty four
pupils under tuition. . . . The most of them were half-breeds. . . . In
a distance of a few miles several other little creeks were passed over upon
tollbridges. One belonged to some frenchmen, who had Indian wives—
They were well-fixed, good farms and a sawmill. . . . [To the east of
Fort Laramie we met] a Frenchman who had found his way into this
distant wild years ago and a Sioux squaw for his *better half*, had established a blacksmith shop in which he was doing well.[42] ♦♦

Troopers, Navahos, and syphilis, Fort Sumner, 1866

♦♦ You can see from my report the vast preponderance
of syphilis over every other disease, and which will always be the case
as long as so many soldiers are around here, because the Indian women
have not the slightest idea of virtue, and are bought and sold by their
own people like cattle. . . . I would recommend you to try to keep the
women as far from the fort as possible.[43] ♦♦

A pathological half-breed, 1863-1873

♦♦ Born June 28, 1835, of a white father and Cherokee
mother, [John B.] Townsend grew to develop a hatred of Indians because several of his relatives had been killed by Comanches in Texas.
The citizenry of northern and central Arizona soon discovered that this

young man had a skill other than ranching—he was an excellent Indian exterminator in their eyes. Those writing of this man seem to agree that he had a pathological hatred for the red man and he hunted them with a grim determination. [From 1863 to 1873 Townsend killed between twenty-five and sixty Apaches before being killed himself.] [44] ◆◆

The role of Blackfoot mixed-bloods, 1892

◆◆ William Jackson, an educated half-breed, who did good service from 1874 to 1879, scouting under Generals Custer and Miles, and William Russell, half-breed, at one time government interpreter at the agency, have both given me valuable assistance. [Also helpful was] Mr. Thomas Bird, a very intelligent half-breed, who has translated a part of the Bible into the Blackfoot language for the Rev. S. Trinett, a Church of England missionary.[45] ◆◆

Mixed-bloods and intermarriage

On the Fort Hall, Idaho [Shoshoni-Bannock] Reservation, 1960

◆◆ . . . approximately 60 percent were completely full-blood while four out of five had three-fourths or more Indian blood. Only seven Indians or 3.1 percent of the principal males and females who responded . . . were less than half Indian. . . . Interestingly there were about 11 percent more females than males who were full-blood Indians. . . . Of the four non-Indian males, one was white, two Mexican, and one Japanese. Of the six non-Indian females, five were white and one was Mexican. There seems to be a greater tendency for white women to marry Indian men (all of the latter were one-fourth or less Indian, however), than for white men to marry Indian women. . . . These mixed marriages appeared to be comparatively well-adjusted. . . . All ten couples had children, although in one case the children were adopted. From the standpoint of economic status, the white women with Indian husbands were much better off than the Indian women with non-Indian husbands. . . . [The four-fifths who are predominantly Indian] exhibit much racial pride; to them a high degree of Indian blood is a symbol of status.[46] ◆◆

Hybrids and assimilation, 1961

◆◆ A strong correlation is noted between Indians who accept the general culture of Yankton [South Dakota] and interracial marriages. They tend to be descendants of a mixed marriage, are themselves married to a member of the white race or had parents who were Indian missionaries or federal employees. In contrast, the [conservative]

. . . Indians come from marriages with members of their own race or
are descendants of race admixture that took place several generations
back.[47] ◆◆

Eurindians in Alaska, 1890-1891

The population of Alaska in 1890 was 21,929.

◆◆ Of those enumerated there were 3,922 white males
and 497 white females; 82 black males, 770 "mixed" males and 798
"mixed" females; and 2,125 male chinese; while the native population
included 7,158 males and 6,577 females. . . . "There are a few Aleut
half-breeds in Sitka. Many of these people talk the Russian language.
. . . One [of the expedition's employees] was a half-breed Tlinkit
[Tlingit] interpreter, "Billy" Dickinson by name, whose mother had
been a Tsimpsean Indian woman and whose father kept the store of
the North-west Trading Company in Chilkat Inlet. "Billy" . . . was a
rather good-looking young fellow of about twenty five. . . . He was as
strong as two or three ordinary men of his build. . . . About eleven
o'clock that night "Alexy," the half-breed Russian interpreter for Ladue
came into our camp in his canoe [near Fort Yukon]. . . . Among the
canoemen who visited us [at an Indian village near the mouth of the
Tanana River] was a half-breed Indian, very neatly and jauntily dressed,
who spoke English quite well, and whom we hired to pilot us to the
Trading station at Nuklakayet. . . . We landed at Upper Nulato . . .
and here encountered a half-breed who spoke tolerable English. . . .
[he was] a neatly dressed young fellow [with a] . . . new "parka" or
reindeer coat for winter wear. . . . Here [Ikogmute Mission] is an old
Greek [Russian Orthodox] church, presided over by a half-breed priest.
. . . The Greek priest is also the Alaska Company's trader. . . .[48] ◆◆

THE PUERTO RICANS

It is likely that almost all Puerto Ricans possess some degree of
Native American ancestry, unless they are descendants of parents who
are recent immigrants from Europe. For the most part, the native ancestry has been thoroughly diluted with African and European stock;
however, the tradition of Indian *mestizaje* remains. In 1880 the population of Borinquén (Puerto Rico) consisted in 324,840 persons of African
or part-African ancestry and 429,473 persons of European and European-
Indian background. "The Gibaros or small landholders and day-laborers
of the country districts are a curious old Spanish stock largely modified
by Indian blood." [49]

The Puerto Rican population, 1915

◆◆ From all we know . . . we must consider [the Puerto Ricans] essentially as descendants of male immigrants who intermarried with native women. It is evident that in early times this must have led to the development of a Mestizo population, in which, however, the amount of Indian blood must have decreased very rapidly owing to the continued influx of Spanish blood. . . . [Negro blood appears to be concentrated near the coast]. . . . There is a popular belief in Puerto Rico that in certain parts of the island, in the so-called "Indiera," Indian types have persisted to a greater extent than elsewhere. I have not been able to find any definite indication of a difference in type; but I have measured only a few individuals from these districts.[50] ◆◆

"Indios Borinqueños" in New York City, 1958

◆◆ There is a good deal of Indian blood, along with European and African among the Puerto Ricans. They run almost the full color gamut. . . . They have produced some special types—including the indio, which has copper skin and sometimes high cheekbones. . . . The various non-European types, including the Negro, make up a high percentage of the crowds one sees in the Puerto Rican ghettos here [New York]. . . .[51] ◆◆

The continued migration of Puerto Ricans to the United States is of considerable biological significance in that these one million Ibero-Americans are enlarging the Native American and African portions of North America's genetic pool. As Puerto Ricans increasingly intermarry with Anglo-Americans they will, of course, diffuse native genes still more widely; and the same will be true of the several hundred thousand Cuban refugees now in the United States.

The diffusion of Native American ancestry into the general population has frequently been overlooked by historians and sociologists. It has been, and is, a significant and continual process, however. Aside from Tribal Americans and Mexican-Americans, resources of Indian genes exist widely among French Canadians, Cubans, Puerto Ricans, other Latin Americans, and American Negroes, and among large numbers of Anglo-Americans and Anglo-Canadians. It can be said that if all people in the United States are not now part native the process of genetic diffusion will soon correct that deficiency.

Notes

1. Franz Boas, "The Half-Blood Indian," *The Popular Science Monthly,* Vol. XLV, October 1894, pp. 761-770.
2. Wilcomb E. Washburn, "A Moral History of Indian-White Relations, Needs and Opportunities for Study," *Ethnohistory,* Vol. IV, No. 1, Winter 1957, pp. 50-51.
3. Magnus, Mörner, "Europe Looks at the Cosmic Race," reprinted from *Americas,* Vol. XIII, No. 1, January 1961, p. 15.
4. Domingo Lázaro de Arregui, *Descripción de la Nueva Galicia,* edited by Francois Chevalier (Sevilla: Escuela de Estudios Hispano-Americanos, 1946) p. 39.
5. Patronato 244, Ramo VII, Archivo General de Indias, Sevilla, Spain; Forbes, *Apache, Navaho and Spaniard,* pp. 127, 135, 138-9, 180; Charles W. Hackett, *Revolt of the Pueblo Indians and Otermin's Attempted Reconquest, 1680-1682* (Albuquerque: University of New Mexico Press, 1942) Vol. II, pp. 322, 329, 337-9, 355; and France V. Scholes, "Troublous Times in New Mexico, 1659-1670," *New Mexico Historical Review,* Vol. XII, 1937, p. 139.
6. Marquis de Altamira al Virrey, July 4, 1744, Biblioteca del Ministerio de Hacienda, Madrid, 975, and Chapman, *History of California, the Spanish Period* (New York: Macmillan, 1921) p. 203.
7. "Reflexiones sobre el reyno de nueva españa," Virreinate de Mexico, II, Biblioteca del Museo Naval, 568, Madrid, Spain.
8. Padrón de Los Angeles, 1781, in Padrones y extractos, C-R9, Carton 3, Bancroft Library, Berkeley, California.
9. Vassili Tarakanoff, *Statement of My Captivity Among the Californians,* p. 27. Reprinted by permission of Glen Dawson.
10. Manuel C. Rojo, "Apuntes Historicos de la Baja California," p. 12. Used by permission of the Bancroft Library.
11. Dana. *Two Years Before the Mast,* pp. 72-3, 157.
12. Thomas O. Larkin, "Description of California," *New Spain and the Anglo-American West* (Los Angeles, privately printed, 1932) p. 109. Reprinted by permission of George P. Hammond.
13. Edwin Bryant, *What I saw in California* (New York: Appleton, 1848) p. 446.
14. Caughey, *Indians of Southern California in 1852,* pp. 18, 23. Reprinted by permission of the Huntington Library.
15. Rose, Jr., *L. J. Rose of Sunny Slope,* p. 51. Reprinted by permission of the Huntington Library.
16. Mrs. M. Burton Williamson, "The Mission Indians on the San Jacinto Reservation," *Historical Society of Southern California Annual Publication,* 1907-1908, p. 142.
17. *Indian Population in the United States and Alaska: 1910* (Washington: U.S. Government Printing Office, 1915).
18. George Stiggins, in Theron A. Núñez, Jr., "Creek Nativism and the Creek War of 1813-1814," *Ethnohistory,* Vol. V, No. 1, Winter 1958, p. 27. This document is in the Draper collection of the State Historical Society of Wisconsin.
19. John K. Townsend, *Narrative of a Journey Across the Rocky Mountains to the Columbia River* (Philadelphia: Henry Perkins, 1839) pp. 75, 114, 172.
20. Burnett, "Recollections," p. 97.
21. Francis Parkman, *The California and Oregon Trail* (New York: George P. Putnam, 1849) pp. 124, 126, 127, 134.
22. Charles D. G. Roberts, *A History of Canada* (Boston: L. C. Page & Co., 1897) pp. 362-3, 365, 384.
23. Humfreville, *Twenty Years Among Our Savage Indians,* pp. 227, 532.

24. Jean H. Lagasse, "Community Development in Manitoba," *Human Organization*, Vol. XX, No. 4, Winter 1961-62, pp. 232-3. Reprinted by permission of the Society for Applied Anthropology, Inc.
25. Robert Beverly, *The History and Present State of Virginia* (Chapel Hill: University of North Carolina Press, 1947) p. 38. Reprinted by permission of the University of North Carolina Press.
26. Foley, ed., *Jefferson Cyclopedia*, p. 420.
27. *Ibid.*, p. 736.
28. Livingston Farrand, *Basis of American History 1500-1900*, American Nation Series (New York: Harper and Brothers, 1906) p. 271.
29. Bradford, *History of Plimoth Plantation*, p. 157.
30. *Ibid.*, p. 328.
31. J. Franklin Jameson, ed., *Narratives of New Netherland 1609-1644*, pp. 72, 106, 174. Reprinted by permission of Barnes and Noble, Inc.
32. Lyon Gardiner Tyler, ed., *Narratives of Early Virginia 1606-1625*, Original Narratives of Early American History (New York: Charles Scribner's Sons, 1907) p. 220.
33. James Truslow Adams, *Provincial Society 1690-1763* (New York: The Macmillan Co., 1927) p. 106. Reprinted by permission of the Macmillan Company.
34. John Spencer Bassett, ed., *The Writings of Colonel William Byrd* (New York: Doubleday, Page and Co., 1901) p. 75.
35. Paul Leicester Ford, ed., *The Writings of Thomas Jefferson* (New York: G. P. Putnam's Sons, 1894) Vol. III, p. 197.
36. Hunter, *Manners and Customs of Several Indian Tribes*, pp. 201-2.
37. Forsyth, "The French, British and Spanish Methods of Treating Indians," p. 205.
38. Catlin, *The North American Indians*, Vol. II, p. 257.
39. Washington Irving, *Fur Traders of the Columbia River* (New York: G. P. Putnam's Sons, 1903) p. 85.
40. George F. Ruxton, *Life in the Far West* (Edinburgh: William Blackwood and Sons, 1849) pp. 265-6.
41. Duflot de Mofras, *Travels on the Pacific Coast*, Vol. I, pp. 245, 247.
42. Paden, ed., *Journal of Madison Berryman Moorman*, pp. 8-11, 28. Reprinted by permission of the California Historical Society.
43. *Annual Report, U.S. Department of the Interior, 1865-66* (Washington: U.S. Government Printing Office, 1867) pp. 150-151.
44. Lenard E. Brown, "John Benjamin Townsend: The Arizona Cherokee," *Arizoniana*, Vol. II, No. 3, Fall 1961, p. 29.
45. Grinnell, *Blackfoot Lodge Tales, the Story of a Prairie People*, pp. xvi, 276.
46. Harry C. Harmsworth and Norman Nybroten, *Human Resources, Relations, and Problems on the Fort Hall Indian Reservation* (Moscow: University of Idaho, 1961) pp. 18-21, 145. Reprinted by permission of the authors.
47. Wesley R. Hurt, Jr., "The Urbanization of the Yankton Indians," *Human Organization*, Vol. XX, No. 4, Winter 1961-62, p. 231. Reprinted by permission of the Society for Applied Anthropology, Inc.
48. Schwatka, *A Summer in Alaska*, pp. 103, 104, 274, 305, 333, 364-5.
49. *Werner Encyclopedia*, Vol. XIX, p. 547.
50. Franz Boas, "New Evidence in Regard to the Instability of Human Types," *Proceedings of the National Academy of Sciences*, Vol. II, (December 1916), pp. 713ff.
51. Christopher Rand, *The Puerto Ricans* (New York: Oxford University Press, 1958) p. 13. Reprinted by permission of the author.

TEN

CONTEMPORARY NATIVE AMERICANS

One of the greatest challenges now facing the United States is the task of integrating Native American and other non-European groups into the mainstream of American life. This challenge is significant not only because it involves almost 30,000,000 persons, but also because it is a test of the ability of the United States to deal fairly and adequately with non-European peoples. As the following selections will show, from New England to Oregon the many Native American groups are far from having a satisfactory relationship with the European-Americans surrounding them. Some are still deeply hostile toward the European "newcomers," and many suffer from social, political, sociopsychological, and economic problems.

Mexican-Americans and California politics

◆◆ There is only one city in the world which has a larger population of Mexican descent than Los Angeles, and that is Mexico City. Of the states in the Union, only Texas has a larger number of people with Spanish surnames—slightly over one million—than California, which in the latest census [1950] counted 760,453 such residents. . . . The mass immigration of Mexicans into California started around 1910. . . . Manpower was needed so badly that the California Chamber of Commerce undertook a large program of encouraging immigration from Mexico. . . . The same Chamber of Commerce [in the depression] . . . started a campaign to send them back to Mexico. By 1932 the Los Angeles Board of Supervisors offered free one-way tickets to Mexico. . . . The younger generation protested, and in many cases stayed behind. . . . Juvenile delinquency increased, and police brutality grew correspondingly. The outbreak of the "zoot suit" riots in 1943 marked the worst period of this development. It was then . . . that the first real attempts were made to remedy this situation. But it took an outside event [World War II] to pave the road to eventual progress. . . . Lack of manpower . . . broke down the job discrimination against minorities. . . . Discrimination in the public schools lessened.

A general rise in living standards among the Mexican-Americans brought about more economic equality, and with it, more social acceptance by their neighbors. . . . Then Mexican-American veterans began to return. . . .

A drive for registration was started by the newly-founded Community Service Organization and results were not long in coming. . . . Edward R. Roybal was one of the founders of the Community Service Organization in 1947. . . . The immediate reason for its foundation was the first, though unsuccessful, effort by Roybal to win the councilmanic seat in the Los Angeles City Council for the Ninth District. . . . In the 1947 campaign Roybal ran third. . . . [then] leaders in the district organized the Community Service Organization. . . . The first order of business was a house-to-house campaign for voter registration. . . . Mexican-American deputy registrars were sworn in only after much resistance. In the end, the result justified all efforts. Some 50,000 voters were registered in 90 days in the 1949 campaign, and Ed Roybal won . . . by a whopping majority of two to one. . . . [Roybal became] the outstanding spokesman of the Mexican-Americans among the by now 17 Mexican-American city councilmen or commissioners in California. . . . [In 1954] he received the unanimous endorsement of the Democratic State Convention in Fresno for lieutenant-governor. At last the great potential of more than 400,000 Mexican-American voters in California has been officially recognized.[1] ◆◆

Roybal was defeated, however, in a close contest. Since 1954 additional political success has come to the Mexican-Americans, especially with the election to Congress of State Senator Henry Gonzalez of Texas and Roybal. Such organizations as the Mexican-American Political Association, the League of United Latin American Citizens, and the C.S.O. have helped, but the Mexican-American, like his Indian and Eurindian brother, suffers frequently from factionalism and apathy, as well as from economic and linguistic problems.

A Navaho between two worlds

◆◆ Lawrence Willie . . . had likewise had contact with whites all his life, living with a white family when he was young and attending public school, he had learned to speak English fluently and had become familiar with many white patterns of life and thought. As a young adult, he lived a life less Navaho than white. His wife and his children all spoke English well.

In 1932, when Lawrence came to Fruitland, he had his first extensive contacts with Navahos. Government agents saw in him what they believed to be leadership qualities. In addition to his knowledge of English, he was informed about the national political situation, and he had expert skill in carpentry. He was given a position with the Civilian Conservation Corps as an interpreter, timekeeper and general contact man between white and Navaho employees.

Soon after farms became available in Fruitland, Lawrence received an assignment and obtained a job with the agency as ditch rider. He put his skill as carpenter to work immediately, built an adobe house, plastered the walls with stucco and moved his family in. Thus . . . Lawrence was living according to non-Navaho standards in his first years at Fruitland. He was the first Navaho employee on the Irrigation Project to impose water regulation by setting the lateral gates with locks. Old residents regarded him with hostility, as following too closely the dictates of the government, though in time they would consider his ways as a subject for humor.

Before Lawrence's arrival at Fruitland, he was already an habitual drinker, and his persistent drinking soon cost him his government job. Now he left the project for long periods, supporting himself at whatever jobs he could find. He returned to Fruitland only long enough to plant his crops but not to harvest them. During the war he rented his farm and home; later he stated that they were badly used.

After his service in the Marine Corps, Lawrence attempted to reestablish himself at Fruitland. He lived with his wife and children and after 1950 worked in town. Although he drank and did not report for work regularly, he was an able enough man when sober to convince his employer that he should be rehired. On the Project, the many who increasingly believed that men with wide knowledge of the American scene should assume leadership positions succeeded in electing him to an office in the local chapter organization.

Lawrence plunged now into the task of developing a community organization to cope with the Fruitlander's many problems. He spoke intelligently and tried to explain the white man's orientation. He gave considerable time at meetings to the discussion of community-development programs and outlined what he had read in the newspapers or heard over the radio. He initiated the move to get wells dug in both Units 1 and 3, and when they proved unusable because of the high alkaline content of the water, he and others called attention to the fact that Indian Service agents had ignored the recommendations of The People in locating the wells.

Another project which he tried to initiate was the building of a community house. He wanted the people to contribute labor, materials, and funds toward the building. But a mission-owned building already started stood in the central location of Unit 1 and the missionary encouraged Fruitlanders to use the building for meeting and general social gatherings. In any event, the people generally did not respond to Lawrence's program as he hoped.

Because of his failure, he became aggressive, particularly toward whites.

He showed his lack of knowledge about Navaho culture and yet expressed some desire to defend it.

"The white people come here to look at the Navahos and call them pagans," he said. "Let me tell you that the Navahos have only one God, it's the spirit. You white people have many Gods and you never know which one to worship. We have only one God and it's the Spirit."

He expressed hostility toward university people as well:

"I know what the university people are, no matter where they come from—Boston University, Harvard University, Cornell University, it is all the same. They are scientists, they try to explain everything by science, science is the only thing to them. They come here and dig holes and find some bones; they say that they are Indian bones. Every time I would try to say something they would interrupt me and wouldn't let me have a chance to answer. White people come here and try to tell us what to do. The Indians are the only true Americans and they were here for a long time before the white people came. We should kick all the white people out of the reservation."

Having spent most of his life with non-Navahos, he had not internalized Navaho role behavior well enough to feel secure in it. Older residents who wanted to achieve the same goals were not to be hurried or pressured, nor were they sure what leadership such an unstable man could give. A circularity was established: Lawrence enthusiastically introduced and promoted suggestions; the people responded casually; Lawrence resented the lack of faith in his leadership. By 1953 he was complaining that his community office was unpaid: "Only the big shots, the people above me . . . get paid for what they do. Why should I work for my own people and spend some money out of my own pocket? I didn't want that job, but they wanted me to be their headman, and to talk for them."

His frustrations caused him to drink more and more. In 1953 and 1954 he was hospitalized several times following automobile accidents.[2] ◆◆

The Navaho population explosion

◆◆ Navaho population in 1919 was estimated to be around 29,000. Today it stands at 80,000; in another five years it will reach the 100,000 mark; and by the year 2,000 . . . it could be somewhere in the neighborhood of 350,000. Yet the resources of the Navaho Reservation, even after full development, will probably never support more than 45,000 people at a level which could be considered really adequate.[3] ◆◆

The progress of Christianity in Arizona

◆◆ Little more than half of Arizona's Indians have accepted the white man's God, and some of those who have declared their faith often have done so with a backward glance at the Great Spirit. . . . The remainder continue with the paganism they have known down through the centuries. . . . Dr. Charles H. Cook . . . who founded a mission at Sacaton . . . in 1871, realized early that the best way to reach the Indians with the Word of God would be through other Indians who would speak the language of their red brothers. . . . After teaching in the government school for 12 years, he finally made his first conversion. It was years after that before he had what could be called a congregation in his little church. . . . [Language and geographical barriers still prevent conversions, and] Navajos, for instance, have a deeply integrated religion of their own and often resent the white man and many of the things he stands for. . . . Indians appear to vacillate on Christian religions. One week they belong to one faith, another week to a different one. This also is borne out by missionaries, who say Indians almost always retain some of their own tradition, regardless of what Christian faith they embrace. A run-down on ten tribes shows the following estimates on the degree of Christianity: Pima, 80 percent; Papago, 60 percent; Maricopa, 85 percent; Navajo, 10 percent; Hopi, 35 percent; Yuma, 50 percent; Apache, 45 percent; Yavapai, 85 percent; Hualapai, 45 percent; and Mohave, 60 percent.[4]   ◆◆

The adjustment of the Klamath

◆◆ Klamath society had never been tightly knit, and reservation culture through the years enhanced tendencies toward separatism and psychological isolation. No saving symbol remained about which they might rally, save an effulgent memory of a native culture that lay well in the past, and their tribal government. In their disunion, Klamath reacted to a felt discrimination entailed in their minority relations with their neighbors and in a resented dependence upon agency bureaucracy, not by dedication to a religious movement (the Shaker Church had but a transient favor) nor by covert witchcraft, but by hostility directed against the outsider and themselves. Law-abiding members of Klamath society often viewed with tolerant amusement the exploits of delinquent youth against the seat and symbols of white power. Clashes with the law were not infrequent: of the 1958 sample of reservation population, 17 percent had been arrested for felony, 43 percent for misdemeanor. At least two tribal leaders have been re-elected to office despite the knowledge that they had served prison sentences for felony. Liquor, forbidden the Klamath before 1951, had led to arrest for 37 percent, and no fewer than 49 percent were judged to have problems associated with drinking. That the bottle had indeed provided a maladaptive instrument is shown by a survey of the causes of death of 139 tribal members who expired in a period of four and a half years: drinking was adjudged to be a contributory factor in no fewer than 57 percent of the deaths.

From this situation, a sizeable number of Klamaths had escaped. Some few had locally embraced white standards and values, although by that measure they estranged themselves from Klamath society. Others had left the reservation. Indeed, as early as 1908 there were well over 100 tribal members living off the reservation, and by 1955, some 40 per cent of the total enrollment were absentee members. Biologically, they were less Indian than those who remained, although even on the reservation a high rate of intermarriage was present: those one-half or less in Indian heritage comprised 72 percent of the reservation enrollment.

The chief political significance of the absentee segment, then, is not a higher rationalization in their approach to political activities, but that, as distant members, they pose difficulties of communication in marshalling voters and their interests have tended to lie rather in the exploitation of tribal resources to yield pro rata shares, in which they might participate, than in the enjoyment of usufruct.[5] ◆◆

The Utes spend their land settlement money

◆◆ The Ute Indian people are living at a standard of living higher than any they have ever enjoyed. Their way of life has been revolutionized by the availability of automobiles, electricity, modern plumbing, household appliances to fit almost every need. The children are going to public schools in good clothing. Their education is being supplemented by a recreational program. These are gains attributable to a regular distribution of capital and are not the product of the effort and industry of tribal members. Indeed, the Ute are more comfortable than they have ever been before and they are enjoying this comfort for the present but they are making little provision for self-support.

Taking everything into consideration, the future development of the Ute appears uncertain and hazardous. Fewer irrigable acres are being used by Indians than before the program started and livestock ownership by Indians of both sheep and cattle is down considerably. Failure to build a firm economic base for future income is the real dilemma facing the tribal members and the tribal leadership.

The Ute Indian people, after the expenditure of over eight million dollars in the past three and one-half years, are still at the crossroads. There are two ways in which economic security can be met. One is through continual distribution of tribal funds per capita, which practice would insure temporary relief and continue the temporary and artificial standard of living presently achieved through unearned income distributed during the past ten years. The outcome of this experience has been that the people dispose of their assets and capital when unearned income in the form of per capita payments ceased to be regularly maintained. Another way to achieve economic security is to build industries and tribal enterprises through the development of reservation resources. . . . However, immediately the Ute do not face a precarious and bleak future since they presently are enjoying the first per capita cash distribution from a multimillion dollar award made in another land claim settlement.[6] ◆◆

The Shoshoni-Bannock of Idaho

◆◆ For several years, leaders and those in a position to know the conditions, have not been satisfied with the progress of the Fort Hall Reservation. . . . per capita income on the Reservation is extremely low. Housing is substandard and overcrowded. . . . relatively few of the Fort Hall youth finish high school. Diseases, especially tuberculosis and venereal diseases, are prevalent. Crime and delinquency rates are high. Many Fort Hall Indians are unemployed. . . . An abnormally large percentage of agricultural land at Fort Hall is leased out to non-Indians, and many of those who till their own property fail to get maximum yield from the soil. . . .

At Fort Hall there were 597 children under five years of age to every 1,000 women age 15-44 inclusive, as compared to 554 in the United States. . . .

[There were] only 17 cases of mental illness, an incidence many times lower than mental illness rates reported for the United States. . . . Females had, on the average, more years of schooling than males. . . . The data showed an extraordinarily high drop-out rate in the ninth and tenth grades. [Of a population of 2,600 Indians at Fort Hall, only seven had attended college and only two had graduated]. . . . In about a fifth of the homes an Indian language is the only spoken, and in an additional fifty percent, Shoshone and/or Bannock is used along with English. On the other hand, in one out of every four homes, English is spoken exclusively. . . . In some instances the language problem creates cleavage in tribal and social affairs.

More than half of the respondents identified themselves with some established Christian Church. . . . [while] a sizeable proportion of Fort Hall Indians . . . belong to the Native American Church, mainly because of the healing powers they attribute to it . . . [and it] is a symbol of Indian culture and a focus of solidarity [but it was observed that religious affiliation had very little, if any, correlation with behavior patterns]. . . .

From the standpoint of group cohesion and cooperation, the most serious weakness at Fort Hall appears to be factionalism. The internal rivalry, suspicion and mutual distrust . . . looms as a major stumbling block to constructive programs. . . . From the standpoint of the individual, probably the most generally recognized weakness . . . seems to be their lack of self-discipline—the self-discipline that enables them to plan, save, and work consistently toward constructive goals.

Decades ago in their native culture, the Shoshone-Bannock peoples exemplified an admirable degree of intra-tribal cooperation . . . and individual self-discipline. It would seem that as these traits can be re-established in the present setting, the solution of community and individual problems will be correspondingly alleviated.[7] ◆◆

Eastern Cherokee passive resistance

◆◆ Today, while most of the Cherokees live in Oklahoma, about 3,200 of them, the Eastern Band of Cherokee Indians, inhabit a small reservation in western North Carolina. . . .

In the 1930's, the most conservative community was Big Cove, then inaccessible by automobile. . . .

Although there was extensive knowledge of the old dances in Big Cove in the 1930's, few of them were still performed. One of the few, however, was the Booger masked dance the nature and fate of which raise certain points pertinent to the thesis of this paper. . . .

The dance emphasizes aggressive obscenity (verbal, in the Cherokee language, and overtly phallic) which is directed by, and sometimes against, the masked dancers. The dancers represent White men, and the leader is a special butt of ridicule because he cannot speak Cherokee without committing grotesque errors.

Both the ball game, which provided a direct means of working off aggression (though not against White men), and the Booger dance were effectively suppressed by Indian Agency personnel before 1940, and no obvious substitutes are in evidence at the present time. It seems doubtful, however, that the motives underlying these activities can have been eliminated so quickly, if indeed they have been eliminated at all. . . .

Between the mid-1930's and 1957, the people of Big Cove lost some more of their few remaining aboriginal traits. Nevertheless, the use of the Cherokee language continues to be widespread. . . .

Is the Cherokee language retained because its use is felt to be an assertion of cultural integrity and identity? It has long been recognized that out-spoken assertiveness may be a rationalization of acute defensiveness rather than an expression of confidence and pride. But among the conservatives there is no evidence of such confidence or cultural self esteem. Quite the contrary in fact. To be sure, there is a recently founded organization of, by, and for conservatives, which has as a rule that meetings must be conducted in the Cherokee language, but its program is not clearly defined, and at present it seems to have become involved, in part,

with the local political activities of non-conservatives. Otherwise, there
is no record of, nor anything now resembling, a nativistic movement.
Indicative of conservative attitudes is the fact that recent revivals of
aboriginal Cherokee culture for tourist exhibition purposes (a life-sized
replica of an 18th Century town, for example) have resulted in no resur-
gence of interest or pride on the part of conservative Cherokees. Rather,
they tend to regard such activities as just another instance of the White
man's taking advantage of them. There is apparently not even any move
to insist that the 'chiefs,' who act as greeters and subjects for tourist
photographers in front of every curio shop, at least be dressed as aboriginal Cherokees would have been, instead of sporting Plains war bonnets
as they do. Even when such opportunities—superficial though they may
be—to assert cultural integrity and identity present themselves, the
conservatives make no such assertion. Defensiveness is the key to conservative attitudes. . . . and they have nothing of their own to assert—nothing, that is, except resistance to any further changes, particularly those
sponsored by Whites who are in positions of authority. . . .

Although conservative resistance is outwardly passive, it is apparent that
conscious hostility toward the Whites underlies it. . . . The active force
of conservative resistance is a demonstrated fact, and so is the conservative
preference for using the Cherokee language. Unable to account satisfac-
torily on any other basis for the persistence of the language, we are led
to conclude that speaking Cherokee by preference is a symbolic, and to
some extent instrumental, act of resistance. This conclusion is further
strengthened when we consider that until 1933, the attempt to eradicate
the language through the school system was an open and painful issue
for all. . . .[8] ◆◆

Tuscarora resistance to assimilation

◆◆ Pressures of acculturation continue to weaken the
cement of Tuscarora tribalism, which so far has held together the retaining wall of social and cultural survival around their reservation community. This is not to presume impending 'disorganization,' but to sug-
gest that the society continues to undergo incisive changes which cut to
the quick of traditional ways of life. Nevertheless, it is apparent from the
anthropologist Anthony F. C. Wallace's studies and those of the present
author, that the Tuscarora, despite what may appear at first glance to be
an almost completely acculturated Indian community, retain a good deal
of their original nonmaterial culture, and have managed to resist to some
degree the tides of culture change.

The Tuscarora have always been a deviant group among the Iroquois,
and despite their acceptance into the Confederacy, have never been emo-
tionally assimilated as blood-brothers by the Five Nations. It would seem
inevitable that they would still be viewed by the other members as some-

thing of a stranger within the gates of the League of the Ho-De-No-Sau-Nee. To this observer it appears that the Tuscarora today still seem haunted with the self-image of themselves as a junior partner in the Iroquois alliance, a mendicant cousin who shuffles with self-consciousness into the peripheral shadows of the council fires.

Such a self-image notwithstanding, there appear to be trends in Tuscarora society toward a renewed interest in their identity as Indians and as an Iroquoian tribe or nation. . . .

Evidences for Tuscarora tribalism are numerous. People identify themselves as Tuscarora and especially as Indians. They constantly differentiate themselves from the White community, whether speaking with injured pride of the sins of history, or with outraged dignity of the current hurts due to actual or supposed discrimination. A Tuscarora will quicken with pride as he talks of the glorious past, but if a discussion ensues it soon becomes apparent that either he knows little about his history, or he has received it more through published sources than intra-cultural transmission. A few persons in the community are actually interested in ancient accounts of their tribe, but sources are usually misquoted or data selected out to validate the image of the noble savage ancestor.

What has carried over from the past is not so much the events of history as the list of historical grievances, which in the eyes of the Tuscarora is as long today as it ever was. These grievances have become the rationale for verbal, and occasionally physical, attacks on Whites. . . .

Many examples of physical attack against Whites, nearly all corresponding to a general pattern of a presumed injustice against an Indian and consequent "ganging up" on one or two individuals were frequently recited in detail for the ethnographer's relish, including the mobbing and near-murder of a state trooper who tried to arrest a young man on the reservation. Lacrosse games, when played against Canadian White Teams, were marked by more than the usual cries for blood, and "Kill the White bastards" could be heard from the pretty teen-age girls as well as the older men. Wallace's account contains many instances of thinly veiled verbal aggressions against Whites, as do the author's field notes. Additionally, the Tuscarora feel strongly about Negroes, and none is allowed to stop on the reservation except as a paying guest at a ball game. The Chief's Council long ago passed a ruling forbidding marriage to Negroes on pain of banishment from the nation and the reserve.

The dynamics of this ethnic-racial prejudice cannot be further discussed here beyond the observation that they seem to be in part a conscious attempt by the Indians to differentiate themselves totally from another disvalued social group.

A large proportion of Tuscarora tribalism, then, is bound up with, and a reflection of, hostility toward Whites, Negroes, the State government, foreigners, Jews and similar categories of people who are different, who in Wallace's apt phrase, come from "off the reservation," and are classed with the unknown, therefore presumably hostile, swamp and forest, as opposed to the clearing, where everyone lives. This negative side of Tuscarora national identification implies: "We are as good as you are, even superior, though vilified, persecuted, and unappreciated. You have wronged us, you have sinned against our forefathers, even now you hold us in contempt. Leave us alone, do not try to buy our lands, do not try to be our neighbors or our friends. You are our enemy." As Wallace has indicated, however, this mask of self-sufficiency slips under slight pressures of economic and social stress, and in its stead we find the traditional dependency which seemed to mark Tuscarora behavior even in the earlier accounts of the historian John Lawson and others. This negative side of Tuscarora identification and its corollaries in the various forms of aggression, need to be more fully explored. It is obvious, however, that among the Tuscarora, as in any group in which aggression is an expression of national identity, its venting results in integrative as well as disintegrative social effect. . . .

Iroquois of the other reservations may have enough cultural security to drop many of the old forms in favor of ones which function more effectively—for example, elective councils instead of Chief's Councils. They may even accept the White man's education system somewhat more easily and agree to school integration with surrounding White communities (which up to 1955, the Tuscarora has resisted stubbornly), since their status as "real" Indians in their own eyes, as well as those of the Whites, seems more assured. They may even consider an at least superficial adoption of the White man's religion, since they rest confident in the knowledge that their native religion is respected by White and Indian alike. (Even Christian ministers who rail against it as "pagan" indicate admiration for its genuineness.)

But the Tuscarora possess none of these securities. They see their sons and daughters becoming less resistant to the allures of White society, and what is more, slowly increasing the rate of intermarriage with Whites. Some of these leave the reservation. They find the federal government ignoring their traditional sovereignty and placing an anti-aircraft installation in the midst of their lands against their protests, acting at times almost as if they had ceased to exist. They look on angrily as the state government takes over many of the responsibilities of the more benevolent government in Washington, and sends in its police to enforce criminal laws made by the White man. The flood of White residences moves to the borders of the reserve and from the century-old farmhouse of one of the older chiefs one may see mushrooming clusters of ranch-houses and pseudo–Cape Cods.

There is, of course, the alternative of cultural defeat, relinquishing identity more completely by replacing tribalism with more complete integration and assimilation. But so far most Tuscarora have taken another road, have sought to reaffirm within themselves and within the tribe important elements of tribalism, though not true nationalism. There is, at any rate, a conscious assertion of dimly known traditions. The instruments for accomplishing this lay within the still not completely desiccated skeleton of past forms of political and social structures. At the same time, they use these customary instrumentalities to resist the temptation of some tribesmen to sell their lands, and thus strive to keep intact the material foundation of the nation. And they continue to resist, by moral suasion at least, the drainage of their numbers through intermarriage and emigration.[9] ◆◆

Narragansett survival after three hundred years

◆◆ In view of the great numerical decline of the Indians of southern New England due to war, disease and westward migrations brought about by the immigration and expansion of the White man for over 300 years, it is of interest to find remnants of formerly powerful tribes still living in the location of their first contact with the Whites. Considering further the tremendous impact of the dominant White man's culture on the constantly dwindling number of Indians, it is also of interest to note the means that are now employed by these remaining Indian descendants for maintaining their identity as a tribe.

An example of such a group is the Narragansett tribe that numbered in the thousands in the mid-1600's and occupied most of the present State of Rhode Island and some adjacent areas. A small remnant (a few hundred) of this tribe now lives in and around Charleston, Rhode Island, in the very area that was in early White contact times the center of their population distribution. At present this remnant successfully maintains its group identity through several cultural means, although its members are deeply acculturated and integrated in the community at large. It is paradoxical and therefore all the more challenging that the practices which now hold the group together and have in the recent past are not expressions of precontact life.

From the early 17th century onward acculturation has been taking place among the Narragansetts to such an extent that it is now difficult to discover any aboriginal traits or values among them. They are also no longer distinct from the community at large in occupation, income level, material possessions, residential distribution, social practices or religion. However most of them live on a relatively low income and educational achievement level. . . .

As far as racial characteristics go, again, the Narragansetts are difficult to distinguish as such. From Colonial times onward so much mixture has taken place between the Indians, Whites and Negroes of Rhode Island that persons of Narragansett descent range in appearance from White to Negro. Most individuals fall between the two extremes, with a few who "look like Indians." The reason for the early Negro admixture is that in

Colonial times Rhode Island contained many plantations worked by Negro slaves. Intermixture between Negro and Indian was furthered by the fact the Indians became virtual slaves to the colonists at various periods as a punitive measure following military defeats. Inasmuch as there are also many people in the community of Negro-White admixture without Indian ancestry, the physical appearance of the Narragansetts as a group is not distinctive.

If the Narragansett tribe is not identifiable by racial type, language, distinct traits of culture or even concentrated residence, we may well wonder by what means they have been able to maintain unity and group identity. This appears to have been accomplished through a combination of institutions, mainly:

(1) The tribal organization itself and its various meetings and social events.
(2) The annual Pow Wow and other similar "ceremonial" undertakings.
(3) The Indian church and its management. . . .

By 1880, when the Narragansetts sold their reservation to the State of Rhode Island the council and its president were regularly elected, managed intra-tribal affairs, and responsibly represented the tribe before the State Legislature and its agents. Important functions of the council prior to 1880 had been giving permission to deserving members of the tribe to cut and sell cedar logs from the Reservation's cedar swamp and the alloting of tribal funds for support of needy members of the tribe.

With formal detribalization and sale of the Reservation in 1880, most of the Council's duties and responsibilities vanished. It was fully expected that the life of the tribe was over and that even the name Narragansett would no longer be mentioned. The Rhode Island Legislature's Committee of Investigation relative to detribalization wrote a sentimental eulogy in its report, to this effect: "There will evidently be a feeling of regret when the name of a tribe so long known in the history of our State passes from existence."

However, the Narragansetts continued to exist, leading an inconspicuous existence, organized in the same pattern as they had been formerly.

In 1934, in accordance with the Indian Reorganization Act, the tribe received a charter and the titles and numbers of officers were changed. For example, instead of the president there is now the chief, and there is a chairman of the sick committee and the social committee, a prophet and a medicine man. The main functions of the present officers are the planning and execution of the Pow Wow, the organization of other social events in the recently built "Long House," and assuming the financial responsibility connected with such endeavors. Occasionally the need for screening individuals for membership arises and rarely, there is a question of the adoption of a White man or an Indian of another tribe to be decided.

Thus, without a known break in time, the tribal government has survived and changed from autocratic hereditary chieftainship to an elected body that behaves in a parliamentary democratic manner. The functions of the governing body likewise have been altered, from complete though temperate power over the tribal subjects to responsibility for the details of social gatherings which in themselves mainly follow an alien pattern.

The second identity-giving institution, the Annual Pow Wow, is likewise an expression of a precontact complex that has been modified over and again, to the point where it is now as remote (if not more so) from its precontact form, as is the tribal government. . . .

Various references to the Pow Wow as practiced during the 19th century give us glimpses of the changes that had been taking place. By the late 19th century athletic contests and cock and dog fights, followed by a trip to the nearby ocean beach, were part of the program. Sale of liquor within a mile of the gathering was forbidden by State law.

Reminiscences written by the present chief describe the summer gatherings as of the early 1900's. At that time the salient feature was the reunion of families and friends, and the wearing of Indian type clothing had not yet been revived.

At present the Narragansett Pow Wow combines several functions. It is very much of a New England church fair, to which is appended what we might call the "Pow Wow" proper. Most members spend much of their time at a Pow Wow, which is a week-end affair, in purely social reunions. A hardworking committee of women prepares and sells dinners and refreshments.

Twice on the Sunday of the Pow Wow week-end services are held in the Indian Church. On Saturday and Sunday afternoons Indian dances and "ceremonials" are performed in the field adjacent to the church. The Christian services, conducted on Sunday by an Indian minister, are followed immediately by "rituals" in which the "great spirit" is invoked; this is accepted as not at all incongruous.

The Pow Wow proper consists of dances and rituals that follow a pattern which has become fairly standard in the northeastern part of the United States. . . .

In the performance of "rituals" there is also opportunity for originality and innovation. A favorite ritual is the conferring of Indian names on little children. This is done by the medicine man in a fashion similar to a Protestant baptism. Another ritual centers on the "peace pipe." A fire is kindled in the center of the circle of dancers and from it a peace pipe is lit by the medicine man. The latter then prays to the "great spirit" and passess the pipe to each male Indian in the circle to take a puff. The present medicine man prays for blessings similar to those which the Protestant minister has invoked inside the church a short time prior to the peace pipe ritual.

It is tempting to think of this as a religious syncretism in reverse from the usual form; in this case we find Christian elements being incorporated in "pagan" worship forms. However, this does not seem to alter Christian beliefs of these people and is practiced only on occasions of this type.

Although the Pow Wow is entirely an Indian-managed, Indian-operated affair, the Indians are sensitive to the impression made by it on non-Indian spectators. It is announced in newspapers and by means of posters in public places ahead of time. A collection is taken from the spectators and there is thus incentive to keep order so that the spectators will remain and come again. There is obvious rivalry between the Narragansetts and other Pow Wow–giving groups in the area; this makes visiting Indians from other tribes all the more welcome for the talent and variety that they add to the local efforts.

Narragansett Pow Wows are conducted and organized entirely by the tribe itself, through officers and committees. There is no help of any sort from the White community; formerly the Whites even expressed hostility, scorn and disapproval of Pow Wows. This is in contrast to the situation at Flagstaff, Arizona, for example, where "Pow Wow, Inc.," a group of business men, organize and arrange the Flagstaff Pow Wow. The Narragansetts not only take the initiative and stage their own Pow Wow, but were able in 1936 to bring enough pressure to secure the passage of a bill proclaiming Rhode Island Indian Day by the State Legislature. . . .

In seeking to explain why such extremely acculturated people should persist in activities that identify them as an Indian tribe, the following reasons seem pertinent: (1) There is a genuine and sincere feeling among some members of the tribe that it is their duty to perpetuate the customs of the past, as they see them. . . . These people bring up their children to hold this attitude, and prod and reward them for performing and wearing a costume. (2) Taking part in the Pow Wow provides an outlet for some creative ability, such as introducing dance innovations, making of articles for sale, designing and making costumes, and the like. (3) Participation in one or all of these institutions discussed provides the opportunity for individuals of Indian descent to enjoy a community life of their own and to assume within the Indian in-group status-giving positions, such as holding an office in the tribal organization or being on the church committee. (4) Participation in the Pow Wow and other events that call for wearing an Indian costume makes it clear to the outside community that the individual is of Indian descent. In the community at large, to be known as a person of Indian descent is an advantage in status over the Negro minority in the community with no Indian ancestry. (5) Membership in a tribe makes an individual more acceptable in other Indian organizations. This is important in travel, schooling and the like, when away from home, or when a family actually moves to another locality. . . . The continuance of these trait-complexes has preserved, as an organized group, a number of people who might otherwise have become an unorganized minority. It is worthwhile to note in this example of group continuity that successful group identity is not necessarily a function of traits and complexes that are highly distinctive or of especially long standing association.[10] ◆◆

A Quaker summary

◆◆ Many Indians are confused, sometimes to the point of hopelessness, in dealing with social and economic problems. Older Indians, particularly, feel keenly the destruction of their culture; they miss the comfort of doing things in the old, familiar "Indian" way.

Many younger Indians, too, are hostile toward the baffling society which surrounds them, feeling, some of them say, like aliens in their own land. They have been told that they must abandon the ways of their forefathers and become "civilized"; but they sometimes find little of lasting value in the kind of civilization they see around them.

The dominant white society insists on conformity. It applauds the melting pot concept, and discriminates against those who do not, or cannot, fit exactly into the popular mold. Indians, like members of other ethnic groups, bitterly resent discrimination, whether it comes in the form of unequal job opportunities or in the unthinking stereotypes of Hollywood movies; but many accept it as the price they must pay for holding on to some vestiges of their culture.[11] ◆◆

The Native American organizes for the future

The secret of success for any group is frequently the possession of an effective and unified organization. The Native Americans of the United States have never possessed an all-inclusive organization but, on the contrary, have split along tribal, linguistic, and cultural lines. Nevertheless, some progress toward the development of a pan-Indian spirit has occurred, stimulated in part by the first Congress on Indian Life at Patzcuaro, Mexico, in April 1940. In 1944 The National Congress of American Indians was founded at Denver, Colorado and the NCAI has achieved a great deal. Nevertheless, this organization represents only Tribal Americans (and not all of them), and it has made no serious effort at recruiting nontribalized Native Americans. This is, of course, a serious flaw, since an organization representing only at best 500,000 persons lacks the raw strength to influence many Anglo-American political leaders.

Mexican-Americans possess a greater political potential than Tribal Americans; however, they too are overly prone toward factionalism. Thus the various Mexican-American organizations (Mexican-American Political Association, Community Service Organization, American GI Forum,

League of United Latin American Citizens, and a host of others) find i
difficult to work together over any length of time.

A new organization that seeks to unify all persons of Native American
ancestry has, however, appeared under the name "Native American
Movement." Whether it will be successful remains to be seen.

A popular type of organization with Tribal Americans is one that
seeks to preserve native dances and cultural traits (and this tendency i
duplicated by Mexican-American "patriotic" and mutual benefit groups)
One such entity is Federated Indian Tribes:

> Federated Indian Tribes is a non-profit corporation dedicated to main
> taining old American Indian cultural patterns. [It is] an organization to pro
> vide a "reservation social atmosphere" for non-reservation Indians and thei
> families. . . . On December 12th, 1958 four Indians from different tribe
> were called together at Dr. Spottedwolf's lodge and F.I.T. was born. . . .
> [Our plans are] to grow, prosper, and to help our fellow red men who are
> interested in preserving their heritage.[12]

Native Americans have not normally cooperated with other minority
groups in the struggle for civil rights and equality. On the contrary, In
dians and Mexicans have sometimes joined with Anglo-Americans agains
Negroes. The Afro-Americans' "freedom now" movement of 1963, how
ever, attracted considerable Native American interest, if not collabora
tion. Stimulated by the Negroes' example, a group of Omahas under th
leadership of Charles Springer left their homes in Macy, Nebraska an
staged a "war dance" in front of the Douglas County Court house i
Omaha. They were protesting alleged discrimination in employment.

The appearance in the mid-twentieth century of a multitude of Nativ
American organizations is indicative of a new awakening within the in
digenous community. Whether this awakening will lead to the develop
ment of an enduring pan-Indian movement or will merely rise tem
porarily and then melt into the sea of assimilation remains to be seen
But in any case, the prophecy of Zane Grey implied in the title of hi
novel *The Vanishing American* has certainly been proven wrong. Th
Native American is not vanishing—he and his part-native brothers ar
increasing faster than any other portion of the population of the Unitec
States.

Notes

1. Martin Hall, "Roybal's Candidacy and What It Means," *Frontier*, June 1954, pp
   5-7. Reprinted by permission of *Frontier* magazine.
2. Tom T. Sasaki, *A Navaho Community in Transition* (Ithaca: Cornell Universit
   Press, 1960) pp. 167-170. Reprinted by permission of Cornell University Press.

3. Address of Glenn L. Emmons, Commissioner of Indian Affairs, April 18, 1957.

4. Dennis Farrell, "Modern Missionary versus Medicine Man," *Arizona Today*, Vol. I, No. 6, December 1962, pp. 7-8, 22.

5. Theodore Stern, "Livelihood and Tribal Government on the Klamath Indian Reservation," *Human Organization*, Vol. XX, No. 4, Winter 1961-62, pp. 173-4. Reprinted by permission of the Society for Applied Anthropology, Inc.

6. Robert L. Bennett, "Building Indian Economies with Land Settlement Funds," *Human Organization*, Vol. XX, No. 4, Winter 1961-62, p. 163. Reprinted by permission of the Society for Applied Anthropology, Inc.

7. Harmsworth and Nybroten, *Human Resources, Relations, and Problems on the Fort Hall Indian Reservation*, pp. 3-4, 28, 34, 67, 147-9, 155-6. Reprinted by permission of the authors.

8. John Gulick, "Language and Passive Resistance Among the Eastern Cherokee," *Ethnohistory*, Vol. V, No. 1, Winter 1958, pp. 61-77.

9. David Landy, "Tuscarora Tribalism and National Identity," *Ethnohistory*, Vol. V, No. 3, Summer 1958, pp. 250-251, 253-5, 271-3.

10. Ethel Boissevain, "Narragansett Survival: A Study of Group Persistence through Adopted Traits," *Ethnohistory*, Vol. VI, No. 4, Fall 1959, pp. 347-59.

11. *The Spirit They Live In* (Philadelphia: American Friends Service Committee, 1956) pp. 6-7.

12. *Federated Indian Tribes: An American Indian Cultural Exchange* (pamphlet).

The Eyewitness Accounts of American History Series